Psychology of Women, Family and Leadership

Psychology of Women, Family and Leadership

Asha Srivastava

MD Publications Pvt Ltd
New Delhi
www.mdppl.com

Published by :

MD Publications Pvt Ltd
"MD House", 11, Darya Ganj,
New Delhi-110 002
Phone : +91-11-45355555
E-mail : contact@mdppl.com
Website : www.mdppl.com

ISBN : 978-81-7533-248-5

Published and Printed by Mr. Pranav Gupta on behalf of **MD Publications Pvt Ltd** at Printext, New Delhi.

PREFACE

Social scientists distinguish between "gender" and "sex." Sex refers to the basic, biologically given physiological differences between males and females. Gender refers to a culture's social construction of differences between the sexes. These include the different traits, roles, behaviors, attitudes, and aptitudes males and females are expected to display. Gender displays reinforce claims of membership in a sex. Expressions such as "gendered practices," "gendered language," and "gendered jobs" are used to emphasize the tenet that gender involves a process of social construction, and to make gender a more central explanation of organizational behavior phenomena such as leadership.

Several reasons are cited for the low proportion of women leaders. One is that females' life aspirations are diminished by their early childhood socialization in the nuclear family. Generally the nuclear family transmits definitions of appropriate gender behavior to children. For girls, this includes submissiveness, passivity, avoidance of aggression and competition, reticence to take risk, and other qualities our culture considers "feminine."

One result of this childhood socialization is the tendency for adult women to be stereotyped as less well-suited than men for leadership roles. Several studies have shown that people perceive successful managers to have the characteristics typically associated with men, though the actual qualities successful managers possess are a combination of masculine (e.g., forcefulness, self-confidence, task orientation, initiative) and feminine (e.g., concern for people, feelings, and relationships) traits. An obvious consequence of this is that a man is more likely to be selected for a leadership position than is a woman of equal qualification. Thus, a woman who aspires to leadership positions must overcome both her childhood socialization, which discouraged development of some essential qualities, and a popular perception of the maleness of leadership—both of which tangibly reduce the chance she will be judged qualified.

Other reasons women ascend to leadership positions less frequently than men are that women most frequently inhabit managerial positions with little power, little advancement opportunity, or where other women are so rare that their presence is attributed to their sexuality or affirmative action, or it is used as a symbol of the organization's enlightenment. Outside their paid jobs, women usually have significant responsibility for the care of their families and home, thereby depleting the energy they might otherwise devote to the pursuit of leadership positions of consequence.

I am very grateful to Mr. Pranav Gupta, Director of MD Publications Pvt Ltd, New Delhi, for his kind cooperation and support for this book.

Asha Srivastava

Contents

1

Psychology of Women, Family and Leadership

An Introduction

Psychology "study of the mind", from "breath, spirit, soul" and "study of" is an academic and applied discipline involving the scientific study of human mental functions and behaviour. Occasionally, in addition or opposition to employing the scientific method, it also relies on symbolic interpretation and critical analysis, although these traditions have tended to be less pronounced than in other social sciences such as sociology. Psychologists study such phenomena as perception, cognition, emotion, personality, behaviour and interpersonal relationships. Some, especially depth psychologists, also study the unconscious mind. Psychological knowledge is applied to various spheres of human activity, including issues related to everyday life such as family, education and employment—and to the treatment of mental health problems. Psychologists attempt to understand the role of mental functions in individual and social behaviour, while also exploring the underlying physiological and neurological processes.

Psychology includes many sub-fields of study and applications concerned with such areas as human development, sports, health, industry, media and law. Psychology incorporates research from the natural sciences, social sciences and humanities and a person who studies or practices psychology is called a psychologist. Psychology is an academic and applied field involving the scientific study of mental processes and behaviour. Psychology also refers to the application of such knowledge to various spheres of human activity, including problems of individuals' daily lives and the treatment of mental illness. Neuropsychology studies the actual neural processes and how they relate to the mental effects they subjectively produce. Biological psychology is the scientific study of the biological bases of behaviour and mental states.

Philosophical and Scientific Roots

The study of psychology in philosophical context dates back to the ancient civilizations of Egypt, Greece, China and India. Psychology began adopting a more clinical and experimental approach under medieval Muslim psychologists and physicians, who built psychiatric hospitals for such purposes. In 1802, French physiologist Pierre Cabanis helped to pioneer biological psychology with his essay Rapports du physique et du moral de l'homme (On the relations between the physical and moral aspects of man). Cabanis interpreted the mind in light of his previous studies of biology, arguing that sensibility and soul are properties of the nervous system.

Though the use of psychological experimentation dates back to Alhazen's Book of Optics in 1021, psychology as an independent experimental field of study began in 1879, when Wilhelm Wundt founded the first laboratory dedicated exclusively to psychological research at Leipzig University in Germany, for which Wundt is known as the "father of psychology". The year 1879 is thus sometimes regarded as the "birthdate" of psychology. The American philosopher William James published his seminal book, Principles of Psychology in 1890, laying the foundations for many of the questions that psychologists would focus on for years to come. Other important early contributors to the field include Hermann Ebbinghaus (1850–1909), a pioneer in the experimental study of memory at the University of Berlin and the Russian physiologist Ivan Pavlov (1849-1936) who investigated the learning process now referred to as classical conditioning.

Psychoanalysis

From the 1890s until his death in 1939, the Austrian physician Sigmund Freud developed a method of psychotherapy known as psychoanalysis. Freud's understanding of the mind was largely based on interpretive methods, introspection and clinical observations, and was focused in particular on resolving unconscious conflict, mental distress and psychopathology. Freud's theories became very well-known, largely because they tackled subjects such as sexuality, repression, and the unconscious mind as general aspects of psychological development. These were largely considered taboo subjects at the time, and Freud provided a catalyst for them to be openly discussed in polite society. While Freud is perhaps best known for his tripartite model of the mind, consisting of the id, ego, and superego, and his theories about the Oedipus complex, his most lasting legacy may be not the content of his theories but his clinical innovations, such as the method of free association and a clinical interest in dreams.

Freud had a significant influence on Swiss psychiatrist Carl Jung, whose analytical psychology became an alternative form of depth psychology. Other well-known psychoanalytic thinkers of the mid-twentieth century included Sigmund Freud's daughter, psychoanalyst Anna Freud; German-American psychologist Erik Erickson, Austrian-British psychoanalyst Melanie Klein, English psychoanalyst and physician D. W. Winnicott, German psychologist Karen Horney, German-born psychologist and philosopher Erich Fromm, and English psychiatrist John Bowlby. Contemporary psychoanalysis comprises diverse schools of thought, including ego psychology, object relations, interpersonal, Lacanian, and relational psy-choanalysis.

Modification of Jung's theories has led to the archetypal and process-oriented schools of psychological thought. Austrian-British philosopher Karl Popper argued that Freud's psychoanalytic theories were presented in untestable form. Psychology departments in American universities today are scientifically oriented, and Freudian theory has been marginalized, being regarded instead as a "desiccated and dead" historical artifact, according to a recent APA study. Recently, however, South African neuroscientist Mark Solms and other researchers in the emerging field of neuro-psychoanalysis have argued for Freud's theories, pointing out brain structures relating to Freudian concepts such as libido, drives, the unconscious, and repression.

Behaviourism

Behaviourism arose partly due to the popularity of laboratory-based animal experimentation and partly in reaction to Freudian psychodynamics, which was difficult to test empirically because, among other reasons, it tended to rely on case studies and clinical experience, and dealt largely with intra-psychic phenomena that were difficult to quantify or to define operationally. Moreover, in contrast with early psychologists Wilhelm Wundt and William James, who studied the mind via introspection, the behaviourists argued that the contents of the mind were not open to scientific scrutiny and that scientific psychology should only be concerned with the study of observable behaviour.

There was no consideration of internal representation or the mind. Founded in the early 20th century by American psychologist John B. Watson, behaviourism was embraced and extended by Americans Edward Thorndike, Clark L. Hull, Edward C. Tolman, and later B.F. Skinner. Behaviou-rism differs from other perspectives in a number of ways. Behaviourists focus on behaviour-environment relations and analyze overt and covert (i.e., private) behaviour as a function of the organism interacting with its environment. Behaviourists do not reject the study of covert or private events (e.g., dreaming), but rather reject the proposition that an autonomous causal entity inside the organism causes overt (e.g., walking, talking) or covert (e.g., dreaming, imagining) behaviour.

Concepts such as "mind" or "consciousness" are not used by behaviourists because such terms do not describe actual psychological events (such as imagining) but are used as explanatory entities hidden somewhere in the organism. By contrast, behaviourism treats private events as behaviour, and analyzes them in the same way as overt behaviour. Behaviour refers to the concrete events of the organism, overt or private. American linguist Noam Chomsky's critique of the behaviourist model of language acquisition is regarded by many as a key turning point in the decline of behaviourism's general prominence. But Skinner's behaviourism has not died, perhaps in part because it has generated successful practical applications. The ascendancy of behaviourism as an overarching model in psychology, however, gave way to a new dominant paradigm: cognitive approaches.

Humanism and Existentialism

Humanistic psychology was developed in the 1950s in reaction to both behaviourism and psychoanalysis. By using phenomenology, intersubjectivity and first-person categories, the humanistic approach seeks to glimpse the whole person—not just the fragmented parts of the personality or cognitive functioning. Humanism focuses on uniquely human issues and fundamental issues of life, such as self-identity, death, aloneness, freedom, and meaning. There are several factors which distinguish the humanistic approach from other approaches within psychology. These include the emphasis on subjective meaning, a rejection of determinism, and a concern for positive growth rather than pathology. Some of the founding theorists behind this school of thought were American psychologists Abraham Maslow, who formulated a hierarchy of human needs, and Carl Rogers, who created and developed client-centered therapy; and German-American psychiatrist Fritz Perls, who helped create and develop Gestalt therapy.

It became so influential as to be called the "third force" within psychology, along with behaviourism and psychoanalysis. Influenced largely by the work of German philosopher Martin Heidegger and Danish philosopher Soren Kierkegaard, psychoanalytically-trained American psychologist Rollo May developed an existential breed of psychology in the 1950s and 1960s. Existential psychologists argued that people must come to terms with their mortality and that, in so doing, people will be obligated to accept that they are free—that they possess free will and are at liberty to defy expectations and conventions in order to forge their own, meaningful paths through life. May believed that an important element of the meaning-making process is the search for myths, or narrative patterns into which the individual may fit.

From the existential perspective, not only does the quest for meaning follow from an acceptance of mortality, but the attainment of meaning can overshadow the prospect of death. As Austrian existential psychiatrist and Holocaust survivor Viktor Frankl observed, "We who lived in concentration camps can remember the men who walked through the huts comforting others, giving away their last piece of bread. They may have been few in number, but they offer sufficient proof that everything can be taken from a man but one thing: the last of the human freedoms—to choose one's attitude in any given set of circumstances, to choose one's own way". May helped to pioneer the development of existential therapy, and Frankl created a variety of it called logotherapy. In addition to May and Frankl, Swiss psychoanalyst Ludwig Binswanger and American psychologist George Kelly may be said to belong to the existential school. Both existential and humanistic psychologists argue that people should strive to reach their full potential, but only humanistic psychologists believe that this striving is innate. For existential psychologists, the striving only follows an anxiety-producing contemplation of mortality, freedom, and responsibility.

Women in Psychology

Understanding the opportunities and obstacles for women in psychology requires an appreciation for how the larger context shapes the contexts and careers of individuals. At the end of the 19th Century, a time when psychology was a newly emerging science, pervasive gender stereotypes shaped educational and employment opportunities for women. Known as the "cult of true womanhood", a conception of femininity as pious, pure, domestic, and submissive was used to justify a societal division of labour congruent with gender stereotypes. As historian Margaret Rossiter observed, women in psychology, like all women in science of the time, were caught between two conflicting classes of stereotypes. First were the stereotypes of women that "linked and limited them to soft, delicate, emotional, noncompetitive, and nurturing kinds of feelings and behaviour".

Second, there were the stereotypes of scientists as "tough, rigorous, rational, impersonal, masculine, competitive, and unemotional". Women in psychology had a special relationship to gender bias and stereotypes, however, as the mantle of scientific psychology was used to justify discrimination against them. As psychological science emerged, psychological theories of female personality and intellect incorporated the myths of gender and race of the time, giving the force of "science" to them. In 1910, pioneering psychologist Helen Thompson Woolley succinctly described the situation with regard to psychology's views of women:

There is perhaps no field aspiring to be scientific where flagrant personal bias, logic martyred in the cause of supporting a prejudice, unfounded assertions, and even sentimental rot and drivel, have run riot to such an extent as here. It was a time when leaders such as G. Stanley Hall, the founder of the American Psychological Association, warned that "mental women" competing with men "in the world" would cause "race suicide" as maternal urges became neglected. The fourth president of APA, James McKeen Cattell, also warned that higher education would endanger women's ability to perform her motherhood role:

Girls are injured more than boys by school life; they take it more seriously, and at certain times and at a certain age are far more subject to harm. It is probably not an exaggeration to say that to the average cost of each girl's education through high school must be added one unborn child. And then, of course, there is Sigmund Freud, whose descriptions of female personality would almost be amusing in today's light were it not for the terrible harm they have done to women.

His phallocentric explanation of psychological development reinforced a societal view of women as inferior to and envious of men and jealous of other women. His construction of reports of sexual abuse by their fathers as female fantasies is one of the great outrages in psychology's history. Psychologists were not the only scientists affected by the myths of time. Charles Darwin, arguably one of the most influential thinkers of the time, used evolution to justify women's subordinate status: With women the powers of intuition, of rapid percept-ion, and perhaps of imitation, are more strongly marked than in men; but some, at least, of these faculties are characteristic of the lower races, and therefore of a past and lower state of civilization. The chief distinction in the intellectual powers of the two sexes is shown by man's attaining to a higher eminence, in whatever he takes up, than can women. As more women entered the field, however, some used their scientific knowledge and skills to challenge gender myths supported by "scientific psychology."

From the field's inception, women psychologists have been leaders in using psychological knowledge and skills to challenge the use of psychology to support a sexist status quo. Thus the contributions of feminist researchers to psychology become an important piece of the picture of women's status and roles in academe.

Sometimes the stereotypes worked to advance opportunities for women in "gender appropriate" domains. Beliefs in women's moral superiority were used to justify women's participation in a wide variety of social reform movement encompassing issues of child labour, prison reform, pure drinking water, free libraries, public sewers, ending prostitution, historic preservation, and peace. Even equal political rights and better conditions of employment were justified as a means for women to reform society. Women's rights were especially linked to child welfare. The confluence of professionalism, progressive education, and child welfare movements engendered a belief in a "professional approach to child care" that was used to argue for women's higher education. As Margaret Rossiter described:

> The rapid development of secondary and then higher education...came only as the result of a shrewd political and intellectual compromise with the prevailing antifeminism; women might be educated, critics acquiesced, but only if it was for motherhood, their basic role in American society.

Women's colleges flourished, providing one of the few places where it was considered appropriate for women to work in all areas of science. Psychological clinics, child guidance centers, and child welfare institutes emerged, providing places for women psychologists to work in keeping with societal conceptions of women's roles.

As higher education expanded, women began to trickle into all fields of science but were particularly likely to go into fields perceived as congruent with gender stereotypes of the time: botany, sociology, economics, applied chemistry in home economics, and psychology. Colleges of education and of home economics provided "womanly" alternatives to psychology departments and homes for the newly emerging fields of counseling and school psychology and child development.

Given limited opportunities for employment in traditional psychology departments and widespread stereotyping that produced gender segregation of psycho-logy's subfields, women became leaders and innovators in newly emerging areas of psychology seen at the time as congruent with women's abilities, including mental development and individual differences, educational psychology, child psychology, and animal psychology.

As more women earned bachelors and master's degrees in the sciences, men became concerned that the presence of women would lower their "prestige"—a new addition to the concept of masculinity of the time. They erected a variety of barriers to restrict women to "women's work" and exclude them from academe, including the requirement of a doctoral degree for employment in the nation's universities. Indicators of prestige, such as "Fellow status" in professional associations and various scientific prizes were developed and then differentially awarded by men to men. These indicators could then be used to exclude women from other activities, including academic employment, based on "merit."

One of the lessons to be learned from studying women's history in psychology is the remarkable resilience and flexibility of women who both made the best of their limited options as well as created new ones. Unwelcome in academe, women in psychology (MAs and PhDs) found employment elsewhere, more in keeping with societal concepts of appropriate roles for women. By 1940, women were 30% of psychologists but held 51% of positions in guidance centers, clinics, schools, educational systems, hospitals, and custodial centers. By 1944 the figure was 60% although the proportion of women in the field had remained stable.

Meanwhile, 26% of positions in colleges and universities were held by women and in the subsequent decades of the 1950s and 1960s, little changed. In 1973, women were one out of every five psychology faculty members, a proportion lower than that found in 1944. It was not until the rise of the women's movement in the 1970s, which grounded its arguments in the importance of the individual, the equality of men and women, and the rejection of gender stereotyping, that the proportions of women began to increase in all of the sciences, including psychology.

Race and ethnicity have erected additional barriers to the full participation of all women psychologists. The curricula in the Black colleges established after the Civil War focused on

Black communities' urgent needs, and psychology in those schools focused on applications and became affiliated with education departments. From 1920 to 1950 only 32 doctorates were earned by Black psychologists, eight of them by women (four EdDs and four PhDs). In 1933 Inez Prosser made history by being the first Black woman to earn a doctorate in psychology—an EdD from the University of Cincinnati. In 1934, Ruth Howard (Beckham) became the first Black woman to earn a PhD in psychology.

Unfortunately for academe, these women did not pursue their careers in academic institutions. Information about ethnic minority women is scarce, and little is known about the history of American Indian, Asian American, and Hispanic American women psychologists, inside or outside of academe. It was not until 1962 that Martha Bernal became the first known Mexican American woman to earn a PhD in psychology. She went on to pursue an academic career and became a leader in the newly emerging field of ethnic psychology. The stories of pioneering ethnic foremothers are still being written today as ethnic women advance in their careers and make inroads into positions previously dominated by White males.

In 1970 APA established a Task Force on the Status of Women in 1970 (leading to a continuing Committee on Women in Psychology [CWP] in 1973), which provided a power base for women psychologists to work for change within the discipline. One of the first efforts of CWP leaders was a successful petition drive to establish a Division of the Psychology of Women (Division 35). Established in 1973, that division provides a power base where feminist psychologists challenge myths and stereotypes and go beyond a reactive stance to generating new theories, methods, and techniques for understanding the development of women and men over the life cycle and in diverse contexts. Ethnic minority women were active leaders in these activities. They have provided powerful critiques of psychology in general and feminist psychology in particular and have been a source of creative energy and insightful vision for the emerging field of the psychology of women.

Because divisions elect members of APA's Council of Representatives (APA's policy-making body), formation of Division 35 enabled women to organize a Women's Caucus of Council, providing a power base for women's issues at APA's highest levels. Today Division 35, the CWP, the Women's Programs Office, the Women's Caucus of Council, and a host of committees and sections on women in other divisions and state associations provide a network of power centers for women's issues within the discipline.

One measure of the power and success of the movement is found in the composition of doctorate recipients in 1996: With women receiving 66.7% of all doctorates (including educational and school psychology), psychology had the highest proportion of women of any field—science and non science—and one of every seven doctorates earned by a woman was in a field of psychology (NRC, 1998). After nearly a century, women's participation in psychology is no longer an issue, and inroads have been made on gender segregation and salary equity issues. It is now time to focus on compensation more broadly and to develop a more sophisticated vision of issues related to power, status, and equity for women psychologists in academe.

Constructing a Women's History of Psychology

To date most of our efforts to "tell women's lives" have focused on biography and autobiography. There are other ways of considering women in the history of psychology, of course. But our primary interest, not unusual for psychologists, has been in the lived experiences of the women in psychology's history. Given this interest in recovering women's experiences and adding them to the history of our field, what is now available for constructing the history of women in psychology based upon their life stories? As for book-length biographies of North American women, there is none written by an historian, although Leta Stetter Hollingworth, Naomi Norsworthy, and Lillien Jane Martin have been subjects of such works. Fortunately, there are shorter biographical studies available in a number of sources.

The most comprehensive of these is O'Connell and Russo's 1990 Women in Psychology: A Bio-bibliographic Sourcebook, which features studies of 36 women. Some of psychology's early women are included in well-known reference works, such as Notable American Women and American National Biography, and several are represented in the series sponsored by Division 1 entitled Portraits of Pioneers in Psychology. Also available is Scarborough and Furumoto's 1987 collective biography of the first 25 American women psychologists, Untold Lives: The First Generation of American Women Psychologists.

For autobiography, the currently available resources are more numerous, although there is only one monographic length work. For shorter autobiographies, there are three multi-volume series. The long-running A History of Psychology in Autobiography and Krawiec's The Psychologists each include a few women. The three volumes of Models of Achievement: Reflections of Eminent Women in Psychology provide a rich collection. However, despite these resources, the gender imbalance in the current availability of full-length biographies of women psychologists raises questions: Was it that women simply did not achieve adequate prominence so as to rank with men? Was that because they did not do remarkable work and make noteworthy contributions? And if so, why was it that they did not achieve and earn honors commensurate with their numbers?

Granted, women have tended to cluster in certain sub-fields, and have been more likely to enter the applied/professional fields as opposed to academic/scientific ones; applied work has been less respected by psychologists and less considered by historians. But a number of the men who have received biographic attention were themselves dedicated to applied work. So might it be that scholars, editors, and chroniclers have simply failed to consider women - either as an oversight or by deliberate decisions to exclude them? Whichever, this situation needs to be corrected! The details of women's lives need to be preserved in archival collections and through careful and inclusive oral history so that future biographers have adequate information to construct the history of women in psychology. The women now included in collections of autobiographies represent a select subset of their cohorts in psychology. They are the eminent, the recognized, the honored. We might even call them deviants or outliers. We do well to applaud and appreciate them. But they constitute only a small subset of those women and men who sought and gained necessary training for entering psychology in the first half of the 20th century. What about the experience and history of the greater number of women in psychology – those who lived unexceptional careers? Only by learning about the less notable, those who dropped out and those who converted their professional tools to labour in non-psychology settings, will we gain an understanding of the range of experiences encountered by our earliest women.

But where will this history take us? So far in the development of this history, we have documented the lack of suitable recognition of women's contributions, but we have not provided much in the way of explanation or interpretation that are to construct a fully-fledged women's history of psychology, we need more than a record of women's life experiences. We need now to determine women's effect on the field. When and how did women's changing status affect the social values and operations of psychology, the science as well as the professional discipline with its organizational and political components? Can we identify a distinct "women's culture" within psychology, perhaps cutting across its sub-fields? If so, when and how did it emerge? Consider this: during psychology's first 80 years, two women held the presidency of the APA, but in the last 30 years, eight women have been elected.

How did that happen? And what might be the effect of the women's terms as APA president? How is it that later women, unlike their predecessors, came to invest so heavily in women's issues and changing women's status? What difference have they made? How might Division 35 and AWP have changed in focus and strategy since their foundings? So, more than just a "for-the-record" reporting, we now need interpretation and analysis. As Eleanor Gibson wrote in her 1980 autobiography, "It is easy to collect material and summarize, but thinking is hard." And it is just that "hard thinking" that might well engage us now as we write a women's history of psychology.

We've come a long way, to be sure, but there are still more questions. There is much yet to explore, much to ponder, and much to understand. Behavioural psychology, also known as behaviourism, is a theory of learning based upon the idea that all behaviours are acquired through conditioning. Conditioning occurs through interaction with the environment. According to behaviourism, behaviour can be studied in a systematic and observable manner with no consideration of internal mental states.

There are two major types of conditioning:

1. Classical conditioning is a technique used in behavioural training in which a naturally occurring stimulus is paired with a response. Next, a previously neutral stimulus is paired with the naturally occurring stimulus. Eventually, the previously neutral stimulus comes to evoke the response without the presence of the naturally occurring stimulus. The two elements are then known as the conditioned stimulus and the conditioned response.
2. Operant conditioning (sometimes referred to as instrumental conditioning) is a method of learning that occurs through rewards and punishments for behaviour. Through operant conditioning, an association is made between behaviour and a consequence for that behaviour.

Cognitive psychology is the branch of psychology that

studies mental processes including how people think, perceive, remember and learn. As part of the larger field of cognitive science, this branch of psychology is related to other disciplines including neuroscience, philosophy, and linguistics. The core focus of cognitive psychology is on how people acquire, process and store information. There are numerous practical applications for cognitive research, such as ways to improve memory, how to increase decision-making accuracy, and how to structure educational curricula to enhance learning.

Psychological Practice with Girls and Women

During recent decades, women and girls of diverse ethnicities, social classes, sexual orientations, and life experiences have encountered dramatic and complex changes in education, health, work, reproductive and care giving roles, and personal relationships. Although many of these changes have resulted in increased equality, opportunity, and quality of life, girls and women are also at risk for a variety of health concerns and life stresses. Stressors in the lives of women and girls include interpersonal victimization and violence, unrealistic media images of girls and women, discrimination and oppression, devaluation, limited economic resources, role overload, relationship disruptions, and work inequities. Violence against girls and women is often predicated in sexism, racism, classism, and homophobia. Salient mental health statistics reveal that women are two times more likely than men to be depressed, and girls are seven times more likely than boys to be depressed.

Women who are subject to group and individual discrimination are even more likely to experience depression. Girls and Women are also roughly nine times more likely to have eating disorders than boys and men. Compared to men, women are two to three times more likely to experience many types of anxiety disorders. The abuse and violence in our society (e.g., abuse, battering, and rape) may contribute to the development of dysfunctional behaviour such as eating disorders, depression, anxiety, and suicidal behaviour, while discrimination against women and girls of colour can result in lowered self-expectations, anxiety, depression, and negative attitudes toward self. In general, the physical and mental health concerns of women and girls are related to complex and diverse economic, biological, developmental, psychological, and socio-cultural environments.

The concerns, behaviours, values, attitudes, and feelings of women and girls also arise from myriad interactions among their multiple identities related to age, race, ethnicity, class, sexual orientation, marital, partnership and parental status, gender identity, ability, culture, immigration, geography, and other life experiences. Although many psychologists and members of the general public may believe that women's issues in psychology were dealt with and resolved in the 1970s and 1980s, the changing and increasingly complex life experiences of girls and women and the intersection of their gender roles with ethnicity, sexual orientation, ability, SES, etc. demonstrate compelling evidence and need for professional guidance for helping psychologists (a) avoid harm in psychological practice with girls and women; (b) improve research, teaching, consultation, and psychotherapeutic and counseling training and practice; and (c) develop and enhance treatment efforts, research, prevention, teaching, and other areas of practice that will benefit women and girls.

In addition, although blatant forms of sexism and racism have decreased over time, researchers have noted the continuing presence of more subtle forms of sexist and racist bias (e.g., ambivalent, symbolic, or unintentional racism/ sexism). Given that the majority of those seeking mental health services continue to be females, special attention to the unique treatment needs of girls and women of diverse backgrounds is warranted. The majority of those seeking treatment remains women and girls, and the demographics of the United States population are rapidly changing to increase more diversity in women and girls needing psychological services. Not only is potential harm reduced, but improved treatment will also likely benefit women and girls, particularly through greater awareness, education and prevention fostered by guidelines for psychological practice with girls and women.

Purpose and Scope

The aim of this document is to articulate guidelines that will enhance gender- and culture sensitive psychological practice with women and girls from all social classes, ethnic and racial groups, sexual orientations, and ability/disability status in the United States. These guidelines provide general recommendations for psychologists who seek to increase their awareness, knowledge, and skills in psychological practice with women and girls. The beneficiaries include all consumers of psychological practice, including clients, students, supervisees, research participants, consultees, and other health professionals. Although the guidelines and supporting literature place substantial emphasis on psychotherapy practice, the general guidelines are applicable to psychological practice in its broadest sense. Rather than offering a comprehensive review of content relevant to all areas of practice, this document provides examples of empirical and conceptual literature that supports the need for practice guidelines.

The "Criteria for Practice Guideline Development and Evaluation" (APA, 2002a) defines the term "guidelines" as "statements that suggest or recommend specific professional behaviour, endeavours, or conduct for psychologists. Guidelines differ from standards in that standards are mandatory and may be accompanied by enforcement mechanism. Thus, guidelines are aspirational in intent. They are intended to facilitate the continued systematic development of the profession and to help assure a high level of professional practice by psychologists". Guidelines may be superseded by federal or state laws. The APA (2002a) also distinguishes between treatment and practice guidelines, noting that treatment guidelines "provide specific recommendations about clinical interventions". In contrast, "practice guidelines consist of recommendations to professions concerning their conduct and the issues to be considered in particular areas of practice".

The following practice guidelines have been written to be compatible with the APA Ethical Principles of Psychologists and Code of Conduct (2002b); the Guidelines for Psychotherapy with Lesbian, Gay, and Bisexual Clients (APA, 2000a); the Guidelines on Multicultural Education, Training, Research, Practice, and Organizational Change for Psychologists (APA, 2003); and the Guidelines for Psychological Practice with Older Adults (APA, 2004a). These guidelines do not refer to practice with transgender individuals. These guidelines are also consistent with the products of task forces on violence and the family (APA,1996) and women, poverty, and public assistance (1998); and with other relevant APA documents such as the Resolution on Substance Abuse by Pregnant Women (APA, 1991), the Resolution on Cultural and Gender Awareness in International Psychology (2004b), the Resolution on Women and Poverty (2000c), the Resolution on Poverty and Socioeconomic Status (APA, 2000b), recommendations of the APA Intimate Partner Abuse and Relationship Violence Working Group (2002c), and the Resolution on Male Violence Against Women (APA,2005).

We strongly encourage institutions, agencies, departments, and/or individuals to discuss ways these guidelines may be applied to their own specific settings and relevant activities. As noted by APA (2002a) criteria, practice guidelines "may not be applicable to every professional and clinical situation". Consistent with APA criteria, these guidelines are not definitive and are designed to respect the decision-making judgment of individual professional psychologists. In addition, these guidelines will need to be periodically reviewed and updated at least every ten years (eight years is recommended) beginning from the year of acceptance by the APA Council of Representatives to take into account changes in practice, research and the effects of changing contemporary social forces and context.

It should be noted that many of the guidelines and recommended practices addressed in this document apply to both genders with diverse social memberships. For example, many of the guidelines encourage psychologists to understand the consequences of gender role socialization and its interactions with other social identities such as race, ethnicity, sexual orientation, and ability as both females and males experience constraints related to their gender and the gender role socialization process, and these processes influence both males' and females' mental and physical health. Hence, the recommendation to integrate an understanding of gender role socialization into the practice of psychology should not be limited to working with girls and women.

Although many of these guidelines are potentially applicable to both genders, this document focuses on the experiences of girls and women for two reasons. First, females in the United States, on average, have less economic, political, and social power than males and therefore have experiences that are more likely to contribute to issues of powerlessness. Women of colour, on average, suffer from at least two sources of discrimination – gender and race/ethnicity, and therefore may feel even more powerless. The average pay gap between men and women has been persistent and significant since statistics about gender and pay have been collected. In addition, a pay gap exists between white women and women of colour, which has widened during the past twenty years.

The impact of such experiences upon the mental health and well-being girls and women needs to be considered as well as the manner in which such experiences affect psychological practice with diverse members of these populations and the obstacles and discrimination with which they may be faced.

Furthermore, compared to what is currently available about boys and men, a much more extensive scientific literature examines the gender role socialization and gendered experiences of girls and women in connection to issues of practice. As research proceeds on boys and men, however, future practice guidelines should expand the scope of our practice guidelines to encompass gender-sensitive concerns over the lifespan for both females and males across all identity categories. The project focusing on males began in the spring of 2005, and that writing group has been invited to borrow freely from this document.

Need

Beginning in the 1960s and 1970s, psychology as a discipline was widely criticized for its biases with regard to gender, race, ethnicity, class, and sexual orientation. A number of classic studies and publications focused on these limitations. This literature challenged the extent to which existing psychological theories were androcentric and did not adequately describe women's psychological development and behaviour including women of colour and lesbians. Scrutiny of a variety of theories of psycho-therapy, research on psychological development, diagnostic systems, assessment procedures and measures found difficulties with non-inclusive versions of mental health and problematic gender and ethnic biases.

Bias in Diagnosis and Treatment

In recent times, gender bias has been observed to be more covert but still a detectable and powerful force in psychological practice. Particular areas of concern include the presence of gender bias as well as bias in other social constructs such as ethnicity, age, race, disability, and social class, within diagnostic criteria and labeling. Women of colour and lesbians may be especially vulnerable to misdiagnosis and other forms of bias. For example, women's and girls' gender role socialization and their economic status, ethnicity, sexual orientation, and disability status as well as biased criteria and perceptions may contribute to inappropriate use and overuse of certain diagnoses such as histrionic and borderline personality disorders, depression, dissociative disorders, somatization disorder, premenstrual dysphoric syndrome, and agoraphobia.

Many symptoms associated with the aforementioned disorders have been conceptualized as exaggerations or stereotyping of traditional female gender roles and behaviours (as defined by mainstream culture) (e.g., overreacting emotionally, attempting to sexually attract men and to preserve romantic relationships at all costs, and placating others by internalizing, denying or inefficiently expressing anger). Misdiagnosis can also occur when a client's problem behaviours are inconsistent with societal expectations such as when an Asian woman, assumed by stereotype to be meek, reacts to discrimination with anger.

In another example, Crosby and Sprock found that when clinicians rated a case of a woman with antisocial symptoms, they were more likely to exhibit biases that were consistent with relying on prototypes (i.e., stereotypes regarding diagnostic categories) rather than actual diagnostic criteria. There is ample evidence that poverty and economic inequality are strong predictors of depression in women. African-American women are more likely to be diagnosed with schizophrenia than White women. Issues of gender identity have been viewed as pathology rather than an alternate form of gender and sexual expression.

In addition, the specific needs and problems of girls may be overlooked and under diagnosed because of girls are more likely than boys to internalize problems or to express problems with less overt symptoms, a problem that may be even more serious if the girl is also from a marginalized group. For example, girls with attention deficit disorders exhibit fewer disruptive behaviour problems than boys but have been found to suffer more severe cognitive disabilities. Problems that coexist with ADHD may also differ for girls and boys and across SES and ethnic groups, further complicating the diagnostic process. Under identification of attention problems in girls appears related to fewer teacher referrals, yet attention problems are associated with lower self-esteem and more frequent peer rejection for girls than for boys.

Inaccurate conceptualization of diagnoses can also be influenced by sampling biases. These biases can occur when diagnostic criteria or prevalence rates are based primarily on symptoms studied only in clinical contexts or are based on empirical studies of a disorder that include the biased representation of males or females, single sex participants, or one ethnic group. Such practices may lead to inaccurate prevalence rates, biased assessment instruments, biased thresholds for diagnosis, and diagnostic criteria that do not reflect the diversity of symptoms that may be associated with a disorder. Hartung and Widiger identified potential gender sampling biases associated with diagnostic categories such as histrionic personality disorder, conduct disorder, somatization disorder, gender identity disorder, and dependent personality disorder.

Problems in diagnosis and tr eatment may occur when the literature on a particular problem is based primarily on a sample of only men and boys, women and girls, or predominantly one ethnic group, and then generalized to all clients. Other data suggest that women and men of colour are more likely to receive psychopharmacological treatment only rather than psychotherapy. Addiction and alcohol dependence research has often been based on male samples and generalized to all clients. However, women and girls metabolize alcohol differently, experience impairment or intoxication after fewer drinks, are at greater risk of dying from alcohol-related incidents, experience more rapid negative consequences of alcohol abuse, and are less likely than men to seek assistance from addiction-specific treatment settings.

Empirical findings have shown gender differences in rates of diagnosis, differential responses to treatment, and differing barriers to treatment for women versus men. There are also gender differences in treatment outcomes and predictors for methamphetamine, cocaine, opiates, and tobacco dependence. Research on criminal behaviour has overly focused on African

American men as subjects. Many assessment instruments have been critiqued for bias that pathologizes people of colour, female trauma survivors, individuals with disabilities, persons with strong religious convictions, sexual minorities, older adults, and those from lower socioeconomic classes and other countries. The unique biological, social, and psychological realities of persons with diverse social identities point to the value of considering how gender and other social identities may affect the expression of a disorder.

Trauma and other Stressors

One important diagnostic issue is found in Posttraumatic Stress Disorder. Despite the greater prevalence and chronicity of PTSD among females, the construct is based on data from male combat veteran experiences, resulting in measurement problems that can affect both research and practice. For example, girls and women may be diagnosed with other Axis I and Axis II disorders when they experience trauma symptoms that do not fit the traditional PTSD profile. Further, women and girls may be misdiagnosed with more stigmatizing and chronic disorders (e.g., borderline personality disorder or schizophrenia) than are men with posttraumatic conditions. Women of colour may experience additional trauma from multiple experiences with discrimination and oppression that lead to further misdiagnosis that does not take into account context.

The experience of African American women with intergenerational trauma and the ongoing effects of a history of slavery have generally not been considered in the diagnosis of trauma. In addition, men and women may experience trauma differently and may respond more effectively to different treatment approaches due to the type of traumas they are likely to encounter; potential differences in neurobiological stress pathways; and cultural and gender socialization experiences that influence self-concept, expectations, and meaning systems and whether the stressor is chronic or a single event stressor.

The Resolution on Male Violence against Women (APA,

2005) notes that more than 20% of women are physically assaulted by a partner and approximately 12% experience sexual assault at sometime in their lives. The effects of these traumatizing events are compounded by ethnicity/race, social class, physical ability, and sexual orientation as the likelihood of assault increases for marginalized groups. Trauma is an important area to consider in more detail because a high proportion of girls and women of all ethnic, SES, sexual orientation, and ability status are exposed to traumatic stressors and their mental health may be severely affected. It should also be noted that psychologists may not be trained to work specifically with trauma survivors, which can reduce the effectiveness of the treatment survivors receive. Not only are a high proportion of women (69%) exposed to a traumatic stressor in their lifetime, women are more than twice as likely as men to develop chronic PTSD symptoms following exposure to a traumatic stressor. Rape and domestic violence seem to account for higher prevalence of trauma in girls and women of all ethnic groups, and survivors have high rates of PTSD. In the 1998 National Violence against Women Survey, 25% of women and 8% of men reported being raped or physically assaulted by a spouse, partner, or date in their lifetime; men perpetrated approximately 90% of this violence. Girls are also raped. Child sexual abuse happens two to two-and-one-half times more often to girls than boys.

Such abuse not only results in immediate psychological symptoms, but also lifetime risk for self-destructive or suicidal behaviour, anxiety and panic attacks, eating disorders, substance abuse, somatization disorder, and sexual adjustment disorders. Rates of childhood sexual abuse are similar for Black, White, Hispanic, and Native American women. Although sexual assault traumas are experienced by women of diverse social identities across the lifespan, the specific issues and challenges of girls and women vary. For example, the presence of stereotyped images of Black women can exacerbate the psychological after effects of rape, can contribute to the marginalization of their concerns, and may increase the likelihood of holding victims responsible for their own assault.

Partner abuse occurs in married, unmarried, lesbian and gay couples, but most of the abuse occurs in heterosexual couples of all ethnic groups and SES level where the woman is at the greatest risk for injury. Battered women have expressed dissatisfaction with mental health treatment and the sensitivity of their therapists and a preference for relying on friends and family. Psychology training programs are not required to provide training in domestic violence and partner abuse, and few do, despite evidence that gender-sensitive training improves attitudes towards and knowledge about women in therapy.

The APA Intimate Partner Abuse and Relationship Violence Working Group (2002c) recently recommended the need for specific training in domestic violence. They stated:...we suggest that those involved in partner violence have special treatment needs and that those who treat them must do so with sensitivity and from a base of knowledge that comes from specialized training. Psychologists who do not have the requisite training potentially endanger their clients, and likely commit an ethical violation. Those who are teaching psychologists-to-be but who do not teach them about partner violence are abrogating their responsibility and risk perpetuating the conditions which foster this problem.

Treatment and Prognosis

Recent research has demonstrated that some therapists and trainees expect a more positive prognosis with male clients, still stereotype women as expressive, and take a more instrumental behavioural approach with men. They may have even lower expectations of outcomes for women of colour, lesbians, and women with disabilities. In addition, studies have found that therapists as a whole interrupt female client's more than male clients. They also may use interventions that do not consider the client's cultural background or ability level. Practitioners also may not perceive the specific external stresses and context of the lives of women and girl and instead emphasize endogenous and/or intrapsychic factors inappropriately and/or detrimentally including not taking into account issues of discrimination and oppression based upon social groupings. Furthermore, some members of the medical and psychological communities have noted that women's physical illnesses contain psychological components that are not expected in men and that gender bias is manifested in advertisements for psychotropic medications and the high use of psychotropic medication prescribed for women.

Inattention to contextual factors may contribute to the lack of recognition of problems of women and girls such as battering and other forms of victimization. Inattention to contextual factors also contribute to lack of recognition of the physical and mental health consequences of battering and other forms of violence. An example is the lack of recognition of traumatic brain injury despite knowledge of the high proportion of injuries to the face, head, and neck during battering. It may also contribute to the under diagnosis of or double standards about problems such as alcohol abuse, and the effects of discrimination on stress and performance.

For instance, research has found that high school girls expect more educational and career barriers than high school boys and perceived barriers (e.g., discrimination) are especially likely if girls are also members of an ethnic minority group. Psychologists may also lack awareness regarding the particular strengths and resources of women and girls that help them deal with stressful issues. For example, many women and girls of colour in the United States live in extended families that create larger communities that provide additional support for their growth and development.

Culture, Ethnicity, and Other Diversities

Another area of gender bias in psychological practice concerns inattention to the ways in which culture and ethnicity influence problems such as depression and schizophrenia in women and girls. Research has demonstrated that therapist insensitivity to racial stereotypes, the interaction of race and gender, cultural values and mores, and social and economic conditions have an impact on women and girls who live in poverty and women and girls of colour. Lesbian relationships and partnerships may also be pathologized through the description of lesbian relationships by terms such as "merged," "fused," or "enmeshed". Social stressors and discrimination from membership in marginalized groups can lead to a variety of internal and external problems.

Sexual Misconduct/abuse by Psychologists

Perhaps the most blatant example of gender bias and abuse in psychological practice occurs when a clinician violates ethical standards in sexual relationships with clients. Despite the APA's *Ethical Principles and Code of Conduct* (APA, 2002), other ethical codes, and increasing awareness through education and training, power abuses, including sexual relationships, still occur in therapy and training. Research indicates that the overwhelming majority of psychologists who have violated professional sexual ethical standards were middle-aged men who had sex with younger female clients. This problem has not only the potential to interfere with treatment efficacy, it also renders women and girls more vulnerable to stress and traumatization.

Women with disabilities

Women with disabilities span across every ethnicity, gender, sexual orientation, SES, and age ever known. One of every five Americans has a disability. Thus, it can be estimated that women with disabilities comprise approximately 10% of our nation's population. It is evident by this statistic that persons with disabilities, particularly women of colour with disabilities, have less access to and availability of mental health services.

Moreover, children with disabilities are a distinct high risk group for abuse and neglect and are, on average, two to three times more likely to be maltreated in their homes and in institutions than are children without disabilities. Beyond increase risk for abuse and neglect, persons with disabilities traditionally have experienced systematic institutional victimization from all aspects of society including, but not limited to, the medical profession, the educational system, and the workforce.

This victimization of women with disabilities, particularly women of colour with disabilities, is especially prevalent. However, disability, gender, and/or culture do not reside solely in a vacuum, and individuals from each social group face struggles within society. Women of colour with disabilities experience simultaneous oppression within society by belonging to three or more marginalized groups (e.g., gender, race/ethnicity, disability, sexual orientation, SES). Persons of colour with disabilities are more likely to have lower educational levels, higher unemployment, and lower incomes. Moreover, these individuals are faced with having to choose which marginalized identity is most salient in what time frame, which can, in it, lead to internal conflicts.

In addition, an individual can be an oppressor, a member of an oppressed group, or simultaneously an oppressor and oppressed, adding to their psychological stress. As the layers begin to mount (e.g., societal attitudes, lower income, physical access, physical pain, accommodating others with being accommodated) the importance of practitioners knowing how to deliver disability and culturally competent treatment becomes evident. The need is overwhelming and only likely to grow. Section 2.01(b) of the APA Ethics Code (APA, 2002b) supports an affirmative need for the profession to develop disability-related competence to deliver optimal care.

2

Contemporary Social Forces

Gender related and multicultural issues relevant to practice will change as the broader socio-cultural context changes. Good practice requires that psychologists remain abreast of new developments in contemporary social forces and their interaction with gender and other social identities. There are many contemporary issues that could be cited here, however, four particularly salient and recent examples include the increasing prevalence of global terrorism, violence, and war in which women are particularly victimized by vulnerability to rape, assault and poverty; the effects of the media in popular culture that portrays an image of woman as thin, white, sexualized, and victimized; bio-psychosocial realities and changes relevant to women's reproductive experiences; and the phenomenon of increasing lifespan with an aging population that consists mostly of women.

Terrorism and War

A contemporary issue that directly affects the welfare and physical and mental health of girls and women of all ethnic/racial groups is terrorism and war. Violence against women and girls is recognized as a global problem. Women and girls suffer the consequences of violence in war through rape, abuse, torture, and the loss of economic security. Violence against women continues as the threat of terrorism and war across the world does not abate. Literature that addresses psychological responses to the effects of terrorism and other traumatic incidents suggests that individuals, both adults and children, who directly experience traumatic incidents that involve perceived threat or actual experience of harm to physical integrity often report symptoms of either acute stress disorder or post-traumatic stress disorder (PTSD) which may be exacerbated if they have suffered earlier trauma in the form of ongoing oppression or discrimination based upon their ethnicity, SES, sexual orientation, ability, etc. Mood disorders, adjustment disorders, phobias and other conditions may also be psychological sequelae for parents and children.

Media

In discussing the influence of contemporary forces, mention must be made of the increasingly powerful presence of the media in modern life. For example, although the terrorist attacks on the United States of 9/11 were confined to the Northeast, many Americans vicariously experienced and observed the horrific events through continuous media exposure. Media coverage of the 2001 terrorist attacks generally emphasized men as victims and experts, rendering women and girls nearly invisible and relegating them to stereotypical support and victim roles. There was brief mention made of the sense of some African Americans that the 2001 terrorist attacks were isolated incidents, differing significantly from ongoing community violence and localized terrorism experienced by African Americans in many urban settings. Media coverage of school shootings has often neglected to emphasize or mention that the perpetrators of the broadcast violence are usually men and boys, with some evidence that misogyny may be one causative factor. The websites of the APA and the National Association of School Psychologists (NASP), among others, provided abundant materials for psychologists and the public to deal with the traumatization of children that might result from watching the repeated news broadcasts related to the planes hitting the

World Trade Center buildings. In general, the media has become an enormously powerful influence regarding access to information; exposure to violence; and conveyor of cultural stereotypes regarding gender, race, ethnicity, and sexual orientation. The media plays a major role in shaping contemporary values and attitudes. As an increasingly important social influence in our society, television often presents idealized images of women that are stereotyped and distorted by emphasizing youth, extreme thinness, and sexuality as well as negative racial, ethnic, and economic stereotypes. There is a large incidence of eating disorders among girls and young women in Western society. Research on the effects of media images and body image disturbance finds that in some young girls and women, increased media attention to the appearance of females on television and in advertising leads to an increased preoccupation with weight, shape, and appearance which varies widely by ethnic groups with the most impact on White and Asian women and less on African American women.

Media images of poor women represent another area of research of importance for practitioners. Women and their children are the largest group of poor individuals in this country, and gender and ethnic stereotypes about poor women can influence both the clinician and the client. Bullock, Wyche, and Williams (2001) found that while print media is sympathetic to poor women, the structural causes of poverty are not discussed. Hence, women, and particularly women of colour, may be blamed for their poverty status. The limitations of the media coverage of poor women as well as a wide variety of constantly changing socio-cultural context factors and their interaction with gender have the potential to affect practice.

Biopsychosocial Aspects of Reproduction

Although reproduction has always been relevant to the lives of girls and women but the recent social developments have also contributed to the significant changes in the complexity and biopsychosocial meanings of reproduction. As the social roles and pressures experienced by girls and women have expanded, the timing of events related to menarche and childbearing have changed. Reproductive technologies and reproductive medical interventions have become more available and sophisticated, and attitudes toward reproductive choice have also changed. From the onset of menstruation, young girls and women are faced with the biological realities of reproduction.

Menarche is associated with a variety of physiological, psychological, and social meanings and changes including changes in appearance beliefs, body image, self-esteem, and peer relationships as well gains and losses in social power, as for instance in ethnic groups in which menarche is seen as a marker of adulthood. The diverse social identities of girls are also related to perceptions of menarche. Although White girls have shown higher depression scores after menarche, no menarche-associated differences have been found in African-American and Hispanic girls. Although a relationship between the timing of menarche and psychological distress is not consistently found, early menarche has been associated with elevated depressive symptoms, eating problems, and substance use and abuse.

As girls mature and gain more body fat at puberty, girls' bodies are less likely to conform to an increasingly thin cultural body ideal. Perceived pressure to be thin and the internalization of a "thin ideal" have been associated with body dissatisfaction or negative body image and depressive and eating disordered symptoms, particularly for White and Asian girls, hence, the biological event of menarche may influence attitudes toward the body. However, those girls who were socialized to think of menarche as a natural event and/or a positive affirmation of womanhood, which is more likely in African American culture, have reported positive experiences. There is also evidence that college women perceive menstruating women as being stronger, more maternal, and more trustworthy. Similarly, issues associated with reproduction and childbirth can evoke a range of feelings from joy to fear in women and girls. Today, women have a greater freedom of choice regarding whether to become a parent and how they want to manage pregnancy and childbirth than they did decades ago. Most women consider pregnancy to be a very positive and joyful experience despite physical and hormonal changes and describe feeling more fulfilled when pregnant as they think about another life growing inside them; however these feelings are not universal. Some feelings of joy that emerge during pregnancy are associated with fantasizing about the future child, experiencing an altered state of being, and imagining a happy and unified family.

Childbirth can also be a biological and psychosocial stressor. An important aspect of pregnancy and childbirth is the evidence of increased violence toward women during pregnancy, particularly Black women. There is also increasing societal concern for the effects of postpartum depression after several high profile cases of women suffering from postpartum depression killing their children. Postpartum depression is characterized by extreme sadness, fatigue, loss of interest in the baby and other aspects of life, and feelings of despair, and women who lack social and/or financial support are particularly at risk for its effects. It affects about 10-15% of women, usually developing six months after the birth, and may last for several months.

Feminists have strongly critiqued a medical care system that does not provide appropriate care and protection for such mothers. While some women experience symptoms of stress and depression in childbirth, other women recognize their personal power, and positively integrate new aspects of identity as a mother. Parenthood can be considered as a developmental stage of both women and men who wish to be parents. Sexually transmitted diseases are a growing societal concern, particularly among girls and adolescents. Women are more vulnerable to STDs than men, and women are more likely to be infected from a single sexual encounter with STDs producing few detectable symptoms.

Women and girls suffer the most severe consequences of STDs, including infertility. Menopause is a biological phenomenon that had been largely ignored until the 1990s. Societal assumptions that menopause is commonly associated with depression, irritability, and mood swings have been refuted as have medical accounts that treated menopause as a deficiency disease. Overemphasis on a biomedical model of menopause has lead to a picture of decline and degeneration rather than the more accurate findings of generally increased and broadened interests in life and greater self-confidence. Voluntary childlessness and desire for an abortion may also be choices for some women.

In the case of abortion, pre-abortion levels of optimism, personal control perceptions, and high self-esteem are related to better post-abortion adjustment. Although motherhood is often viewed as desirable, joyful, and fulfilling, a view which varies by ethnic group and SES, satisfying female gender roles are not necessarily linked with motherhood. Individuals who choose not to be parents may cope with social pressures and negative stereotypes (e.g., selfish or desperate) in various ways, including the use of a new more positive term to reflect their status: "childfree".

Many women and couples who wish to conceive children are unable to do so. Such women and couples must confront fertility issues and experience loss, grief, and mourning due to reproductive challenges. Changes in attitudes and practices toward adoption are also relevant. Also, although early literature on adoption focused on negative experiences in adoptive children and ignored the common practice in some ethnic groups (e.g., African American) of extended family adoption, more recent research is focusing on the full adoption "triad" (i.e., adoptees, birthparents, and adoptive parents) and on both positive and negative aspects of the experience.

Recent research on maturation and change regarding reproductive capacities reveals that these aspects of women's and girls' identities, bodies, and lives are associated with both strengths and potential problems. The research cited in this section suggests that an integrated biopsychosocial approach to understanding both the resources and difficulties that all girls and women experience in many aspects of their lives is likely to contribute to positive psychological practice.

Elderly Women

Our society has an increasing proportion of older individuals, and since significantly fewer men than women survive into very old age (80s, 90s and beyond), the elderly in our society are primarily women. Women are more subject to problems with financial resources, racial and ethnic bias, and bias against individuals with any specific disability associated with aging. The typical victim of elder abuse is a woman over 75. Few psychologists have taken courses in aging as part of their professional training. By the year 2030 older adults are expected to account for nearly one fourth of the population. Since women tend to marry older men and live longer than men, and men are more likely to remarry, many older women are widows and single.

Single rates are even higher for African American women who may depend more upon extended family for support than a spouse. Hence, older women are single than older men. Older women are affected by poverty or low financial security, special health issues, and belonging to a disenfranchised or marginalized group. In addition, more negative stereotypes of aging have been directed toward women than men (e.g., witch, hag, and crone). In fact, psychologists are more likely to rate older women as less competitive, less competent, less assertive, and less willing to take risks than young women.

Culture also affects the view of the aging process. For example, in cultures or subcultures in which older women are valued as mature and wise (e.g., some Native American tribes), older women may experience positive effects including new freedoms and renewed sexuality. Elderly African American women have been found to be active in community organizations such as a church and closely involved in the lives of their grandchildren.

Many members of both the profession and the public are not aware of the benefits of aging for women in the United States including feeling freer of gender role stereotypes and gendered roles. On average, women experience more years of good health than men; however, they are also more likely to live with chronic illnesses such as chronic fatigue syndrome, fibromyalgia, arthritis, thyroid conditions, migraine headaches, anemia and urinary incontinence. These factors have an impact on the psychological identity and lifestyle of women. Older women can be especially at risk for depression and alcohol problems because they are more likely than men to outlive their spouses and to face other losses that can lead to loneliness and depression.

This effect is less likely for women, such as African American women or others from communal cultures, who have depended upon extended family systems for their life-span. Women are also at greater risk for alcohol-related health problems as they age such as harmful medication interactions, injury, liver and cardiovascular disease, cognitive changes and sleep and memory problems. As women age, outlive their spouses, and experience increasing dependency and mental and physical health issues, their primary caregivers also tend to be women, many of whom try to balance caring for both their children and elderly parents or parents-in-law while in full-time employment.

Numerous studies have indicated that caregivers experience significant emotional, physical and financial stresses. These issues have caused such concern among psychologists that APA has endorsed and published a separate set of guidelines for older adults (APA, 2004a). These introductory pages have provided a foundation for both establishing a public need for these *Guidelines for Psychological Practice with Girls and Women* for girls and women of all social groups and the evidence of their variable, and too often, inappropriate treatment. Issues that need to be addressed include bias in diagnosis and treatment, differences in environmental stressors and trauma, and the multiple diversity intersections of ethnicity, age, sexual orientation, SES, and disability.

Psychological Perspectives on Sexual Orientation

The unavoidable increased interaction with the nation's diverse populations, the profit -driven aggressive marketing of all manner of goods and services to the nation's 'growth demographics' – which increasingly are dominated by people of colour, and the increased tolerance associated with the breakdown of isolation and boundaries among nations, cultures, and social groups, all serve to promote the social-psychological concept of 'multiple identity groups' as one that popular culture views as almost hip and chic. Ambiguity of race, ethnicity, gender, and sexual orientation increasingly is peddled as an entry level requirement for 'the beautiful people'. But of course, in reality, issues of multiple identify are far less glamorous and far more complex.

In this Special Section, we are pleased to present a series of brief articles/essays that examine, through a psychological prism, the meaning and challenges of sexual orientation in communities of colour. Specifically we seek to promote better understanding of the cultural variations in both the meaning given to lesbian and gay status, and the unique issues confronting both ethnic minority communities related to sexual orientation, and lesbian and gay persons of colour. For example, our multicultural counseling theories inform us of the high value most communities of colour place on family connectedness, religiosity/spirituality, and respect for elders.

Political and social scientists inform us that many communities of colour can be characterized as 'socially conservative' and politically liberal'. Community and social psychologists often emphasize the positive and negative effects of the stigma, oppression, marginality, disempower-ment and limited resources that to varying degrees characterize communities of colour. The authors in this Special Section dissect the challenges presented to lesbian and gay persons of colour by these and other characteristics of communities of colour, as well as those challenges presented by the issues of power, privilege, and social domination that often characterized majority White community settings and populations.

The Rock of Ethno-racial Identity and the Hard Place of Heterosexism

This section considers the lives of lesbians and gay men of colour as a distinct heterogeneous group that contributes to the diversity of people of colour. Lesbians and gay men of colour are a large heterogeneous group that is represented in all locations on the spectrum of ethnicity, age, social class, disability, religious and spiritual orientations, sex and gender roles. Lesbians and gay men's ethnic group membership and sexual orientation are only two of the multiple identities that group members have however all of their identities will influence their experience of being lesbian or gay person of colour in a racist and heterosexist society. Like their heterosexual counterparts, their identities are shaped by both dominant cultural imperatives, dynamics unique to their families and their relationships, as well as the cultural practices and values associated with their ethno cultural group membership. However, lesbians and gay men of colour are often invisible in the psychological literature, as well as in popular media representations of both communities of colour and lesbian and gay communities. More often than not, lesbians and gay men as a group are selectively represented by members of the dominant culture who tend to be better educated and have higher incomes than is the norm even for lesbians and gay men as well as for people of colour. Hence lesbians and gay men often appear to people of colour to be a group that is predominantly white, male and economically well off. In research, this can be a function of selecting those who are easiest to find in what has been regarded as a hidden population.

As long as people are punished for being lesbian or gay, many will not divulge that aspect of their identity to others as well as themselves; nor will they attend gatherings where their presence would identify them as lesbian or gay. For lesbians and gay men of colour there is the clear risk of losing family and community support, essential to surviving racism, if they are "out" as lesbian or gay in their ethnic communities. Furthermore, limited depictions of lesbian and gay identities fuel views of lesbians and gay men as an affluent group that is undeserving of protection from discrimination and harassment. Minority sexual orientation comes to be seen as a chosen inconvenience when compared to the protracted and systemic hardship of racism. Such views however understate the realistic magnitude of the harm done to lesbians and gay men of colour by heterosexist attitudes and practices. People of colour have long histories of discrimination and are aware on a personal level of its corrosive and toxic effects. It would seem that they would be less likely to adopt heterosexist values and practices whose rationales and mechanisms for enforcement are alarmingly similar. It is not only permissible to discriminate against lesbians and gay men, in some cases it is legally required, not unlike practices that have historically targeted people of colour, women, people with disabilities and others. However, many people of colour resent the comparison between racism and heterosexism in part because of their history of having their struggles with racism appropriated when it is convenient for majority identified persons to do so, and then abandoned by majority persons when it becomes difficult or when they are rewarded for their silence about racism.

These views are reinforced by the diminished visibility of lesbians and gay men of colour as the "gay community" is seen as "white" and by definition more privileged than people of colour. Such beliefs among people of colour may be understandable but they actively contribute to intensifying the hostile environment faced by lesbians and gay men of colour as well as the harm done to them. Such practices weaken rather than solidify communities of colour and display the failure to grasp the unique challenges faced by the lesbians and gay men of colour in their own communities and among their own families. Just as lesbians and gay men are presented as if they are all white and affluent, people of colour are presented as if they are all heterosexual.

Research on members of ethnic minority groups across a range of areas rarely acknowledges differences in the sexual orientation of group members. Lesbian and gay men and women of colour may find their ethnic communities to be a very different experience of "home" than their heterosexual counterparts. The relative invisibility of lesbians and gay men of colour in the psychological literature as well as in media representations has a range of negative consequences. For people of colour who need to deny their presence among group members, their relative invisibility can make it easy to do so and facilitate the pathologizing of those who choose to be visible. Another negative consequence of their invisibility is that there is no exploration of the complex interaction between sexual orientation and ethnic identity development. The realistic consequence of membership in more than one socially marginalized and disparaged group is an important component of gay and lesbian and ethnic identity formation.

The complexity of identity formation is not adequately taken into account in attempts to understand the lives of both lesbians and gay men or people of colour in ways that accurately represent the full range of diversity of both groups as well as the overlap between them. For example, understanding the vicissitudes of racism and ethnoracial identity in intra- and interracial couples of the same sex and its effect on their relationships is not possible in the context of a narrow focus on heterosexual relationships that is found in the literature on relationships and couples therapy among people of colour. There is an equally narrow focus on predominantly white couples and relationships in the gay and lesbian literature.

When lesbians and gay men of colour are included in research it is in such small numbers as to hardly be representative or they become a focus of attention only when the discussion turns to HIV treatment and prevention efforts and men on the "down-low". For example, when men on the "down -low" are viewed as the chief causative factor in rising rates of HIV infection in Black communities, other likely sources of infection that are a function of heterosexual relationships and drug use do not receive the attention that is warranted in an epidemic of a such serious proportions. To compound the bias inherent in such research, published studies lacking representative numbers of lesbian and gay people of colour as participants rarely state the limited generalizability of their findings to either heterosexual people of colour, or to white lesbians and/or gay men, nor do the titles of those papers specify the group the study actually represents.

When this occurs it perpetuates the problem of presenting data on dominant group members as if it were representative or as if it should be considered normative. The invisibility of lesbian and gay men of colour in research on psychotherapy leaves practitioners ill equipped to address their clinical needs with cultural sensitivity, literacy and competence. Responses to and perceptions of lesbian and gay men and women of colour will vary depending on the individual dynamics and characteristics of the family in the broader context of their ethno racial group membership and, for some group members, the social climate during the course of their development.

These are but a few of the factors that influence what are perceived to be appropriate gender roles, sexual behaviours and attractions, who is family and who is not, and a host of other issues that affect the experience of lesbians and gay men of colour. Families may also be influenced by their religious or spiritual beliefs which may also vary as a function of their ethnic group membership. There is a wide range of diversity among people of colour in the religious denominations they belong to and the degree to which any given denomination is more or less homophobic. What is important to remember is that they are not homogeneous.

While religious and spiritual values can shape attitudes toward lesbian and gay people of colour, those values and proscriptions are not absolute determinants of those attitudes. Religious beliefs are always interpreted within a cultural context. When the context is heterosexist, sexist, racist, or classcist, scriptural text is often interpreted in manner that is consistent with the prevailing dominant cultural status quo.

However, most people of colour are affiliated with religious groups that have a history of either an active articipation in or endorsement of racist ideology and practices, or of at the very least failing to challenge such practices at times that represented the height of persecution of group members. People of colour in faith communities have demonstrated an ability to separate aspects of religious teachings that could be used to support racism and their exploitation from others that have been useful in developing liberation theology in their struggles with racism.

Those who wish to embrace the broader spiritual doctrine that encourages the use of religious belief to bring family and community together despite differences or conflicts can clearly use such beliefs to do so.

However they may also use those beliefs in the service of splitting, scapegoating and persecuting members of society who are unpopular, elicit discomfort or for whom there is a desire to exploit. Religious values therefore should be scrutinized for how they are used against any vulnerable population rather than simply what certain scriptures may literally espouse. When they are used to harm they cannot be considered benign or infallible.

Other factors to consider in understanding lesbians and gay men of colour more fully include the degree of acculturation or assimilation of the individual or family into the dominant vs. ethnic culture, and the history of discrimination or oppression which the particular group has experienced from members of the dominant culture. Another important dimension is that of sexuality. Sexuality and its meaning is contextual.

Therefore what it means to be a gay man or lesbian will be related to the meaning assigned to sexuality in the culture. It will be important to explore the range of sexuality which is sanctioned, in what forms it may be expressed and by whom, and the consequences for compliance or failure to comply.

An exploration of the role of ethnic stereotypes in the creation of sexual mythologies about ethnic group members is another important part of this inquiry. Despite similarities in the histories of members of ethnic minority groups, generalized descriptions of their cultural practices may never be applied with uniformity across the spectrum of people of colour, nor to all members within any ethnic group. While there is much diversity between ethnic groups and the dominant culture, there is great diversity within them. Practitioners will need to explore every client's cultural heritage in the context of the client's experience and uniqueness.

Three Types of Research

Causal Research

When most people think of scientific experimentation, research on cause and effect is most often brought to mind. Experiments on causal relationships investigate the effect of one or more variables on one or more outcome variables. This type of research also determines if one variable causes another variable to occur or change. An example of this type of research would be altering the amount of a treatment and measuring the effect on study participants.

Descriptive Research

Descriptive research seeks to depict what already exists in a group or population. An example of this type of research would be an opinion poll to determine which Presidential candidate people plan to vote for in the next election. Descriptive studies do not seek to measure the effect of a variable; they seek only to describe.

Relational Research

A study that investigates the connection between two or more variables is considered relational research. The variables that are compared are generally already present in the group or population. For example, a study that looked at the proportion of males and females that would purchase either a classical CD or a jazz CD would be studying the relationship between gender and music preference.

Theory and Hypothesis

A theory is a well-established principle that has been developed to explain some aspect of the natural word. A theory arises from repeated observation and testing and incorporates facts, laws, predictions, and tested hypotheses that are widely accepted.

A hypothesis is a specific, testable prediction about what you expect to happen in your study. For example, a study designed to look at the relationship between study habits and test anxiety might have a hypothesis that states, "This study is designed to assess the hypothesis that students with better study habits will suffer less test anxiety." Unless your study is exploratory in nature, your hypothesis should always explain what you expect to happen during the course of your experiment or research.

While the terms are sometimes used interchangeably in general practice, the difference between a theory and a hypothesis is important when studying experimental design. Some important distinctions to note include:

- A theory predicts events in general terms, while a hypothesis makes a specific prediction about a specified set of circumstances.
- A theory is has been extensively tested and is generally accepted, while a hypothesis is a speculative guess that has yet to be tested.

Effect of Time in Psychology Research

There are two types of time dimensions that can be used in designing a research study.

1. Cross-sectional research takes place at a single point in time.
    - All tests, measures, or variables are administered to participants on one occasion.
    - This type of research seeks to gather data on present conditions instead of looking at the effects of a variable over a period of time.
2. Longitudinal research is a study that takes place over a period of time.
    - Data is first collected at the outset of the study, and may then be gathered repeatedly throughout the length of the study.
    - Some longitudinal studies may occur over a short period of time, such as a few days, while others may take place over a period of decades.
    - The effects of aging are often investigated using longitudinal research.

Feminist Perspectives on Collaborative Research and Action

In their commitment to reflection on the processes and methodologies used to create and apply knowledge, feminist geographers have devoted considerable attention to the politics of research, emphasizing such issues as reflexivity, relations with 'subjects,' representation, and voice, particularly to concerns about power. Most research questions continue to be defined by the single researcher, and publications to appear in a single authorial voice. Nevertheless, some feminist geographers have discussed how they involved community women in shaping research agendas and collecting data, and a few have taken up questions of collaboration with research assistants. In this chapter, we introduce additional considerations that arise when collaboration involves partnerships between researchers and community organizations and/or cross-national partnerships.

Drawing on our experiences with colleagues and community health agencies at the Mexico-U.S. border, we consider themes of differences in conceptual and methodological orientations, access to resources, expectations about publication of results, and modes of communication. In the process, we reflect on motivations, building relationships of trust, the importance of flexibility, institutional reward systems, and 'turf.'

We invite readers to reflect on how such issues can be particularly construed from feminist perspectives. Methodological issues clearly generate much interest in feminist geography. Over the years, our attention has emphasized the politics of research, power relations, and ethics, particularly relationships between the researcher and the researched, issues of positionality, reflexivity, representation, what it means to be 'in the field,' the places of qualitative and quantitative research, and the significance of context.

The geographic work draws on and complements feminist literature from other disciplines, such as the works by Haraway (1988), Harding (1987), Oakley (2000), Roberts (1981), Maynard and Purvis (1994), and Wolf (1996). We will not review this substantial literature but will rather turn to a theme that we consider being still, and somewhat surprisingly, under explored: perspectives on collaboration. 'Collaboration' has become something of a buzz word in agencies that fund three types of work - international research, projects that link universities and communities, and programs designed by community services agencies to address complex, interrelated problems. However, beyond the priorities of funding agencies, we see collaboration as consistent with long-standing feminist goals of challenging hierarchical relationships and of conducting research that is directed toward changing society. As academics who have been engaged in the Transborder Consortium for Research and Action on Gender and Health at the Mexico-U.S. Border for the last several years, we are interested in examining what collaboration means both conceptually and empirically. This chapter is a beginning effort in that direction. Our interest in collaboration spans several levels - among researchers who are working in multi-person projects, in relationships that cross national and disciplinary boundaries, and in those that link researchers and workers in community agencies. We also think that more consideration should be given to the roles of players in the research endeavour other than the principal scholar(s). These include people who, to varying degrees and in diverse ways, serve as facilitators and/or gatekeepers of our endeavours - research assistants, librarians, clerical staff, editors, reviewers, and funding agency personnel.

A few feminist scholars have drawn attention to some aspects of such working relationships. Huntley and Logan examine gender dynamics in a multi-disciplinary project, including those within the team and with the project sponsors; Gaskell and Eichler reflect on their relations as foreign "experts" in a project with Chinese women academics and Kelly *et al* engage in a conversation about their inter-personal relations as senior researcher, junior research fellow, and administrative assistant in a research team. In the paper that follows we first review existing feminist geographic writing that addresses processes of collaboration, then turn to literature from other fields that explores meanings of the concept.

We next use our experiences in the Transborder Consortium as a case study to explore the evolution and challenges of a collaborative endeavour that crosses national and university-community boundaries. By and large, feminist geographic research continues the male tradition of the discipline in which research questions are defined by a single scholar and published in a single authorial voice. Yet even in those research and teaching works that are co-authored, we have noted that discussions of positionality and methodology, either by intent or default, are often presented as individual accounts, while discussion of collaborative processes is brief or missing. Two examples serve to illustrate this point. In the Women and Geography Study Group collaboratively-authored text (1997), one short paragraph is devoted to the 'hows' of the collaboration among the authors, but ten individual accounts explore how they came to feminist geography in order to demonstrate the significance of context and 'difference' in shaping scholarship.

In their co-authored research volume, Linda Peake and Alissa Trotz devote several pages of their chapter on methodology and reflexivity to separate, parallel accounts. They note that they constantly interacted with each other in the writing process, and that their work involved members of Guyanese women's organizations in several key capacities, including serving as interviewers and as reviewers of draft questionnaires. Though Peake and Trotz provide an insightful account of how their own "racialised and national identities and subsequent (never fixed) positions on the sliding scale of insider/outsider" shaped differences in their individual work, they do not elaborate on how their interactions mediated the research as a whole or influenced their interpretations of material collected by others.

A few pieces by feminist geographers do reveal more about collaboration and group methods. Most attention thus far has been paid to the implications of working with research assistants. Susan Hanson and Geraldine Pratt acknowledge that their student research assistants cannot be regarded as interchangeable bodies in their relations with subjects and that interviewers are neither passive nor transparent conduits of information, but rather are engaged in conversational performances which have implications for the ways in which questions are interpreted and answered. They report that their assistants challenged the project directors' interpretations and research practices, though assistants also acknowledge that experiences of working in the project affected their own developing research interests.

Louise Johnson, situating her remarks within the context of the increasing pressures in Australian universities to conduct externally-funded team research, reveals her anxieties as a socialist feminist of being placed in an employer-employee relation with research assistants. She reflects on the difficulties of knowing whom to hire, how to supervise, and most especially, her concerns over the boundaries between employer-employee versus collegial relations with a research assistant.

She asks to whom the projects do and data belong and laments the loss of both the pleasures and stresses of doing one's own work in the field. Isabel Dyck, Judith Lynam, and Joan Anderson take up the layering of power relations in a project that involved research assistants conducting in-depth interviews in a health-related study with Chinese Canadian and Indo-Canadian women. In particular, they explore the roles of research assistants as mediators between the researchers, clinic personnel, and women being interviewed.

Interviews in institutional clinical settings, for example, exposed the vulnerabilities of the immigrant women. In other cases, the involvement of the assistants as translators for the women in their encounters with clinical personnel cast the assistants in varying positions — as resources by the women, as colleagues sharing the power of the clinic staff, or as neutral bystanders. When follow-up interviews were held in the women's homes, additional aspects of interpersonal dynamics emerged – for example, in the ways in which the interviewers adapted the interests of the researchers to the context, took on responsibilities for serving as advisors, or were subject to specific social placement by the women being interviewed. In another paper, Dyck raises concerns about the ethical difficulties that arise when a project puts research assistants in emotionally stressful positions with women being interviewed.

J.-K. Gibson-Graham from a different perspective has described how workshops with community women recruited as interviewers prompted her to rethink an essentialist category ('miners' wives'). While interactions in the workshops revealed the diversity within the group, they nevertheless permitted Gibson-Graham to find points of partial identification with and among the women. This recognition helped her to transcend the pessimism and immobilisation that post-structural perspectives about differences among women can generate in the researcher. Additionally, she indicates that the encounters among the women built a sense of group identification that supported their subsequent actions in the community.

Finally, Janet Townsend addresses aspects of her collaboration as a peer with Mexican colleagues. Their backgrounds in different disciplines influenced not only the questions asked, but also tended to be displayed in the diverse skills team members brought to approaching specific topics such as sexuality. Overall, however, this feminist geographic writing focuses on collaboration by individual researchers and a relatively small number of other people in supporting roles. We are interested in such relationships, but think it is also important to address collaboration that crosses organizational boundaries. As Huxham points out, such work is not only increasingly desired and expected, it is difficult: "It is a non-trivial practice because of a number of inherent hazards."

Defining Collaboration

To this point, we have addressed collaboration without acknowledging that the concept itself needs to be examined. One source we have found helpful in clarifying our own thinking on differentiating the forms of working jointly is Mattessich *et al*, The authors distinguish collaboration from other forms of joint effort which they label 'cooperation' and 'coordination' on the basis of how they differ in four key areas: their vision and relationships; their structure, division of responsibilities and styles of communicating; their understanding of authority and accountability; and the way they manage resources and rewards. In this schema, cooperation is the least demanding way of interacting in that it "is characterized by informal relationships that exist without any commonly defined mission, structure, or planning effort".

An intermediate form of interaction they call 'coordination': characterized by more formal relationships and an understanding of compatible missions. Some planning and division of roles are required, and communication channels are established. The most complex form of interaction they label 'collaboration', which "is a mutually beneficial and well-defined relationship entered into by two or more organizations to achieve common goals. The relationship includes a commitment to mutual relationships and goals; a jointly developed structure and shared responsibility; mutual authority and accountability for success; and sharing of resources and rewards". Arthur Himmelman defines a similar schema in his work which draws on his study of different organizations in the field of health care. He identifies a continuum of change strategies of increasing levels of complexity and commitment, and three common barriers to working together successfully – dealing with time, trust, and turf. However, his schema includes an additional category which we consider a helpful refinement. At the simplest level, he says, is *networking* – "exchanging information for mutual benefit." He sees it as involving "an initial level of trust and commitment among organizations and... best done when connections or linkages are made person-to-person rather than organization-to-organization". This seems a useful distinction to us in this 'information age' when information is regularly shared at will, rather than on an as-needed basis among actors who may never interact beyond such interest-based contacts. Himmelman's other categories roughly parallel those of Mattesich *et al*,, though he inverts the definitions of coordinating and cooperating while making similar conceptual distinctions.

Himmelman also draws attention to the importance of power in decision-making and ownership within these relationships. There is relatively little literature to guide or analyze how such relationships might be created, maintained, or analyzed. A recent report from the Social Science Research Council notes "a fuller understanding of collaboration as a field of social action is long overdue". Mattessich *et al*, evaluating studies of collaboration among community social service agencies in the United States, outline twenty factors that might be considered to assess 'success,' grouping them within six domains: environment; membership characteristics; process and structure; communication; purpose; and resources. Their work led us to several studies of collaboration between universities and local communities, especially those involving urban planning, that highlighted the importance of building trust and of making efforts to negotiate across differences in organizational cultures.

Within the context of scientific cooperation between researchers and institutions of the 'North' and 'South,' the Social Science Research Council's (2000) examination of international scholarly collaboration identifies seven aspects of cases to review: agenda setting, goals, personnel, process, institutional structure, who pays, and results. In a similar vein, the Swiss Commission for Research Partnership with Developing Countries has proposed eleven principles: deciding on objectives together, building up mutual trust, sharing information and developing networks, sharing responsibility, creating transparency, monitoring and evaluating the collaboration, disseminating the results, applying the results, sharing the profits equitably, increasing research capacity, and building on achievements.

An earlier study by the Commission (1998) described some of the more common barriers to forming genuine North-South research partnerships: the tendency to neglect issues of social importance to the South; the resistance to recognizing the validity of participatory research; the bias of funding sources towards 'hard' sciences and technical fields over social science questions or methods; and the lack of attention to capacity building as a reciprocal and sustainable goal. Such considerations point to a history of the fundam-ental lack of appreciation of the agency and abilities of nominal partners from the South, and serve as clear examples of the kinds of assumptions which work against building the trust necessary for authentic collaboration. In assessing our own experiences in hindsight, we find all these frameworks useful. In what follows, as we analyze the work of the Transborder Consortium, we will draw on aspects of each.

The Integration of Feminism

The purpose of this chapter is to examine various ways in which feminist theory integrates with qualitative research methodology. In my research on the lived experiences of teachers' in inclusive classrooms, my feminist perspective addresses the importance of the relationship between myself as a woman researcher and the subjects of my research who are primarily women. It emphasizes the complexity of interpersonal relationships, and locates value in women's' lived experiences. In this chapter, how feminist scholars present this perspective and how this perspective influences my decisions regarding the qualitative methods of data collection and analysis in my research.

Feminist Theory

Although feminist theory, like other theories, such as critical theory or post-modern theory may be understood by its defining principles; it seems a deeper meaning may be found in examining the beliefs and actions of feminist scholars and the practices of feminist researchers. In my own journey of exploring how my feminist theoretical perspective influences my work as a qualitative researcher have found it challenging to examine this complex theory as it is so embedded in my being. But then again, is that not feminism?

Hester Eisenstein in her introduction to the text Contemporary feminist thought explains that from her perspective the term "feminist" holds an element of "visionary and futuristic thought". She then goes on to relate her understanding of feminism to that of Juliet Mitchell. She agrees with Mitchell who purports that in addition to the elements of women, their condition, and their experiences; men and an opportunity for social change are essential to our feminism.

The feminist qualitative research which includes teachers' lived experiences (women along with their male colleagues) and the knowledge which they draw upon through reflection on these experiences provides the opportunity for social change and reform in education. Luke and Gore in their work on poststructuralist feminism continue to acknowledge that the focus is to move beyond the deconstruction of the male position and give voice to marginalized groups, including women.

In so doing feminists pursue the work of social justice. Confirming this belief, teachers whom I interview often comment that the opportunity created through my research to reflect upon their work in teaching has prompted action or further analysis on their part, resulting in subsequent change.

Types of Feminists, Feminisms

There is no one type of feminism and that having a feminist theoretical stance is complex and dynamic. Multiple feminist theories including liberal feminists, socialist feminist and radical feminism to name a few, have been identified. Liberal feminists have been described as those feminists whose focus is on access and success, and equality with men. Socialist feminists are those who focus is on exploiting social practices which have marginalized women. Radical feminists are those whose focus is on promoting the positive characteristics of women, such as empathy, passion and creativity.

Combined with the common epistemological theories of positivism, realism, critical theory and constructivism, feminist perspectives have resulted in multiple ways of constituting knowledge. Feminist empiricism incorporates post-positivist realism with liberal feminism to provide a space in which to explain the objective existence of a social world without gender bias. Feminist empiricist researchers seek to ensure their work is free from gender stereotypes, research participants are representative, and results are not over generalized beyond the participants represented. Feminist standpoint theory incorporates post-positivist critical theory with radical and social feminism to provide a space in which to claim there is no objective truth.

Scholars working with this theoretical stance acknowledge that an individual's position in relation to the dominant group provides them a unique understanding of reality, and must reflect upon how their own social status influences their interpretation of data. Lastly, feminist postmodernists incorporate post-positivist constructivism with radical feminism in creating a space which denounces the existence of a single truth or reality. These scholars view the world as endless stories of different knowledge's which may or may not sustain or disrupt the status quo. It is clear to me now that being feminist, having a feminist perspective or doing feminist research has many meanings, only some of which have been summarized in this brief section. Although there are commonalities in the underpinnings, beliefs and commitments of feminist scholars, they too hold sacred their individualities.

Feminist Research

Contemporary feminist research emerged from an initial purpose of "consciousness-raising" exemplified in the work of Catharine MacKinnon and the recognition that there are multiple knowledge's identified in the work of Patricia Hill Collins.

Liz Stanley and Sue Wise describe this transformation as moving from a "reactive stance" to exploring and envisioning what "feminist knowledge' could look like". Now more than ever, feminist research embodies the theoretical complexities of social relationships and situated experiences and calls for a re-examination of research methodologies which allow for the representation of women's voices as sources of knowledge. A critical examination by both theorists and researchers resulted in a clearer articulation of the foundational elements of this continually evolving research practice.

Five features of feminist research have been identified for consideration:

1. The giving voice to women's experiences
2. The moving away from dichotomous and other forms of simplistic thinking
3. The incorporation of reflexivity
4. The adoption of a collaborative approach and
5. The use of research as a tool for emancipation

In reflecting upon the elements of feminist research, it is important to acknowledge that not all research by or about women is inherently feminist. As noted above feminist researchers consider many elements including being reflexive in their work which requires an acknowledgment of the influence of contextual values including the values and assumptions which they hold. Inherent in feminist research is the understanding that knowledge and awareness does not remain fixed requiring feminist researchers to continue in the work of analyzing new knowledge's gained through their research.

Feminist Qualitative Research

Contemporary feminist researchers agree that both qualitative and quantitative research methodologies may be feminist in their theoretical stance and are necessary in fully understanding women's lives. In my research on the lived experiences of teachers in inclusive classrooms, I employ a qualitative research design which combines data collection methods (participant observation with resultant field notes and in-depth interviews) with analysis through the use of the constant comparative method resulting in grounded theory through conceptual specification. This integration of feminist theoretical perspectives with qualitative research design is now commonly referred to as feminist qualitative research.

Those researchers seeking a more feminist research methodology have shifted to a more humanistic relationship in which the interviewer reveals feelings and allows for a reciprocal question and answering. It is thought that these new practice which allows for more open ended responses to questions provides greater insight into the lives of the respondents. Feminist qualitative interviewing practices require an open, trusting, and often long term relationship between the interviewer and the subjects. The purpose of such a relationship is clearly articulated in the conclusion of their chapter The Interview: From structured questions to negotiated text, in which Andrea Fontana and James Frey simply state "to learn about people we must treat them as people, and they will work with us to create accounts of their lives".

Marjorie Devault in her reflections upon the relationship between researcher and subject acknowledged two intersections between qualitative research and feminism. The first is the relationship between the researcher and her subjects. The second is the belief that a feminist perspective allows for movement beyond a simplistic description of a complex relationship by including the lived experiences of the participants. In my research, conducting informal, semi-structured interviews is a way to provide a more relaxed atmosphere, one which facilitates a closer relationship between researcher and subject. At the same time, however, that informality may concern participants, who are unaccustomed to considering a "conversation" to be "research." Belenky, Clinchy, Goldberger and Tarule distinguish women's more conversational style of interviews as "relatively unstructured rather than bound by more or less explicit rules. Women have been practicing this kind of conversation since childhood".

DeVault describes how this feminist form of interviewing affected her respondents in a study on household routines:

Chatting about the household routines is a way of finding out what someone else does, reflecting on one's own practice, getting and sharing ideas or solutions to common problems. Sometimes, in fact, my respondents were uncomfortable because our talk didn't seem like an interv-iew: several stopped in mid-sentence to ask, "Is this really what you want?" "Are you sure this is helping you?" They were prepared to translate into the vocabulary they expected from a researcher, and surprised that we were preceding in a more familiar manner. The point here is that feminist topics go beyond standard labels and apply to other kinds of research as well. Feminist qualitative participant observations also require unique practices and perspectives on the part of the researcher. The observer's participation in the social situations within the world being studied must acknowledge observers' presence as collaborative participation. This means of feminist observation allows for a richer understanding of the constantly changing human relationships while requiring from the participant observer a more apparent commitment and caring, inherent in feminist research practices. Feminist qualitative researchers not only find their participation in the context of the study of particular interest but also their understandings of their perception of power in participants' social interactions. Feminists' are aware of power relations in all aspects of qualitative research.

The relationship between the researcher and participant is one source of reflexivity on power relations. Yet, another is through observations. In observations, the feminist researcher is keenly aware of power relationships and holds a commitment to focus on the empowerment of women in relationships. So too must they acknowledge the role they may play and the power they possess as a participant in the observation. Hsiung encourages feminist researcher to look beyond a binary view of observations which positions two participants, or a participant and researcher, in relation to one another, but to think more in multidimensional power relations. It is in this way that we yet again, explore the complex richness of women's lived experiences. This is true certainly in the observing the lives of teachers. They find themselves in multiple relationships simultaneously with parents, students and colleagues and the decisions they make effect those they are in relationship with in varied ways.

Over the last several decades, feminist scholars have become increasingly more reflective with regard to the research process. Addressing the issue of what makes a particular piece of research specifically 'feminist,' they find that it includes incorporating gender, privileging subjectivity, avoiding exploitation, and empowering women. From these characteristics, they conclude that there are no feminist research methods, but that there is one feminist methodology.

The outline these methods and methodologies and then call on future research to expand these approaches in order to produce better accounts of gendered lives.

Over the last several decades, feminist scholars have become increasingly more reflective with regard to the research process: in addition to undertaking studies related to women and gender, they have offered numerous perspectives on the nature of feminist research itself. More specifically, in their efforts to identify new questions – or to approach traditional topics in novel ways – they have outlined a range of differences between feminist and mainstream approaches to social science, most notably in sociology, political science, anthropology, and history. Most conclude that there are no feminist research methods in terms of specifically feminist research techniques.

At the same time, however, many also argue that there is a common feminist methodology, in the sense that feminists share a similar philosophy about the means and ends of social investigation, even when they employ a wide range of research tools. This apparent consensus, contradicts the broader statements made by these scholars that there are multiple ways of doing feminist research. Rather, taken together their work suggests - albeit implicitly - that there are not only actual feminist methods, but also several distinct feminist methodologies. Embracing the conventional wisdom thus comes at a sharp cost, preventing further elaboration of feminist alternatives to mainstream approaches to social research.

Seeking to clarify the potential of these contributions in this chapter, review and discuss the literature on feminist research methods in order to show that feminist scholars have not only adapted existing techniques to the demands of a feminist mindset, but have also devised new methods and perspectives for analyzing various kinds of research questions. In the first section, find that central contributions in feminist methods and methodology converge on a number of key features of feminist research, which include incorporating gender, privileging subjectivity, avoiding exploitation, and empowering women.

Although these scholars subsequently conclude that these characteristics mean that there are no feminist research methods, but that there is one feminist methodology, argue that their work supports the idea of feminist methods, as well as multiple feminist methodologies. In the second section, discuss some examples of how feminists have adapted existing research techniques in order to make them more consistent with feminist concerns, as well as ways in which they have created their own research methods in order to answer certain research questions. In the third section, elaborate five feminist methodologies and one hybrid approach that react to different aspects of (social research) in order to present various alternatives. In the final section, conclude that feminist researchers should focus on expanding these six approaches in order to produce better accounts of gendered lives.

Perspectives on Feminist Research Methods

Feminists writing on research methods have thought extensively about what constitutes a feminist research project. Although many assume that feminist research involves female scholars writing on issues of women and gender, most do not limit their scope to these kinds of studies. Rather, they focus on how the means and ends of the research process might be made more or less 'feminist.' Despite variations in their arguments, they generally identify the same key features, which include paying attention to the importance of gender as a central element of social life, challenging the norm of objectivity to incorporate subjectivity into research, avoiding the exploitation of women as goals that are usually informed by extensive reflexivity throughout the research process subjects and objects of knowledge, and empowering women through social research.

As these goals are sufficiently broad, they argue, many different research techniques may be employed in a manner consistent with feminist values. Indeed, many note, a particular strength of feminist research is its largely 'problem-driven' nature: feminists as a group experiment with various types of methods when seeking to answer certain types of questions, and as individuals select different methods as they take on new research topics. For this reason, they insist that feminist work can and should utilize both quantitative and qualitative techniques, even though many associate qualitative methods more closely with feminist research. These features combined with a diversity of research tools lead scholars to conclude that there are no feminist methods, but that there is one feminist methodology. Although often used interchangeably, these terms are in fact quite distinct, with important implications for evaluating feminist approaches to social research. Strictly speaking, methods refer to "techniques and procedures used for exploring social reality and producing evidence." They encompass various processes for gaining knowledge, like life histories, interviews, participant observation, archival research, content analysis, experiments, and surveys.

Feminist Methods

At a practical level, feminists use many of the same methods as other researchers, but adapt them in ways that make them more consistent with feminist concerns. Although relatively few of these scholars reflect explicitly on their methods and methodologies, many experiment with existing techniques as they try to answer specific research questions. In many instances, this involves adjusting the content and implementation of particular methods to incorporate gender, privilege subjectivity, avoid exploitation, and empower women. In the use of interview techniques, for example, feminists have often been careful to involve research subjects in the construction of data about their lives.

In the process, they have become conscious of particular challenges inherent in generating feminist insights - or simply remaining consistent with feminist goals - when interviewing across age,18 race,19 class, 20 gender, 21 and political differences.

Similarly, when engaging in ethnographic fieldwork, feminist researchers have sought to gain a more complex understanding of their subjects at the same time that they document their lives, activities, experiences, and social contexts. Some have reflected on how different theories of 'gender' may influence research findings, while others have addressed the ethical dilemmas in ethnographic work that, they argue, become particularly acute in light of feminist goals to avoid any exploitation of their research subjects.

Feminists have also discussed ways in which other techniques may be employed to feminist ends: archival research - or even starting a group's own archive - can help promote knowledge of many different kinds of women; internet research can reach women who are geographically dispersed but 'virtually' connected in order to study how they share knowledge or mobilize collectively; content analysis can provide insights into discursive and visual representations of gender through non-traditional research materials like artwork and other cultural artifacts; and surveys and statistical analyses can reveal that gender inequalities do in fact exist, affording often crucial leverage for feminist activists in their efforts to influence public policy.

In other cases, feminist researchers create new methods in the pursuit of better knowledge of gender relations. The quintessential method of this type is consciousness-raising, a crucial tool in second wave feminism, which typically involves small groups of women who meet to discuss their personal experiences. These gatherings, which may also take the form of 'speak-outs' and 'write-ins,' help participants recognize the hidden and taken-for-granted aspects of their lives that not only enable personal transformation, but that also provide insights for devising strategies for change.

Other innovative techniques developed by feminist researchers - usually invented in the course of asking questions whose answers are difficult to access through traditional methods - include: dramatization through role play, which allows research subjects to collaborate in research and to find their own voice; genealogy and network tracing, which draws on the networks in which individuals are embedded; multiple person stream-of- consciousness narrative,

Which removes the voice of the author by offering multiple perspectives to communicate possibly conflicting research findings; conversation, which presents multiple voices as a way of gathering and displaying data; identification, which 'breathes life' into the person being studied through the personal reflections of the scholar doing the study; use of unplanned personal experience, which begins as a study of other people's experiences but eventually draws in the author, who unexpectedly finds herself part of the group being examined; structured conceptualization, which entails synthesizing information in the form of a map in order to display how ideas are related to one another; photography, which compiles images of the research subjects to tell a visual story of their lives and experiences, sometimes involving their participation in the presentation of findings; and taped self-interviews, which enable respondents to answer questions at their convenience in the privacy of their own homes.

These original solutions, combined with extensive feminist adaptations of existing techniques, suggest - contrary to the conventional wisdom - that there are in fact feminist research methods, consistent with different definitions of 'feminism' and various feminist goals in the research process. Indeed, these various innovations have sparked renewed interest among feminists in theorizing how their work speaks to the limits of traditional techniques, as well as how their experiences in the field point to new ways for conducting social research.

Of course, feminists are not unique in challenging established research procedures: scholars in various fields of social science have developed a range of new methods for tackling issues related to the conceptualization, measurement, ethics, and impact of different kinds of research. However, this particular literature pays very little attention to questions of gender. At the same time, feminist innovations have made few inroads into the conduct of mainstream research. Promoting a dialogue across this divide requires more explicit elaboration of feminist alternatives that in many ways supplement - but also challenge - foundational aspects of social inquiry.

Feminist Methodologies

At a theoretical level, feminists develop a number of alternative methodologies through various experiments in feminist knowledge production that reverse key tenets of traditional research. Their starting point is the 'scientific method' - often used as a synonym for conventional approaches - which they argue comprises at least five overlapping claims:

1. The mind is the only reliable source of knowledge,
2. The knower must not be influenced by his or her social context,
3. Reason is the only means to gain knowledge,
4. The knower is an individual, and
5. The knower must stand at some distance from the research subject. In response, they outline at least five approaches – and one 'hybrid' approach – that react to different aspects of the scientific method in order to produce what they claim are better accounts of gendered lives. All six methodologies may be considered 'post-positivist,' in the sense that they question whether 'reality' is directly accessible through the scientific method.

Nonetheless, they cannot simply be subsumed into postmodernism: while they share a similar stance regarding the political power of knowledge claims, feminist approaches uphold the category of 'women' and believe that feminist knowledge is possible, ideas that are fundamentally undermined by most versions of postmodern thinking. Like some postmodern theorists, however, the first methodology inverts the mind-body dualism and views bodies as a source of knowledge. These researchers argue that the 'body' is not only closely associated with the feminine, but also that feminists can talk of 'women' as an oppressed group only by reference to the female body and its place in women's experiences.

As the 'body' is embedded in a complex matrix of power relations, they assert, it can become a source of knowledge in at least four ways: the embodied knower, the body as the subject of inquiry, the body as a category of analysis, and the body in relation to the material. This approach may take a number of different forms, ranging from 'writing women's bodies' to reveal the conditions for the repression of difference,38 to analyzing how bodies are socially produced and culturally variable to gain insight into subjectivity and identity in particular places and times.

Overlapping with some of these concerns, the second methodology replaces the context-free knower and introduces experiences as an alternative basis of knowledge. These scholars suggest that studying women's experiences has a number of important advantages for linking ideas and reality: as a research strategy, it provides data that otherwise does not exist about gendered lives and power relations, fosters knowledge about many different kinds of women, pinpoints 'extra-discursive' realities that do not yet find expression in existing theories and language, and identifies common features of gendered lives that connect one woman's experiences with those of others.

Although some feminists question the authority of experience on the grounds that individuals may construct the same event in different ways, proponents privilege the partial and intuitive knowledge that comes from a subject situated in a specific social context, arguing that women must be able to speak for themselves about their everyday lives, especially when they occupy a position of multiple marginalization.

The information gained can then be used to analyze the language in which these experiences are expressed in order to paint a more inclusive picture of the diversity of women's lives. Delving into one particular aspect of experience, the third methodology focuses on emotions as a source of knowledge, rejecting reason as the only valid path to the study of social life.

Although women have historically been excluded from generating authoritative knowledge on the grounds that they are not rational but emotional, these scholars propose that emotions can play a valuable role in developing critical theory, despite perceptions that they simply disrupt rational thought. This is because people learn what their culture defines as appropriate responses to certain situations, not only influencing their ability to neutrally observe social facts, but also identifying emotions that do not conform to these social expectations. These 'outlaw' emotions - experienced, for example, by people of colour when they hear a racist joke, or by women when they are in a group of men engaged in sexual banter - lead to individual confusion, which arises from a social position that makes them unable to generate a conventionally prescribed response like laughter.

Placing emotions at the center of analysis thus helps theorize how social life and basic facts about it is constructed through relations of power that remain invisible through an exclusive focus on 'reason.' Rethinking the means and ends of the research process, the fourth and fifth methodologies recommend expanding the number of people involved in generating knowledge, although for two quite distinct reasons. The fourth suggests replacing the single, individual knower with collective, interactive knowledge production, on the grounds that all social research implicitly involves many individuals.

Although they appear to be individual activities conducted in isolation from other researchers, even typical applications of the scientific method, like testing hypotheses and running experiments, form part of a broader process that entails the continual modification of existing theories. These feminists simply advocate making this dialogue more explicit through collective research projects that

1. Foster 'transformative criticism' through public debates that engage conflicting perspectives on particular research problems,49 or
2. Establish group-generated expertise through a process that assembles the knowledge of many different types of women.

In contrast, the fifth methodology seeks to overcome the separation between the researcher and the research subject, as well as between the researcher and the research results, through what its proponents call 'participatory action research,' which invites research subjects to participate in the research process and connects the value of research findings to political goals. Although this type of approach may take a number of different forms, it basically aims to involve research subjects in order to empower disenfranchised groups in a way that promotes social change. In some cases, this entails a continuous set of feedback loops, whereby researchers solicit collaboration but also hope to change their subjects' behaviour as they go about collecting data.

In others, it involves drawing on participatory research to present new solutions to policy-makers in a way that directly affects the research subjects. In many instances, however, the experience also changes the researcher in a very personal manner, in the sense that he or she comes to realize how widespread a particular problem is, what intended and unintended effects specific policies have, and how simple lack of information keeps certain groups marginalized.

Publishing in both popular and scholarly venues, these scholars maintain that all attempts to produce knowledge of social life are political, and thus that political commitment is an inextricable part of social investigation, despite more traditional efforts to present research as an alternative to political action.

The sixth methodology, finally, is a 'hybrid' approach known as feminist standpoint theory, which is grounded in women's experiences but also draws on knowledge of their bodies and emotions for political action purposes. At its core, this approach reverses 'perspectival hierarchies' by focusing on the lives of marginalized people rather than the views of the 'neutral' observer, who is often implicitly a member of the dominant group as the best starting point for developing 'general' knowledge. As such, it undermines beliefs that women are not able to 'know' by legitimating women's ways of understanding the world, at the same time that it challenges the idea that detachment and reason alone lead to the correct research conclusions.

Feminist standpoint theory thus embodies three

simultaneous goals: to incorporate new information into social research (based on the bodies, experiences, and emotions of marginalized people), to develop new standards for collecting and evaluating evidence (focused on subjectivity rather than objectivity), and to empower marginalized groups through the research process (centered on promoting participation and a political purpose). Despite these innovations, standpoint theory is often criticized by feminists and non-feminists alike as a research strategy on the grounds that 'women' as a category are not unified or fixed, 'experience' does not have a consistent meaning across all individuals, partial visions are not all equally valid, and the problem of 'false consciousness' may preclude political action.

Nonetheless, feminists have developed several distinct versions of standpoint theory that reflect at least partial solutions to these objections. The first argues that, due to the sexual division of labour, women experience life differently than men. However, anyone committed to transforming gender relations men included can access this experience through conssiderable struggle in order to uncover gender inequalities, expose them as unjust, and devise a plan for change.

The second elaborates how 'black feminist thought' as a type of standpoint theory has actually developed in practice, as black feminist intellectuals have negotiated their 'outsider within' status to analyze race, class, and gender inequalities. Themes common to this standpoint include the self-definition and self-valuation of black women; the interlocking nature of oppression, especially for groups like black women who occupy multiple contradictory positions vis-à-vis white male power; and the importance of a black women's 'culture.'

The third focuses on how to theorize embodied knowledge through a strategy of 'strong objectivity,' which entails studying multiple - and possibly conflicting - experiences of marginalized people, often in collaboration with members of more privileged groups, in order to gain a better understanding of society as a whole.

3

Feminist Perspective on Science and Technology

Certain feminist perspectives on technology establish technology as a distinctly masculine product. As a result, women are seen to be alienated from technology. A societal level view of this feminist critique of technology emphasizes this anti-technological perspective. Within this perspective women are seen as having two potential roles; they must either incorporate technology designed and implemented by males into their work, which often results in deskilling or they can resist or reject the technology. Yet within this broad societal view, everyday, in organizations, women must successfully accept and use technology in the accomplishment of their skilled work.

Our research seeks to understand how a feminist technological viewpoint actually plays out in a given setting – a bank. Using dramatistic analysis we develop how this feminist perspective accounts for the lived experience of using technology during moments when it 'fails' by examining tape recorded interactions between bankers and the help desk technicians they call for help. At these points in time both bank workers – roles played by both genders - assume a particular relationship with technology which current feminist perspectives do not quite explain. We explore these anomalies and discuss the implications they have for a feminist critique of technology. Certain feminist perspectives on technology establish technology as a distinctly masculine product. Technology, technical skill and masculinity are "intimately entwined" with much of technology being associated with masculinity. Within this vision technology is conceptualized in terms of men, excluding women from almost all levels except as having one of two potential roles; they must either incorporate technology designed, implemented and controlled by males into their work, which often results in positions for females which are "deskilled, degraded, and devalued" or they can resist or reject the technology and thus not participate in the economy built around the new technologies.

Our research seeks to understand this feminist critique by examining how it plays out in the everyday setting of work conducted in a bank. Bank work is now almost exclusively carried out using information technologies by workers of both genders. There are moments during everyday use in which technology is called into the 'present at hand' - when technology fails to work in the intended way, or the technology user is unable to accomplish their tasks and requires help. In these moments, the technology and its usage come into the foreground in ways which can serve to broaden our understanding of these tools, the individual's work relationship to them and importantly, how they are implicated more broadly in work life at the organizational level. Thus our research seeks to understand what is revealed about sex, gender, work and organizing when the technology implicated in that work suffers temporary failures.

In this research we use the ontological inspiration of Burke's dramatism and methods to analyze audio-taped technical support calls to the technical help desk of a large financial institution. These are crisis events in which a user's work is interrupted and halts while technical problems are attended to in concert with help desk technicians. These events create a hermeneutic rupture - an interruption in the normal ebb and flow of everyday work life. They allow us to focus on the implications of technology for the individual but they also form the route into focusing on the organizational system as a whole. By examining tape recorded conversations of help desk calls, situations reflecting moments where technology assumes a more conscious role in work life, we hoped to be able to develop a more detailed picture of scope and trajectory of female reactions to technology.

As we examined our data and looked for the presence of the culturally bounded relationship between masculinity and technology to deepen our understanding of this relationship and its impact on organizations in an everyday setting, we realized we were uncovering relationship and identity transformations that may have dramatic impact on organizations and technology. Our analysis uncovered how the agency of technology imposes relationships, both of conflict and of partnership, upon the individuals in the organization. The background for this research which is presented next examines the organization and individual level work within which our research is situated. We seek to briefly outline the broad perspectives which have been influential in establishing the ground work for studying technology in organizations, while then narrowing down to how we have sought to understand the role of gender and technology in the life of the individual worker.

Our methods section discusses dramatism as the ontological position of this work and as the methodology which we deployed. We explain both the broad positioning of dramatism within its particular paradigm and then our application of it to our research site and data analysis. Our analysis section reviews our analysis and findings. We conclude with a summary of the depiction of organizational life with technology which is revealed in this work and the implications this has for current thinking about organizing. The present research examines, with a feminist lens, data which had been collected for another research project. Interested in exploring the role of technical support in individual users' experience with technology, we collected the data outlined below. In exploring that data we came to realize that both men and women participated as bankers requiring help and as technicians who provided help and determined to re-examine the data set for purposes of exploring the feminist critique of technology.

The recent research in the relationship between technology and organizations has attempted to fully understand the role and perspective of the technician. This research focuses on the professionalization of role of technician within the organization and the contradictions that this causes within the hierarchy of the organization. However, to the best of the authors' knowledge this research has not focused on the role of sex and gender in understanding this relationship. Adam et al approach the relationship between gender and IT by highlighting a new need within organizations to have women stay in the field of information technology. Earlier within this field of research the issue of women in technology was approached as a problem that could be solved by attracting more women into IT work.

It has only been recently that the issue of keeping women in IT work has appeared. Adam et al, reported that a large number of women are leaving IT in the UK. They identified this situation as an opportunity to approach the relationship between gender and technology through exploring the actual experience of women working in the field of information technology. Drawing from Adam et al, the feminist view we adopt here is that technical skills have a strong link to our society's views of what it is to be masculine. Therefore the experience of women in IT is inherently problematic. Additionally, this view highlights our society's valuing of traits, occupations and behaviours that are equated with being masculine are considered of higher value than occupations and behaviours that are equated with being feminine.

Through this perspective Adam et al, identified several coping strategies in which females in IT attempt to solve this problem. For example, they identified that female IT workers often do not identify themselves as being in IT or attempt to take on a gender neutral role. Informed by this approach and within the context of technical problems and gender experience we explored the users' experience in working with ICTs and what this understanding revealed about the relationship of sex, gender, technology and the organization.

Feminist Perspectives to Science and Mathematics Education

Feminism is clearly not a unitary movement. Though there is a basic desire for equality and the end of discrimina-tion, there are many feminist groups including radical feminists, socialist feminists, Marxist feminists, lesbian separatists, women of colour, post-modern feminists, feminist empiricists, and so on; all of which have a different definition and viewpoint. "Feminism is the refusal to define all women and therefore all human beings solely in terms of sex". It is an active desire to change women's position in society. A feminist believes that women suffer discrimination because of their sex, that they have specific needs that remain negated and unsatisfied, and that the satisfaction of these needs would require a radical change in the social, economic, and political order.

Feminism is an effort to bring insights from various female experiences together with research and data gathering to produce new approaches to understanding and ending female oppression. There are several ways to categorize feminists and feminist theory, and critiques depend in part on the perspectives taken. The goal of this chapter is not to look at all the different feminist perspectives, but to look at a general view of feminism and the underlying attitude a feminist would have toward science, mathematics, and mathematics education. Feminist theory is based on the underlying belief that we live in a male-dominated culture in which men have developed the guidelines for society. They have drawn on their knowledge, perspectives, and visions to create and construct the prevailing theories, history, and values that have become important. Even our major educational institutions were developed by men, for men. Later, when girls' schools and women's colleges were developed, they were patterned after the male institutions.

The belief was that this would give women an education equivalent to that of men. Little attention has been given to the modes of learning, knowing, and valuing that may be common in women. Common acceptance of stereotypes of women's thinking as intuitive, emotional, and personalized has most likely contributed to the devaluation of women's minds and contributions.

In a culture that values rationalism and objectivity, it is assumed that intuitive knowledge is more primitive and thus less valuable than objective knowledge and objective modes of learning. For many women, the real and valued lessons in life did not grow out of their involvement with academics, but rather their involvement in their relationships with family, friends and teachers, life crises, and the community.

Women often feel alienated in academic settings. They see formal education as irrelevant and far from their central interests and development. Also, some women are "left behind" in their understanding of academic concepts because many faculty members assume that the pedagogical techniques that are appropriate for men are also suitable for women. A study by Fennema and Peterson showed that competition in a classroom did not facilitate girls' learning, but cooperative learning had a great impact on the girls' learning. Yet there are many classrooms that thrive on competitive learning situations. In order to design an education appropriate for women, we must first learn about the academic experiences of ordinary women.

Feminist Theory and Science

Recently, feminists have convincingly argued that there is a masculine bias at the very heart of most academic disciplines, methodologies, and theories. Feminists are beginning to articulate the values of the female worlds and to reshape the disciplines to include the woman's voice. Take for instance the academic subject of science. First, one might ask why there are so few women scientists. Science has been defined as a masculine activity of which women, because of the qualities associated with femininity, are incapable. Society has accepted science as masculine, and those values have been passed on to women. In the 1960s there was a great deal of attention placed on the subject of women in science.

The low representations of women in science, particularly in the upper levels of the scientific community, were discussed. In an article enumerating the various impediments confronting women in science, Keller sugges-ted that the one that was perhaps the most powerful was the widespread belief in the intrinsic masculinity of scientific thought. These beliefs are kept alive by widely held myths about science that abound in society and are often looked upon, by women as well as men, as truths. A sample set of myths given by Keller (1983) is as follows:

1. "Science is impersonal; women are personal".
2. "Science deals with things; women deal with people".
3. "The male way of knowing in its highest development is objective, analytical, scientific investigation. The female way of knowing in its most complete sense is the mother's intuitive knowledge of her baby".
4. "Science is reason, unalloyed by feeling. Feeling is a female element while thinking is a male element".
5. "Science is 'hard' and tough-minded; women are 'soft' and sentimental".
6. "Science seeks power; women seek harmony".

Masculine epistemology and knowledge have an emphasis on the domains of cognitive and objective rationality, on reductive explanation, and on dichotomous partitioning of the social and natural worlds. This masculinist knowledge has produced today's science, which seeks to relegate women and women's knowledge to the realm of nature. The epistemology of science is based on dualisms such as nature/culture, subject/object, and knower/known. The dichotomy of science leads to hierarchies and control, which is typical of our male-dominated society. Thus science has an androcentric bias and a bias in research methods. This has led to a bias in the choice and definition of problems with which scientists and science have concerned themselves. The potential for bias on the part of male scientists is also heightened by the recurring tendency to select exclusively or predominantly male samples for research.

Studies are done, conclusions are made, and what has been learned from the study of men is generalized and transferred to the lives of women. If and when scientists turn to the study of women, they typically look for ways in which women conform to or diverge from patterns found in the study of men. Although feminists agree on the present masculinity of science, they have not agreed on a definite alternative. In contrast to a masculinist epistemology, a feminist epistemology evolves from women's lives and experiences. It is centered on the domain of inter-connectedness and affectual rationality. It emphasizes holism and harmonious relationships with nature.

A number of feminist critiques of science and masculinist epistemology argue that we should replace the masculinist epistemology of science with a feminist epistemology. Three epistemologies that are designed to accomplish this task have risen to the forefront of feminist theory. They are feminist empiricist epistemology, feminist standpoint epistemology, and feminist post-modern epistemology. Feminist empiricism is a critique of science that concentrates on the exclusion of women from science and what they could contribute if they were included. It seeks equality with men and hence is considered a first generation feminism. It argues that sexism and androcentrism are social biases and feminist scientists, men as well as women, are more likely than non-feminist scientists to notice this bias.

It assumes that the laws and methodologies of science are correct, but if attention is paid to the inequities of participation, the problems that have arisen in the conduct of science will start to be resolved. All in all, the problem lies not in science itself, but in a "bad science" - a science that is distorted by masculine bias in problematics, theories, concepts, methods of inquiry, observations, and interpretations of the results of research. Feminist empiricism has some flaws that need to be considered. First, if strict empiricism were correct, the laws and methodologies of science would be such that the gender of the researcher would be irrelevant. But feminist empiricism claims that feminists are more likely to produce objective and unbiased results than are non-feminists. Secondly, a key origin of androcentric bias can be found in the selection of problems for inquiry.

Feminist empiricism insists that its methodological norms are meant to apply only to the "context of justification" not to the "context of discovery" where the problems are identified. Thus the attempt of feminist empiricism to reform a "bad science" has resulted in what have been called "empirical inadequacies in empiricist epistemologies". A second theory that offers hope for changing science is feminist standpoint epistemology. Recognition of the incoherence of feminist empiricism led to the development of this philosophy. Feminist standpoint epistemology purports that women, because of certain aspects of their makeup, possess a privileged position that provides them with a unique perspective.

Women can know the world in ways not available to men because they are less bound to the norms of science and are better able to examine it. This theory is consistent with second generation feminism in which individual qualities are embraced and assimilation into the male world is rejected. Feminist standpoint epistemology is based on the idea that knowledge begins with women's lives and experiences. Thus multiple feminist standpoints exist, all of which are different but not necessarily disjoint. Hence feminist standpoint epistemology allows for a multiplicity of ideas and truths.

A major defect of feminist standpoint theory is that the many ways in which women divide themselves in the world are overlooked. How can a single feminist standpoint exist in this situation? Does there need to be a feminist standpoint for every division of race, class, and culture? Or, does this mean that one person or group will dominate the whole?

The final epistemology that is at the forefront of research is feminist post-modern epistemology. This theory celebrates the diversity of women's being and expresses a profound doubt toward the universalizing of claims about existence, nature and powers of reason, progress, language, and science. Feminist postmodernism would attack the roots of masculinist science and strive for a transcendence of dualistic thought. It would use race, class, cultural differences, and gender as categories of analysis. What passes now for gender-free and objective is exactly in line with a masculine view of the world. It appears to be objective to most men because it labels men as the norm, but it leaves the women feeling excluded.

Feminist postmodernism would also avoid generalizing beyond the scope of the data. Attention would be given to individuals, and thus a science that is de-centered, pluralistic, and non-hierarchical would be developed. Feminist post-modern epistemology is the start of third generation feminism.

In third generation feminism, "women seek equality with men... they embrace their own special qualities and reject uncritical assimilation into the male world...and seek solutions that arise out of a careful synthesis of old and new questions". Feminist post-modern epistemology is aware of its inconsistencies and faults and does not claim to have a "lock on truth". From this perspective, feminists' claims seem more plausible and less distorting since they are grounded in the solidarity of the diverse identities of women.

Though feminist post-modern epistemology seems to have the most hopeful future of the three epistemologies due to its awareness of the plethora of women's voices, it has some inconsistencies. Unlike the feminist standpoint theory, we may ask ourselves "can we afford to give up the necessity of trying to provide one, true feminist story of reality"? Feminist theories about science in general have been well documented, but little attention has been given, in comparison, to explicitly focusing on a feminist view of mathematics. The early research in gender and mathematics was grounded in feminist empiricism. Noted researchers such as Fennema, Fox, and Sherman began by addressing the gender problem and outlining the research agendas for future, less sexist studies.

A number of studies that focus on females' achievement in the mathematics classroom have been conducted. The results of these studies have produced a persistent theme in the study of gender and mathematics. This is that females excel at lower level computational skills while males excel at higher level problem solving skills. This result gives the impression that females understand mathematics at a lower level than do males. Many of these studies were based on the need for a comparison of females to males using males as the norm. The studies tried to explain why females' mathematical achievement was not as high as males' and why females did not elect to participate in advanced mathematics courses or in mathematics related careers to the extent that males did. This male bias, however, has only compounded the difficulty of exposing the full implication of mathematics achievement for females. To learn about the mathematics achievement of females, we must study females in and of them.

Introducing a feminist standpoint epistemology to mathematics would require "a willingness to abandon beliefs about the nature of mathematics and how it must be taught and learned in order to be open to the 'nature' of mathematics as it is experienced". A major part of this experience for women takes place in general society. The relationship of most women to mathematics is constructed by the receipt of messages about mathematics. For women, a recurring message is that it is important to learn mathematics, but it is not important for women to learn mathematics. Thus a woman who continues to pursue higher level mathematics must continually reject her "natural" position. A feminist post-modern view and movement toward third generation feminism can be seen in recent research. A study of Mr. Martin's middle school mathematics class, performed by Stanic and Hart (in press), concerned it with both gender and race.

Though this alone would be considered first generation feminist thought or even feminist empiricism, Stanic and Hart looked past the categories of gender and race to make important conclusions about individual differences. We began our case study with the objective of looking at sex and race differences in mathematics attitudes and the achievement-related behaviour of persistence. The fact of the black students scoring higher than the white students on the paper-and pencil measures of attitudes and persistence notwithstanding, we found that the most productive level of group analysis required looking at sex and race simultaneously. Even this group analysis was limited to the extent to which individual students showed unique configurations of interacting characteristics, which confirmed for us the importance of considering archetypical students rather than just demographic groups. Our work points to the need to qualify group differences by studying individuals over time and attitudes and behaviours in interaction, using multiple measures of achievement (in press).

A model proposed by Reyes and Stanic concerns itself not only with gender and race, but also with socioeconomic status (SES). The goal of this model is to explain group differences in performance by using variables such as societal influences, school mathematics curricula, teacher attitudes, student attitudes, achievement related behaviour, classroom processes, and student achievement. Much has been studied about the mathematical achievement of students as related to race differences, gender differences, SES, and other differences as individual entities. The intent of this model is to bring all of these variables together to more fully explain achievement differences and thus to attain equity for all students. As stated by Reyes and Stanic, "There is clearly much work to be done to prove that group differences in mathematics achievement we now see do not reflect the natural order of things".

Another study that moves toward a solution by examining pedagogy was performed during the 1987-88 academic year by Zelda Isaacson. In this study, Isaacson taught a mathematics course to a group of 24 women. These women were generally in their twenties and thirties and were well-educated in humanities, languages, or social studies, but not in science, technology, or mathematics. In talking with the women, Isaacson learned that many had joined the course because their life experiences had given them confidence in their practical and technical skills, but that they were much less confident in their ability to learn mathematics Mathematics classes need to become places where originality, independent and creative thinking, and imagination are valued. Individuals' contributions and ideas must be welcomed, not rejected. Common sense knowledge should be validated and built upon, rather than relegated to the category of irrelevant and unimportant knowledge.

All this implies using an investigative open ended approach whenever possible. Mathematics classrooms should also be places where pupils come to have fun and to be intellectually stimulated rather than to be filled with rules. Fear and anxiety are wholly negative, damaging emotions that should have no place in mathematics classrooms. Teachers need to be fully aware of how easy it is to engender these feelings - and how important it is, instead, to strive to create a relaxed supportive, non-competitive environment where pupils can gain and maintain confidence in their mathematical abilities. And last, but not least, mathematics classrooms need to be places where talk is encouraged and where collaborative, cooperative work is the norm. From the study of these 24 women and their trials with mathematics, implications for classroom practices were formed by Isaacson. These measures would improve mathematics classrooms for all pupils, but especially for girls.

In a 1987 study at Potsdam College in New York, it was concluded that in an environment hat is genuinely open to and supportive of all students and in which the style of teaching is true to the nature of mathematical inquiry, women are attracted to mathematics and are just as successful as men. Though no solutions are offered, research like this is beginning to move closer to outlining a clearer picture of a feminist view of mathematics teaching. These studies bring me to ask the questions "Is there truly a feminist mathematics or just a feminist pedagogy? Is mathematics itself discriminatory or does the discrimination lie in the attitudes of society towards women in mathematics?" It is my opinion that mathematics is a beautiful science and no longer a male domain. Girls and women need to be told that they can succeed in mathematics. Research needs to focus more toward teaching methods, the ideas of students in the classroom, and how well teachers are able to identify these ideas, interact with them, and help students improve on them.

Assessing Psychological Gender Differences

Reviews of research on psychological gender differences began with Woolley's and Hollingworth's and extended through Maccoby and Jacklin's watershed book The Psychology of Sex Differences, in which they reviewed more than 2,000 studies of gender differences in a wide variety of domains, including abilities, personality, social behaviour, and memory. Maccoby and Jacklin dismissed as unfounded many popular beliefs in psychological gender differences, including beliefs that girls are more "social" than boys; that girls are more suggestible; that girls have lower self-steem; that girls are better at rote learning and simple tasks, whereas boys are better at higher level cognitive processing; and that girls lack achievement motivation. Maccoby and Jacklin concluded that gender differences were well established in only four areas: verbal ability, visual-spatial ability, mathematical ability, and aggression. Overall, then, they found much evidence for gender similarities. Secondary reports of their findings in textbooks and other sources, however, focused almost exclusively on their conclusions about gender differences.

Gender meta-analyses generally proceed in four steps:

a. The researcher locates all studies on the topic being reviewed, typically using databases such as PsycINFO and carefully chosen search terms.
b. Statistics are extracted from each report, and an effect size is computed for each study.
c. A weighted average of the effect sizes is computed (weighting by sample size) to obtain an overall assessment of the direction and magnitude of the gender difference when all studies are combined.
d. Homogeneity analyses are conducted to determine whether the group of effect sizes is relatively homogeneous. If it is not, then the studies can be partitioned into theoretically meaningful groups to determine whether the effect size is larger for some types of studies and smaller for other types. The researcher could ask, for example, whether gender differences are larger for measures of physical aggression compared with measures of verbal aggression.

Meta-Analysis of Sex Differences in Smiling

Research on nonverbal behaviour confirms that women are both better encoders and decoders of emotion. In fact, three expressive domains—namely, smiling, general expressiveness, and decoding accuracy—have been well examined and show relatively large sex differences. In particular, one of the largest and most reliable findings of behaviour research is that men smile less than women. Nonetheless, there is considerable debate as to what factors account for this difference. In what follows, we briefly review several hypotheses advanced by J.

A. Hall and others in meta-analyses of sex differences in smiling. We revisit some of their conclusions as well as present a number of new hypotheses in light of what is now a substantially larger body of empirical findings.

Prior Meta-Analyses of Sex Differences in Smiling

In 1984, J. A. Hall published the first meta-analysis on sex differences in smiling, which showed women smiled more than men. Based on 20 published studies, the effect size (d) she reported was a moderate 0.63. In a follow-up report, J. A. Hall and Halberstadt (1986) added seven new cases and reported a somewhat lower weighted effect size of 0.42. In the latter report, three moderators were considered to moderate the size of observed sex differences in smiling. In their meta-analysis, studies were coded to assess the degree to which various moderators were associated with the observed sex difference in smiling.

Level of acquaintanceship was a moderator to test the warmth-affiliation hypothesis; status was a moderator for the dominance-status hypothesis, and comfortableness was the moderator for the social-tension hypothesis. Each moderator was correlated with the size of the sex difference as well as analyzed with a series of multiple regressions.

These analyses led J. A. Hall and Halberstadt to conclude that the social-tension hypothesis (three moderators) received "strong support," that the warmth affiliation hypothesis (three moderators) received "weak" support, and that the dominance-status hypothesis (one moderator) was not supported by the data. Several explanations for the link between social tension and sex differences in smiling were considered, including the possibility that smiling in situations of high social tension represents an attempt to be cheerful in spite of the tense situation or an effort to ease the other person's discomfort.

Aims for the Present Meta-Analysis

The present meta-analysis takes another look at the literature examining the relationship between gender and smiling. The reasons for this second look are several. First, it is occasioned by the availability of what is now a substantially larger set of relevant research reports. Sex differences in smiling have been measured in a large number of studies published since the J. A. Hall and Halberstadt analysis, even when that particular relationship was not the central question for the research. We included in our meta-analysis unpublished studies such as conference papers and theses, as well as previously unanalyzed data that were not included in their prior meta-analysis. Second, we explored the influence of several moderators derived from work in other areas of sex difference research. Theory suggests, for instance, that the sexes tend to present themselves in more or less gender-stereotypic ways in response to environment cues that make gender salient.

For example, in classic studies by Zanna and his colleagues, women exhibited more or less stereotypically feminine behaviours depending on how they thought a male interviewer or potential date viewed women. Even incidental exposure to gender-relevant cues such as advertisements in fashion magazines has been shown to increase gender self-stereotyping. Such effects occur because by the time individuals reach their teen years, they are well versed in what constitutes expected gender-normative behaviour. Consequently, we contend that norms for gender-appropriate expression—in particular, that of calling for women to smile more than men—are activated when participants believe that their behaviour is being monitored or evaluated in some way. In addition, there was reason to consider the possibility that the size of the sex difference in smiling might vary across cultural groups. Although little research has addressed the joint impact of culture and gender on expressive behaviour, findings indicate that sex differences in expressiveness are larger in some cultures than in others.

Joshi and Maclean reported that Indian preschool girls

were more inclined to report facial masking of negative emotion than either Indian preschool boys or British preschoolers of either sex, a finding they attributed to the greater emphasis on decorum and deference to adults in the socialization of Indian girls. Among adults, Frymier, Klopf, and Ishii compared American and Japanese responses on an affect scale. They noted no sex differences for Japanese participants but substantial sex differences for the American sample. Although much of the available research on sex differences in smiling has focused on Western cultures, a large database of studies on gender and smiling allows us to determine whether there are nationality differences and ethnic differences within the United States. The third goal for the present meta-analysis was to conduct a more fine-grained analysis of several moderators previously considered by J. A. Hall and Halberstadt but which could not be fully tested at the time because of a relatively modest database.

For example, like J. A. Hall and Halberstadt, we examined the impact of tension and nervousness on the size of the sex difference in smiling, but we considered the possibility that there are different kinds of tension. Specifically, we distinguished between social tension, as might occur when an interpersonal interaction is strained in some respect, and task tension, which could be precipitated by anticipated evaluation of one's performance. In addition, our larger database permitted a more complete test of a controversial moderator of sex differences in smiling, namely, status or power differences. As noted above, J. A. Hall and Halberstadt concluded that the dominance-status moderator was uncorrelated with the size of the sex difference. However, their sample did not include studies in which participants could be coded as occupying a low-status position. In the present review, we were able to locate 69 cases that could be coded for low levels of social power. We turn now to a discussion of the moderators we propose for the present meta-analysis and our theoretical rationale for their inclusion.

Theoretical Perspectives on Sex Differences in Smiling

This chapter begins with the premise that smiling is a significant social behaviour that shows a reliable sex difference. Drawing on several "wide-lens" theories of sex differences as well as recent research in the area of nonverbal communication, we propose that the degree to which sex differences in smiling are found depend on social surroundings and social standards. Specifically, we propose three core contextual factors are key to understanding sex differences in smiling. These are gender based norms, situational constraints, and emotion salience.

Perceptions and Age Differences

The developmental period of adulthood covers a large time span, from age 18 or 21 to death. A variety of strategies for dividing this long period into shorter age-based periods have been recommended. For example, Erikson's theory of psychosocial development includes distinctive stages defined by personality developmental tasks; for example, young adulthood (the 20s) is characterized as a time of concern with identity and intimacy issues, whereas middle age (the 40s) is characterized as a time of concern with generativity. Other theorists have emphasized the notion of "executive personality" in middle age, or a confident sense of command. Older adulthood in Erikson's theory is characterized as a time of personality integration in which the key accomplishment is a sense of integrity. Recent theorists have noted that these issues (identity, intimacy, generativity, and integrity) preoccupy adults to varying degrees at all ages, although they may be particularly intense during specific periods and may take different forms at different adult ages. In addition, increased average life spans have challenged both aging adults and developmental theorists to articulate new age boundaries for these stages, and to explain when the process of integration resulting in integrity might be expected to occur and when it may be reflected in an early stage of more inchoate "concern about" aging. Stewart, Ostrove, and Helson found that four aspects of personality originally theorized as central to young adulthood (identity certainty), middle age (generativity and confident power), and older age (concern with aging) were all perceived to be more salient for women in later middle age than in early middle age (the early 50s vs. the 30s and 40s), implying that there was growth on all of these dimensions during a 20-year period within middle age (30s to 50s).

Other research has demonstrated that aspects of personality develop over longer periods of adulthood. In our study we used cross-sectional data from college-educated women to consider the possibility that adult development may be better conceived as composed of elements that have different developmental trajectories, rather than as a series of relatively bounded stages. There are many ways to study personality development, and each design has different advantages and disadvantages. Some researchers have gathered data from a well-defined sample over a long period of time. To ensure that findings are generalizable beyond a single sample, and to begin to disentangle age from cohort effects, it is especially valuable to use longitudinal data over the course of adulthood from multiple birth cohorts.

In fact, though, only a small number of longitudinal studies that follow individuals over the course of adulthood exist, and these data sets take a long time to yield evidence for all ages. A second approach is to use cross-sectional data drawn from individuals who are in different life stages at a given time (e.g., McAdams et al,). Although this method is much quicker, birth cohort is confounded with age, and it is impossible to examine within person change. Finally, it is possible—as in this study—to use data from a single time point, with a combination of retrospective and prospective views of other life stages. Some of the literature on subjective personality change that involves retrospective and prospective evaluations of personality has demonstrated that personality is perceived to change in ways that are consistent with developmental personality theories such as Erikson's (1950;

people expect to be most generative during midlife).

Moreover, this literature also shows that other aspects of personality that are expected to be stable in adulthood (e.g., impulsivity) indeed are not perceived to change. We, in turn, combined in our study cross-sectional data from three cohorts of women (currently in their 20s, 40s, and 60s) with their retrospective and prospective views. Five Domains of Women's Personality Development In this chapter, we examine five domains of personality, and consider their potentially different developmental trajectories in adulthood. One domain (personal distress) is generally considered in the research literature to be equally important in adulthood at all ages, although its developmental course has not been examined often. Three domains (identity certainty, generativity, and confident power) were predicted to be tied to particular life stages, and thus have developmental trajectories that rise and fall with particular periods, defining relatively discrete stages.

Finally, one domain (concern with aging) was expected to continue to gradually increase over the life course. We also review the theoretical background for each of these domains in terms of the developmental stages with which they have been most associated. According to Erikson, the main psychosocial task of adolescence is identity development. The job of the adolescent is to sort through previous identifications in childhood, including those adopted unthinkingly from authority figures, and integrates them into a coherent whole. This should result in a strong sense of self that includes commitment to a particular occupation, political ideology, and religious perspective, and lays the groundwork for establishing intimate relationships. Erikson suggested that identity certainty might come later for women than for men, in the context of their intimate relationships. Indeed, Kroger and Haslett found that women were likely to develop achieved identities in interpersonal domains more quickly than in vocational domains.

Arnett argued that the period of identity solidification has recently extended well into the 20s for both men and women, and Kroger suggested that there is a wide scope for identity development into middle and later adulthood. In a combined sample of men and women, Whitbourne, Zuschlag, Elliot, and Waterman found that identity scores increased throughout the 20s, declining only after age 31. Thus, it seems possible that although identity may first emerge in late adolescence, a sense of identity certainty might actually increase, especially for women, over the course of adulthood. Stewart et al, found, in fact, that identity certainty increased, or was perceived to increase, for women over the course of midlife. For that reason, we predicted, contrary to a more stage-based model, that identity certainty would be expected or recalled to increase from the 20s to the 40s to the 60s for all three cohorts in our study.

Though we expected identity certainty to develop in women beyond young adulthood, we did anticipate that young adulthood has some particular stage-related features. Although some longitudinal studies have shown that psychological distress declines during the college years, young adulthood has nonetheless been characterized in the recent literature as a period of unusually high levels of personal distress for many individuals. Jones and Meredith found that for two cohorts of men and women, psychological health increased across adulthood from age 30 to age 60. A number of developmentalists have pointed to the increasing length of time between childhood and commitment to adult roles, as years of education, age at marriage, and age at childbirth continue to increase in developed nations.

Arnett has labelled the span between 18 and 25 as "emerging adulthood," a period that is differentiated from both adolescence and young adulthood. There is evidence that this period is characterized not only as one of identity development, but also of distress. This may, in part, be a cohort-related phenomenon, because the early 20s have become more and more a time of moratorium in recent decades. There is also greater financial strain on young people today. Ortner and Eskilson and Wiley suggested that young adults are appropriately pessimistic about their financial futures because jobs offered to college graduates have been declining and they have little hope of matching their parents' financial status. Ronka and Pulkkinen suggested that the recent trend of the transition to adulthood becoming more extended, individualized, and discontinuous makes heavy demands on individuals' abilities to cope. There is evidence, however, that older cohorts also suffered widespread distress as young adults.

In one study that examined women who graduated from college in the late 1950s, Pals concluded that the 20s were a turbulent time in which women were attempting to organize their lives and establish themselves in adult roles. Furthermore, young adulthood was found to be the time of greatest emotional difficulty in a U.S. national sample studied more than 30 years ago. Thus, we predicted that feelings of personal distress would be high for women currently in their 20s, and that these women would anticipate a decrease in these feelings over the life span as adult roles become more stable. It remains to be seen whether this contemporary cohort of young adults is significantly higher on personal distress than previous cohorts recalled having been at the same age. Middle age has been characterized as dominated by both generativity and confident power. Generativity is the ability to care for and contribute to the next generation and to the larger world outside of oneself. This can be accomplished by caring for one's own or other children, but also by producing important and lasting work, caring for the environment, and so forth. Stewart et al, found that generativity was higher for women in their 50s than they recalled it being in their 30s and 40s.

In contrast, some studies have shown that generativity peaks in middle age. Stewart and Vandewater argued that the confusing picture presented by cross sectional studies might result from measures that do not differentiate among three components of generativity: desire, felt capacity, and accomplishment. They suggested that Erikson pointed to felt capacity as characteristic of middle adulthood, whereas desire might emerge earlier and accomplishment might peak later and, in fact, contribute to subsequent adult integrity. Stewart and Vandewater also suggested that the appearance of a midlife "peak" is the result of measures that combine items assessing desire, capacity, and accomplishment. The measure we used in this study included elements of desire and felt capacity, but few of accomplishment. Therefore, we expected that generativity would be higher for women in their 40s than for those in their 20s, but would level off or even decline for women in their 60s.

Confident power grows out of Neugarten's work on the executive personality, which she and her colleagues suggested was a hallmark of midlife personality and characterized by feelings of mastery and competence. Women in the three cohorts studied by Stewart et al, described themselves as higher on confident power in their 50s than in their 40s and in their 40s rather than in their 30s. We expected women in their 60s—who are still mostly involved with major work, community, and family roles—would score higher on confident power than women in their 40s, who, in turn, would score higher than women in their 20s. Stewart et al, found the exact same pattern for changes in women's concern with aging, probably the most common conception of what people become preoccupied with during middle age and beyond. Some researchers have suggested that the transition to midlife and increased preoccupation with becoming old will be particularly salient for women because of the premium placed on women's youthfulness in U.S. culture.

We, therefore, expected to find that women in their 60s would score higher on concern with aging than women in their 40s, who, in turn, would score higher than women in their 20s. Stewart et al.'s research, although an important foundation for our work has several limitations. First, it was limited to personality change within the course of midlife (30s to 50s), and second, it relied in part on retrospective ratings. In this research, we improved on their design by studying women in three different stages of adulthood: young adulthood (20s), middle age (40s), and older age (60s). Thus, we had direct data from women while they were in each of these distinct life stages and were able to ask questions about the periods that preceded and followed middle age.

In addition to having women rate their feelings in the present, we also asked them to rate the other two ages prospectively or retrospectively. Thus, our data allowed us to perform cross-sectional analyses between cohorts and to examine recalled or anticipated change within cohort. We tested two hypotheses and predicted the following outcomes. Personal distress would be higher in the 20s than in the 40s or 60s. These different patterns would, of course, result in distinctive clustering of preoccupations within each period, but would not, in our view; resemble bounded stages, with steep rises and declines in a single period. Within each cohort, there would be similar patterns, with women expecting or recalling increases in the domains of identity certainty, confident power, and concern with aging from their 20s to their 40s to their 60s, and generativity increasing from the 20s to the 40s, but not to the 60s. Women would also expect or recall a decrease in feelings of personal distress from the 20s to the 40s.

Stereotype

A stereotype is a preconceived idea that attributes certain characteristics (in general) to all the members of class or set. The term is often used with a negative connotation when referring to an oversimplified, exaggerated, or demeaning assumption that a particular individual possesses the characteristics associated with the class due to his or her membership in it. Stereotypes can be used to deny individuals respect or legitimacy based on their membership in that group. Stereotypes often form the basis of prejudice and are usually employed to explain real or imaginary differences due to race, gender, religion, ethnicity, socio-economic class, disability, occupation, etc.

A stereotype can be a conventional and oversimplified conception, opinion, or image based on the belief that there are attitudes, appearances, or behaviours shared by all members of a group. Stereotypes are forms of social consensus rather than individual judgments. Stereotypes are sometimes formed by a previous illusory correlation, a false association between two variables that are loosely correlated if correlated at all. Stereotypes may be occasionally positive. The term "stereotype" derives from Greek (stereos) "solid, firm" "blow, impression, engraved mark" hence "solid impression". The term, in its modern psychology sense, was first used by Walter Lippmann in his 1922 work Public Opinion although in the printing sense it was first coined 1798.

Effects, Accuracy, Terminology

Stereotypes can have a negative and positive impact on individuals. Joshua Aronson and Claude M. Steele have done research on the psychological effects of stereotyping, particularly its effect on African-Americans and women. They argue that psychological research has shown that competence is highly responsive to situation and interactions with others. They cite, for example, a study which found that bogus feedback to college students dramatically affected their IQ test performance, and another in which students were praised as very smart, congratulated on their hard work, or told that they scored high.

The group praised as smart performed significantly worse than the others. They believe that there is an 'innate ability bias'. These effects are not just limited to minority groups. Mathematically competent white males, mostly math and engineering students, were asked to take a difficult math test. One group was told that this was being done to determine why Asians were scoring better. This group performed significantly worse than the other group.

Possible prejudicial effects of stereotypes are:

- Justification of ill-founded prejudices or ignorance
- Unwillingness to rethink one's attitudes and behaviour towards stereotyped group
- Preventing some people of stereotyped groups from entering or succeeding in activities or fields

The effects of stereotyping can fluctuate, but for the most part they are negative and not always apparent until long periods of time have passed. Over time, some victims of negative stereotypes display self-fulfilling prophecy behaviour, in which they assume that the stereotype represents norms to emulate. Negative effects may include forming inaccurate opinions of people, scapegoating, erroneously judgmentalism, preventing emotional identification, distress, and impaired performance.

Stereotyping painfully reminds those being judged of how society views them. Sometimes "stereotype" and "prejudice" are confused. Stereotypes are standardized and simplified conceptions of groups, based on some prior assumptions. Stereotypes are created based on some idea of abstract familiarity. Prejudices are more specific - they are predispositions to differential behaviour patterns.

Gender Stereotypes of Women Managers

The lack of studies on gender stereotypes of women managers in India despite the dismally low number of women in the top tiers of Indian organizations prompted this study. Managerial gender stereotypes held by both sexes in Indian organizations are explored in this study. 105 men managers and 93 women managers separately rated one of three managerial sets (men managers, women managers and successful middle managers) of the modified Schein Descriptive Index. While results for the male sample differed from previous studies for worse, results for the female sample were positive.

Women managers showed significantly increased associations between middle managerial success and women managers, as compared to the western context about two decades ago. Twenty managerial gender stereotypes relevant to the Indian context were identified. Even today, the majority of the managerial workforce in organizations consists of men. Given that the inclusion of more women in the workforce has been strongly promoted in recent times, we still have very few women in the middle and top tiers of management in organizations. In 1971 women occupied 38% of the total workforce in the United States.

The percentage of women in middle and top managerial positions was insignificant. In a quarter of a century from then, only women managers occupied 40% of the managerial workforce in the US. In 1997 The United States and Canada had two of the highest ratios of women to men in managerial positions (67 and 68 women for every 100 men, respectively). In New Zealand there were 48 women for every 100 men in managerial positions. In most other countries, the numbers were far lower. In Poland the number was 18 while Japan had 9 women managers for every 100 men managers. In India, however, that number was found to be abysmal 2 women managers for every 100 men managers. Why are there so few women in our organizations' top tiers? Does a manager's gender, determine the way in which s/he behaves and/or is treated? How can the treatment women managers receive in organizations be explained? - These are some of the commonly researched questions in the field of "gender issues in management".

Perspectives in Literature

Five theoretical perspectives have been advanced in gender literature to answer the above questions, the person-or-gender-centered perspective, the situation-centered or the organization-structure perspective, the gender-organization perspective, the gender organization-system perspective and the gender-context perspective. The first perspective, the person-or-gender centered view was first advocated by Horner, in her study of low achievement among women, and in Hennig and Jardim's book on successful women in management. According to this perspective, the attributes individuals perceive they possess vary according to their sex and women's limited corporate progress is attributed to factors that are internal to women. Gender-centered theorists have promoted that their biological and/or socialization pattern has prompted women to exhibit traits and behaviours that are not conducive to their becoming successful managers. The second perspective, the situation-centered or organization-structure perspective was advocated by Kanter and further promoted by other researchers like Fagenson and Mainiero.

According to Kanter, individuals' positions in the organizational power hierarchy shape their perceptions, attributes, traits and behaviour. According to this perspective, there are two types of situations in organizations: advantageous and disadvantageous. Lower level positions in organizations offer little power to individuals, making them more dependent on others. This encourages lower level individuals to perceive themselves as being more feminine (understanding, aware of others' feelings and helpful to others) or "other focused" than upper level individuals. Traditionally women have been found to occupy lower level positions than upper level ones and hence the difference. The third and fourth perspectives make use of additive and non-additive combinations of the two above-mentioned perspectives to advance their viewpoint. Fagenson studied all four perspectives, and found some support for the first two perspectives.

However, she found no support for the third or the fourth perspective. The last perspective, the gender-context, is influenced by three streams of research: gender proportions, gender-ascribed status and gender stereotyping. Schneer suggested a conceptual combination of these three streams into one perspective, and labeled it "gender context".

According to these streams of research, it is not only a proportion of a certain gender present in a situational context that is important in determining differences, but also the ascribed social status of that group. As Falkenberg and Rychel (stated, women are stereotyped as having traits associated with a homemaker, which has created the second stereotype that women do not have the necessary traits to enter perceived masculine and/or high status occupations. Compounding this stereotype is the perceived higher value of men and masculine traits over women and feminine traits.

One conclusion from the studies pertaining to the gender-context perspective indicates the importance of 'perception' as compared to 'actual behaviour'. Significant differences have not been found to exist between men and women managers when factors like age, education and level in organization, are controlled. Women managers possess the personality traits and the motivation to manage and also have the leadership skills, etc. that are required to be successful managers. However they are perceived as not in possession of such skills. Thus if one has to improve upon differences in the situations of women and men in management, one should work on the 'perceptions' that prevail about women managers. Therefore, research, which probes perceptions, rather than that, which probes gender differences, would be far more suitable in explaining why the differences still exist and how such perceptions could be changed.

The gender-context approach is more useful in this respect. It deals with the phenomenon of 'gender stereotyping'. Stereotyping is a common phenomenon and humans are known for their dependence upon stereotypes to reduce information processing demands. Unfortunately, this dependence creates a number of problems for organizations and individuals when inaccurate stereotypes are formed, which in turn create barriers in the advancement of minority status individuals like women. The topic of human differences, real or alleged, and responses to these, is a key one in the social sciences. Social psychologists tend to discuss it in terms of 'stereotypes'. Stereotyping is the process by which people use social categories (e.g., race, sex) in acquiring, processing, and recalling information about others. Walter Lippmann introduced the term "stereotype" to represent the typical picture that comes to mind when thinking about a particular social group. Stereotypes are the traits and roles associated with certain groups or categories.

Within a social cognition framework, stereotypes function to reduce information processing demands, define group membership, and/or predict behaviour based on group membership. Stereotyping often has a negative connotation because it is often a source or excuse for injustice, based on relatively little information, is resistant to change even with availability of new information, and is rarely accurately applied to specific individuals. Gender Stereotyping has already been seen to lead to a number of inaccuracies resulting in negative consequences. Women managers are perceived as not possessing the traits/characteristics that are thought necessary for success in the managerial context, even though they have been found to actually possess such managerial traits. This study considers as gender stereotypes those managerial characteristics, on which there is a high association between managerial success and either man managers or women managers.

Gender Stereotyping and its Negative Effects

Research studies document the many negative effects of gender stereotyping in the workplace like role-status incongruence; career immobility, including recruitment and evaluation differences; power differences; differences in training and developmental opportunities; feedback differences and job segregation. One of the consequences of inaccurate gender stereotyping is that women are less likely to be chosen for traditionally male positions, such as those in senior management. This occurs because the perceived lack of fit between the job requirements and the stereotypic attributes ascribed to women managers leads to expectations that they will fail. Perhaps because of the expectations that they will fail, women are less likely to be chosen for assignments involving risk or working in unfamiliar areas of the business. Thus, another consequence of gender stereotyping is that women managers receive fewer developmental opportunities than men managers. Most organizations use performance evaluations in one way or another to decide salary increases and promotions to be given to employees.

Women's achievements tend to be devalued or attributed to luck or effort rather than ability or skill, which may reduce the organizational rewards, they receive. It has been observed that academic work produced by men may be valued more highly than that of women. A female student may have to outperform her male peers to be taken seriously by her professors. This general tendency to devalue women and their work is illustrated by Nieva and Gutek's study, in which two groups were asked to evaluate articles, paintings, resumes, and other similar products. The name on each item was clearly masculine or feminine. The sex of the originator of each item was switched for the second group of evaluators. Regardless of the type of item evaluated, those ascribed to a male were rated higher than those ascribed to a female. Stereotypes, however, cannot be eliminated, therefore making it imperative for organizational behaviour researchers to first identify stereotypes that are commonly held of women managers, and then promote conditions that propagate more accurate stereotypes.

Even before emphasizing on increasing gender diversity and recommending diversity benefits to counter negative effects of gender stereotypes, there is a need to assess what stereotypes are held of women managers. Stereotypes held of women managers have often been measured in the western cultural context. There being a dearth of such stereotype-assessment studies in the Indian context, such a study was long overdue. Gender stereotypes are held by both men managers and women managers. The need for assessing the stereotypes held by men managers of women managers was considered more important, as men still dominate organizational positions from which they recruit, assess, and develop women managers. The need was also felt for assessing gender stereotypes held by women managers themselves, as women are increasingly going to occupy important positions in organizations and will equally share employee assessment and recruitment functions with men managers in the not so distant future.

This stereotype-assessment issue in the Indian context was addressed in part by Bhatnagar and Swamy, when they explored the relationship between "interaction" with women managers, and "the attitudes toward women managers" as measured by a 22- item WAMS scale, the sample being male managers from a single bank. Results showed little relation between the extent of interaction and attitudes towards women managers. However, the "attitudes towards women managers" were not separately explored. It was felt that the 22 items in the modified WAMS instrument were not enough to capture the entire stereotypical picture of women managers in the Indian context. A more comprehensive list with exhaustive managerial characteristics as items was needed. Schein's Descriptive Index (henceforth referred to as SDI), fitted the requirements of the study better, despite issues of cross-cultural applicability. The BSRI was also considered, but rejected, as the characteristics (items in the instrument) were found to be too general in applicability and not as managerially-oriented in nature as the SDI.

As in Heilman et al.'s study, here too, the interest lay in the managerial sub-set of gender stereotypes of women, as this sub-set is more relevant to the managerial context in organizations, than the overall stereotypes held of women in general. Towards the end of the period 1987-1996, the ratio of men to women in all managerial positions in the USA in was 1.4 to 1. At the very top level of salary, however, the ratio of men to women was 20 to 1. A Catalyst survey in 2003 revealed that women held only 7.9% of the highest titles of the Fortune 500 companies. In the Indian context, the absence of such studies leaves little room for factual verification of the same phenomenon. Only one Indian company appears on the Fortune 500 list. Even without equivalent data for the top 500 companies in India, one can safely conclude that the percentage of women at the very top would not be high.

However, given that management schools across India are churning out fresh women managers who represent about 7-10% of the total fresh graduate managers at the junior organizational levels, it cannot be expected that the percentage of women managers in the top tiers in India would exceed any significant number. Evidently, more women enter the managerial workforce at the junior levels. It is at the middle managerial level that they stagnate, resulting in a dismal number graduating from the middle to the top. Therefore, the third set in the SDI solicited ratings of 'successful middle managers', the other two sets referring to 'men managers' and 'women managers'. It was expected that not only men, but women too would associate men managers with success, more than they associate women managers with success. Moreover, the numerical proportions fuelled expectations that gender stereotypes associated with women managers and success, would be characteristics which are not usually associated with performance related measures.

Men-Managers' Sample

For the exclusive male sample, the respondents' ages ranged from 22 to 57 years (mean = 33.86 years, median = 30 years). Managerial experience ranged from less than 1 year to 36 years (mean = 8.84 years, median = 6 years). This is quite comparable to the Heilman et al, (1989) study, in which the age range was from 24 to 63 years; and managerial experience ranged from and 'less than 1 year' to 42 years (median = 6 years). As mentioned earlier, the respondents were practising managers from three levels of management (junior, middle and senior) in different industries, and from all over India. The sample comprised of 28.57% junior, 41.9% middle and 29.53% senior level managers.

Intra-class Correlation Coefficients

To determine the degree of correspondence between ratings of successful middle managers and men managers, and that between successful middle managers and women managers, two intra-class coefficients (ICCs) were computed. This was done to compare the similarity of respondents' ratings of successful middle managers and women managers and successful middle managers and men managers, as reported on the Descriptive Index. Thus, a high ICC would reflect a similar description of each set of descriptors or characteristics (successful middle managers and men managers or successful middle managers and women managers) and a low ICC would reflect a difference or dissimilarity in the descriptions of each set. The intraclass correlation coefficients in this study show a large and significant relationship between ratings of successful middle managers and men managers, but no significant relationship between ratings of successful middle managers and women managers.

Women-Managers' sample

For the exclusively female sample, the women respondents' (n = 93) ages ranged from 22 to 46 years (mean = 29.78 years, median = 29 years). Managerial experience ranged from less than 1 year to 15 years (mean = 5.46 years, median = 5 years). This is somewhat comparable to the Schein study, in which the age range was from 24 to 64 years; and managerial experience ranged from 1 to 40 years. As mentioned earlier, the respondents were practising managers from three levels of management (junior, middle and senior) in different industries, and from all over India. The sample comprised of

49.46% junior, 45.16% middle and 5.38% senior level managers.

Results related to Stereotypes

Stereotypes with negative connotations, which perceptually hamper the progress of women managers in India, would be those managerial characteristics on which successful middle managers are rated closer to men managers than to women managers. The other stereotypes held of women managers would be those characteristics on which successful middle managers were rated closer to women managers than men managers. However, any stereotypical characteristic would not have much effect on further studies, if there were an absence of associations of success along with that characteristic. Thus, for a stereotype to be considered as important for further studies, two things have to be considered: 1. Managerial characteristics, which are considered necessary for managerial success and are also, associated more with men managers than with women managers. These would be 'masculine-positive' stereotypes. 2. Managerial characteristics, which are considered necessary for managerial success and are also, associated more with women managers than with men managers. These would be 'feminine-positive' stereotypes.

Male Managerial Sample ANOVA

A series of one-way ANOVAs was conducted on each of the 92 Descriptive Index items. ANOVA was conducted on the male respondents' sample to determine which of the 92 items were rated differently, to a significant extent, across the three sets/groups: women managers, men managers and successful middle managers. For each ANOVA an alpha level of 0.0005 was used as the criterion of significance to maintain an overall alpha level of $p < 0.05$ for all ANOVAs. In our study a significant effect was found for 35 items, as compared to 79 items in the Heilman et al, study. To identify the specific items that were seen as more descriptive of successful middle managers and men managers than of women managers, and the items that were seen as more descriptive of successful middle managers and women managers than of men managers, a Duncan's multiple-range was done on each of the 35 items for which significant effects were found in the ANOVA analysis.

In the previous studies, masculine stereotypes were determined by those descriptors on which men managers and successful managers were rated closely and on which women managers were simultaneously rated significantly differently. Similarly, feminine items were those items on which women managers and successful managers were rated closely, and men managers were simultaneously rated differently.35 items, were found to be significant (as compared to 31 out of 79 in the earlier Heilman et al, study. For 18 of the 35 significant items, ratings of successful middle managers were more similar to men managers than to women managers, and for 2 out of the 35 significant items (as compared to none out of the 79 items in the earlier study), ratings of successful middle managers were more similar to women managers than men managers. There were 15 items, on which no significant differential associations were made with successful managers.

It is disheartening to note that none of the two items on which women managers have been rated closer to successful managers, are actually thought of as "required" for success. In other words these two characteristics (as opposed to characteristics like 'analytical ability' and 'skilled in business matters') would not usually contribute towards success as translated in hard performance terms. Before proceeding to the next table of items, it is necessary to explain the inclusion of the word "less" in the above. The rating scale of the SDI is a five-point scale, in which 1 represents "Uncharacteristic" and 5 represents "Characteristic". There is a neutral point 3 in the scale, which represents "neither characteristic nor uncharacteristic". 5 – Characteristic 4 – Somewhat characteristic 3 – Neither characteristic nor uncharacteristic 2 – Somewhat uncharacteristic 1 – Not characteristic After performing the Duncan's multiple range test for the characteristic of 'vulgar', a close look at the three means (from the three different sets....women managers, successful managers and men managers) reveals that both successful managers and women managers have been rated closely no doubt, but on the lower side of 3, i.e., towards 1, while men managers have been rated highly, i.e., towards 5.

Gender Stereotypes and the Socialization Process

The term gender does not exist still in many languages through the world and it is not easy to make understand even to educate people what is the subtle difference between gender and sex and why we are talking now about gender and not about sex. Gender equality has been and still is perceived in many societies as something concerning only women, invented for women and implemented by women. Women are struggling for gender equality, what about men? Do they need it? Will they allow it? Will they accept it? The stereotypes concerning both genders are so deeply enshrined in our minds that sometimes even the strongest advocates for gender equality are stepping back unconsciously and are paying tribute to their stereotypical thinking. This is maybe the reason why the gender equality cause was perceived only as a "women's" cause and men were more or less isolated from this process.

There are some major events that paved the way to gender equality and gave more arguments to the movement that supported it. Starting with the Vienna Conference in 1993 and the UN International Conference on Population and Development (ICPD) in Cairo in 1994 we came to Beijing in 1995, whose Platform of Action and Declaration became major program documents that fuelled the struggle for women's rights and gender equality for many years on. In the Beijing Declaration, adopted by the Fourth World Conference on Women in 1995, governments expressed their determination to encourage men to participate fully in all actions towards gender equality. The Declaration emphasized that equal sharing of responsibilities and a harmonious partnership between women and men were critical to their well-being and that of their families as well as to the consolidation of democracy. The Platform for Action emphasized the principle of shared power and responsibility between women and men at home, in the workplace and in the wider national and international communities. It stressed that gender equality could only be achieved when men and women worked together in partnerships, and that the principle of equality of women and men had to be integral to the socialization process.

Specific actions aim in particular at promoting harmonization of work and family responsibilities for men and women; at encouraging men to share equally in child care and household work; and at promoting programmes to educate and enable men to assume their responsibilities to prevent HIV/AIDS and other sexually transmitted diseases (STDs).

When and where starts the socialization process? It starts with the opening of the eyes of the small baby. She or he understands very quickly the difference to be female or male, to be poor or to be wealthy. Although in different cultures in the world the attitudes toward boys and girls show some nuances, girls are taught since the very early age that they have to obey, and boys - that they have to be strong and to be leaders. Girls are playing with dolls, they are learning to prepare food and clothes and everything that is associated with "women's duties" and boys are playing with small cars, weapons, are encouraged to practice different sports and are taught to be the "masters of the world". What is sad is that, these first lessons, children are receiving from their mothers, who are usually "contaminated" by the same stereotypical thinking and it is really difficult to get out of this vicious circle. Too often it seems that boys learn early on that their interests are opposed to those of girls and women. This is based partly on a defensive insecurity, but it is also based on the fact that material relations (access to resources) actually have been structured in a way that benefits men and harms women. So, when women organize for equality, often men react defensively.

The next environment that children are entering is the school, where a conscious socialization is happening. Again, looking through the school books from the very beginning gender stereotypes is present and reinforced. The images that small kids receive from these books are women with babies in their hands, or women preparing food, or women working in the field, or, at the high end - women nurses, women teachers. In the same time men are usually soldiers, playing some prestigious sport, executing some heavy job, and, of course, leaders. Somehow the perception that being a soldier and carrying weapons is more important than giving birth and taking care of life is induced in the minds since the very beginning of the conscious life of children. And this leads to further divisions, stereotyping and to the perception that women have to give and to accept and men have to take and to impose. Looking again at school manuals we will find images or small texts, where boys are those, who are good in mathematics: they are "helping" their little sisters in solving the problems and girls - they are good in reading, singing, etc. When the teaching practical skills of the boys will be of learning to operate machines or computers and girls will be taught to be dactylos or similar.

The process of socialization starts even before school - with tales and toys. It was strange to discover during and literature exercise with boys that tales for the smallest were full of violence and gender stereotypes. And if stereotyping was more or less understandable, the discovery of violence was shocking. Somehow children become familiar with violence and the tales since the early childhood help them to accept as something normal the coercion, the harassment, the cruelty and the violence. When [within the exercise] the students had to think and discuss this theme, they themselves discovered, that the society unconsciously was imposing a way of thinking, leading to easier acceptance of violence and gender division. The patriarchal society is a violent one. But violence is something that is learnt. And to combat it we need learning and a space for discussing it openly. This space is missing both to boys and girls. In order to change these patterns, it is necessary a complete rethinking of the process of socialization and initial education and much more attention to be paid to teaching equal values both to boys and girls.

Boys also can cry, and girls need to be strong. Therefore the engagement of men and boys in achieving gender equality requires much greater attention to gender stereotypes and expectations about men's roles and responsibilities, and how these expectations influence male behaviour. Such stereotypes continue to place greater emphasis, as well as greater value, on the role of men and boys in public life and in the work place, as opposed to women's role in unpaid famlly labour, care giving and community work.

The World of Work and the Family

The growing interest in the role of men and boys is due as well to the shift in the work for gender equality from a focus on advancing women's status to a focus on gender relations, i.e. the relations between women and men. The gender approach allows for clarification of the roles commonly associated with being male or female in public and in private life, and provides a basis for identifying differences and inequalities between women and men in responsibilities assigned, activities undertaken, access to and control over resources as well as decision- making opportunities. A better understanding of gender roles and related structural inequalities increases opportunities for policy measures and other actions aimed at overcoming such inequalities. Changing patterns of production and reproduction are also indicative of changes in gender relations which challenge traditional images and expectations associated with men's - as well as women's - roles, such as those of breadwinner, care giver, or head of household. Therefore there is a need for a re-assessment of the roles and responsibilities of women and men, of stereotypical and traditional gender roles, and of existing power relations between women and men.

The question of unequal power relations between men and women as an obstacle to gender equality is crucial, especially with regard to violence against women. Another crucial point is the role of men in preventing HIV infection among women and girls, especially having in mind the asymmetric power relations between men and women and women's subordination and vulnerability to discrimination. Peer pressure, socialization processes and belief systems influence adherence to gender specific stereotypes. Ideas of the inferiority or superiority of either of the sexes, and of stereotyped roles for men and women not only limit progress in achieving gender equality, but also perpetuate inequalities and can constitute obstacles to men's abilities and opportunities for redressing gender inequalities. There is the deep stereotypical thinking that only women can take care of children, therefore, when talking about equality in the family life, men usually cannot take advantage of paid leave for rearing a child. Almost nothing is done to make men choose to stay at home and take care of children.

The state policy is failing to create interest towards this issue and help in achieving equality. There are a lot of men willing to do so, but peer pressure and stereotypical thinking stop them from being equal. We need to reinvent the roles of both genders and make men and boys play a substantial role in promoting and achieving gender equality. This is a responsibility of the entire society that concerns and engages equally women and men. There is a need to combat persistent gender stereotyping, which had led to insufficient sharing of tasks and responsibilities by men for care giving within families, households and communities, and unequal power relationships between women and men.

In the contemporary world the percentage of single parent female-headed households is higher than that of male-headed. The percentage of female- headed families with two parents is also increasing. High levels of underemployment and unemployment for both women and men, especially in the countries of transition mean that men often cannot play the role of breadwinner sufficiently. In this context the household as a workplace is very typical example for gender inequality.

Unpaid workers, overwhelmingly women through their caring work support education of children and the paid employment of men. There is a strong belief that power is associated with physical strength. The deep stereotyping concerning this belief makes difficult to change the mentality of men and boys. But they have a number of reasons for not wanting change in gender arrangements, and sometimes face difficulties if they do want, or support change: they are brought up with the expectations of being cared for, they lack of skills in domestic work and practice in caring work; the public policies and practices make it cheaper or easier for families to maintain old breadwinner/housewife patterns, which means that still in many countries the "family friendly" measures are available only to mothers. However this is gradually changing with the new legislation being adopted in the EU and with the obligation for the accessing countries to comply and implement the acquis communautaire. But the fear of social stigma or loss of dignity still exists if men depend on women's earnings. It happens when men resist women's involvement in paid work with the arguments how they would feel insulted if the wife earns.

It is not exactly the case in Eastern Europe, where women have long lasting tradition in sharing the responsibility of bread winning of the family. However the stereotype exists here as well in a more subtle level: there is a division between women's jobs and men's jobs, where women are usually employed in low paid positions or are encouraged to enter professions that have lost their prestige because of the big number of women exercising them.

In the same time, a shift in men's perception of masculinity could be noticed and there are many reasons why men and boys would like to move towards equality as well. One of them is the negative impact on men's' life and health of the 'breadwinner' model. Men have more and more difficulties in meeting the expectations to be the only breadwinners and these impacts negatively their self-confidence and the family climate.

This is especially true in the countries of transition, where social values have dramatically changed. In this part of the world women have been caring the burden of bread winning on equal footing with men during long years. However the political changes impacted both women and man - women becoming progressively the poor of the society and men carrying the psychological burden of not being able to meet the expectations of the family to be the only bread winner.

Therefore the younger generation should be motivated to change. The European legislation provides for a compulsory parental leave for at least 15 days for the father and more on will. Unfortunately the economic motivation is too weak for men and hampers their desire for more active fatherhood.

The Difference in the Perception of Sexual Relations and HIV/AIDS

In the man's world there are certain things that men don't question: the bravado, the lust for experiment and adventure, the way men pursue their sexual desires. This and other male icons are closely connected to "the right to be a man". In the man's world there are also certain things you do not talk about: the mistakes, love, hesitations, social failures, weaknesses that are often associated with femininity. Sexuality and love have deep roots in the creation of an experience of personal identity. For young men the teenage years are an age of denial of weaknesses which is connected to what is considered feminine. There is also the wrong perception of socialization: socialization doesn't necessarily mean sexual relationship or sexual activity. Men are differently positioned in relation to the HIV/AIDS pandemic and these differences need to be recognized when developing strategies.

The specific customs and ideas about sexuality are also relevant. Asymmetrical ideas of men's and women's sexuality encourage unsafe sex among young people. There is evidence of a strong belief in men's sexual initiative among youth. The very way sexual relationships are constructed may be important. There is a general need for educational action towards gender equality and a specific need for HIV and safe sex education directed towards heterosexual men. To the extent men control sexuality; they have the capacity to change sexual practices. Men can take a more active role in reproductive health generally, and research is needed and policy support for this. Providing services to men and boys are an important venue for work around gender equality principles and practice, including:

- Sexual and reproductive health services and programmes, especially those that deal with issues about sexuality and fatherhood;
- General health services;
- Education programmes by NGOs which address men;
- Develop further strategies for combating HIV/AIDS pandemic and male involvement in achieving girls' and women's sexual and reproductive rights.

Strategic Opportunities

There is a gradual shift of opinion towards gender equality, especially among younger men. This arises from a broad commitment to social justice and human rights, which are acknowledged by men and boys. There are elements in most men's consciousness that a program for equality can address. Men are not a homogenous group. There are divisions of interest among men, which align some groups of men or some issues with women, or specific groups of women.

For many men, the gain from patriarchy is more symbolic than material, may even be illusory. A more gender equal society will not be to the advantage of all men compared with the world we now live in, but it may be to the advantage of a majority of men. However, there are sometimes alliances between women and men - fighting for health care, government support for families, equal access to education etc. But the group of men who are working in the alliance for gender equity, equal health care and education, equity at work or in decision-making is too small in number. Something more: they are marginalized in their own community and often intimidated as though they are feminine in kind.

These sorts of intimidation result in a kind of silence among men that lets the access of gender discrimination in a subtle way. Though the developed world often prides itself on achieving gender equality, there is more gender inequality than most people believe, and gains of the past are not secure for the future. The content of mass media in the developed world still presents to young people exploitative images of women, violent images of men and reactionary ideas about gender equality. There has been a movement in Bulgaria initiated by women's NGOs to stop discriminatory advertisements. Phone cards have been advertised using the size of women1s breast. Other media images have been attacked as well showing women only as objects of sexual desire or as stupid females whose only taught goes to washing products or similar. This stereotypical representation is acting unconsciously on the attitudes and perceptions of young people - both boys and girls. These images provoke unrealistic beliefs concerning the roles of genders in the family and in the social life. Men's partnerships with anti-violence women's groups are critical. They enable men to learn from existing efforts rather than reinventing he wheel *(BGRF programmes)*. They lessen the risk that men will collude in, or be complicit with dominant and oppressive forms of masculinity. They are a powerful and practical demonstration of men's and a woman's shared interest in stopping violence.

Men's partnerships with women are an inspiring example

of cross-gender collaboration, a form of activism which reaches across and transforms gender inequalities. It is also a matter of experience that men (as well as women) attempting to change gender relations and definitions of masculinity can be subject to ridicule, harassment or intimidation from other men defending the status quo.

Possible benefits to men and boys are not necessarily at the expense of women and girls. The belief that what one gender gains and the other must necessarily lose is both damaging and false. However, to achieve equality there must be a redistribution of income and prestige, certainly, in which men's relative advantage will decline. But there are ways in which men specifically stand to gain, including better work/life balance, better diet and health, less vulnerability to occupational stress and injury. Many of the benefits of gender equality are shared benefits between men and women, especially the reduction of the level of violence.

Gender Roles and Stereotypes

Gender roles are "socially and culturally defined prescriptions and beliefs about the behaviour and emotions of men and women". Many theorists believe that perceived gender roles form the bases for the development of gender identity. Prominent psychological theories of gender role and gender identity development include evolutionary theory, object-relations theory, gender schema theory and social role theory. Evolutionary theories of gender development are grounded in genetic bases for differences between men and women. Functionalists propose that men and women have evolved differently to fulfill their different and complementary functions, which are necessary for survival. Similarly, sociobiologists suggest that behavioural differences between men and women stem from different sexual and reproductive strategies that have evolved to ensure that men and women are able to efficiently reproduce and effectively pass on their genes. These evolutionary-based theories share similarities with the essentialist and maximalist perspectives discussed previously.

In contrast, object-relations theorists focus on the effects of socialization on gender development. For example, Nancy Chodorow emphasizes the role of women as primary caregivers in the development of sex differences. Chodorow asserts that the early bond between mother and child affects boys and girls differently. Whereas boys must separate from their mothers to form their identities as males, girls do not have to endure this separation to define their identities as females. Chodorow explains that the devalued role of women is a product of the painful process men undergoes to separate them from the female role. Gender schema theory focuses on the role of cognitive organization in addition to socialization. This theory postulates that children learn how their cultures and/or societies define the roles of men and women and then internalize this knowledge as a gender schema, or unchallenged core belief. The gender schema is then used to organize subsequent experiences.

Children's perceptions of men and women are thus an interaction between their gender schemas and their experiences. Eventually, children will incorporate their own self-concepts into their gender schema and will assume the traits and behaviours that they deem suitable for their gender. Alice Eagly offers yet another explanation of gender development that is based on socialization. Eagly's social role theory suggests that the sexual division of labour and societal expectations based on stereotypes produce gender roles. Eagly (1987) distinguishes between the communal and agentic dimensions of gender-stereotyped characteristics.

The communal role is characterized by attributes, such as nurturance and emotional expressiveness, commonly associated with domestic activities, and thus, with women. The agentic role is characterized by attributes such as assertiveness and independence, commonly associated with public activities, and thus, with men. Behaviour is strongly influenced by gender roles when cultures endorse gender stereotypes and form firm expectations based on those stereotypes. As Eagly suggests, gender roles are closely linked with gender stereotypes. Stereotypes are "over generalized beliefs about people based on their membership in one of many social categories". Gender stereotypes vary on four dimensions: traits, role behaviours, physical characteristics, and occupations. For example, whereas men are more likely to be perceived as aggressive and competitive, women are more likely to be viewed as passive and cooperative.

Traditionally, men have been viewed as financial providers, whereas women have been viewed as caretak-ers. Physical characteristics and occupations have also been considered consistent or inconsistent with masculine or feminine roles.

Traditional gender stereotypes are most representative of the dominant (white, middle-class) culture. Hope Landrine asserts that although race and social class may not be mentioned when inquiring about gender stereotypes, most people will make assumptions about these categories. Her research suggests that when race and social classes are specified, different gender stereotypes emerge.

Gender roles and stereotypes affect couple and family interaction. Often, for example, the division of household labour is based on gender.

Traditionally, white women in heterosexual couples remained at home and completed most of the domestic labour, while their male partners worked outside the home to provide the family income. Although women have increasingly joined the workforce over the past thirty years, they continue to do the majority of the household labour. Lawrence Kurdek studied white, heterosexual, gay, and lesbian couples without children.

He found that heterosexual and gay couples were more likely than lesbian couples to divide household labour so that one partner did the majority of the work. Lesbian couples were most likely to share domestic tasks or take turns doing the tasks.

Gender roles often become more differentiated when men and women become parents. Overall, women provide more direct care for and spend more time with children. This care includes taking responsibility for the mental work of gathering and processing information about infant care, delegating the tasks related to infant care, and worrying about infant health and well-being. In sum, the unequal division of both household labour and childcare, with women doing the bulk of the work, is thought to contribute to the reported lower marital satisfaction for women. Gender roles and stereotypes affect men and women in other ways.

Specifically, men and women may be judged by how well they conform to traditional stereotypes. In his theory of masculine gender role strain, Joespech Pleck asserted that boys and men are pressured to fulfill a standard of masculinity. Boys and men, for example, who do not fulfill the standard often, suffer from low self-worth.

Other lifelong consequences befall men who experience traumatic socialization practices such as rites of passage that entail violence.

Even men who successfully fulfill the standard of masculinity suffer psychologically or emotionally from rigid constraints on acceptable parenting roles for men. Richard Lazur and Richard Majors contend that gender role strain is pronounced with men of colour. Men of colour must balance the dominant standards of masculinity with their cultures' standards of masculinity in an effort to fulfill both satisfactorily. In addition, men of colour must overcome prejudice and other obstacles to fulfill the standards of masculinity. The result is increased gender role strain for men of colour. Likewise, white women and women of colour may be constrained by standards of femininity, such as the pressure to have children.

Gender stereotypes can also affect men's and women's

performance. Stereotype threat is defined as "an individual's awareness that he or she may be judged by or may self-fulfill negative stereo-types about her or his gender or ethnic group". Research indicates that stereo-type threat can negatively affect performance by increasing anxiety. For example, Steven Spencer, Claude Steele, and Diane Quinn found that women performed significantly worse than men on a math test when the participants were led to believe that the test would probably produce gender differences.

In contrast, women and men performed equally well when the participants were led to believe that the test did not produce gender differences.

These findings suggest that negative stereotypes can and do negatively affect performance even when the stereotype has not been internalized or incorporated into the view of the self.

4

Woman's Choices and Changes

Women who turn 40 today have a lot more going for them than those who reached that milestone a generation ago. Many still have young children at home, having started their families later than their mothers did. And, because so many of them work outside the home, they have a wide range of interests and activities in addition to their home life. While Mom may have agonized over what she would do when the kids left home, today's woman is more likely to wish them well and then to launch a new career or concentrate on putting the romance back into her marriage. Reaching 40 does not signal the end to her satisfying sex life and, for an increasing number of women today, "mid-life crisis" is not even in their vocabulary.

If sex has been an important and enjoyable part of your life during your younger years, there is no reason to expect it to change because you have suddenly crossed an arbitrary age barrier. In fact, it might just get better; inhibitions often disappear once the fear of pregnancy is gone and, with the "nest" empty, there may be time for more leisurely lovemaking. One of the more important ingredients for a healthy sex life after 40 is unquestionably good communication with your spouse. During the middle years, there are a number of physiological changes that take place in a woman's body.

Some can be modified; some can be controlled; but none can be avoided altogether. The important thing is to realize which is which.

Since no one yet has found the Fountain of Youth, there is no magic formula to ward off aging. While science continues its search for the genes that decide how people age, we know that to a large extent how a person ages is strongly influenced by some controllable lifestyle factors: exposure to sunlight; whether or not they smoke; whether or not they exercise and eat well; how they handle stress; and their overall outlook on life.

Today, women appear to have chosen to think of menopause as a threshold that signals a time in their lives when they are free to do all those things they have waited a lifetime to do. This is really not a new phenomenon. Anthropologist Margaret Mead is credited with saying, "There is no greater power in the world than the zest of a post-menopausal woman." It appears that a great many Baby Boomer women believe her with their "lead, follow, or get out of the way" attitude.

In recent years, it appears that American women are experiencing the symptoms of menopause earlier than the previous average age. Research suggests that women who fall into the Type A personality style — who are constantly on the go and who are often under considerable stress — often experience early menopause. Generally speaking however, the "average" age of menopause is 51. Somewhere between the ages of 45 and 55, women begin to experience a year or two of irregular periods, fluctuations in body temperature, and some other unfamiliar and vague physical or emotional symptoms. The biological impact of the change does not happen overnight, it is a gradual process that may cover as much as ten years. After a woman has gone for an entire year without menstruating, the process is considered complete.

Just as it is impossible to predict when it will occur, there is no way of knowing ahead of time exactly how the process will affect a woman. Some are virtually unaware of any change at all, and others find themselves suffering from a wide range of unpleasant and frightening symptoms. As the hormonal changes begin to occur, it is not unusual for a woman to feel "strange" and even a little off balance. The "classic" symptom of menopause is the hot flash – or medically speaking, vasomotor instability – when the skin temperature rises, then falls, and is accompanied by sweating and heart palpitations, nausea and anxiety. Research shows that three out of four women experience them. An important thing to understand is that until a woman has been without a period for a year, she may still be ovulating. That means that –, unless a pregnancy is desired – contraception is still needed. While there are a number of options for birth control during this time, many women are concerned about taking the "pill" because they say they remember warnings about risks when taking the pill over age 35.

Women's Health in Middle and Later Life

Evidence exists in literature about the problems of women approaching their later years. There is sufficient coverage at an international level in terms of the transitions women face in later life including physiological changes. Aging in the West has prompted the recognition of the individual as deserving of attention to delay morbidity and maintain quality of life.

Health care for the older woman is visualised by urging promotion of a healthy lifestyle, physicians' attention in diagnosis and prevention of disease and addressing the various psychological and psychosocial issues that older women face. Amongst these hormones replacement therapy is advised in these developed countries to alleviate certain physiological symptoms of distress, as well as risks of certain diseases such as osteoporosis. The other transition that women undergo is from a reproductive to a non-reproductive stage of life with menopause emerging as a striking feature within it. A review of the state of knowledge prevailing about menopause, suggests that there was limited data on age at menopause especially of non-European populations. Data was also insufficient and hence there were recommendations for studies to establish any relationship between age at menopause, and marital status and occupation, parity, smoking, use of oral contraceptives, weather and altitude, or socio-economic factors, as well as the impact on it in different socio-cultural settings. Studies have also demonstrated the association of vasomotor and psychological symptoms with the cessation of menstrua-tion, as well as a few enquiries about the variations in sexuality.

Our concerns, however, veer down to rural women's lives in India. The problems of the aged, studied in some rural situations in India have highlighted some of the special needs that the aged required fulfilled. While many of the aged were relegated to a subordinate status within their families, almost a third of those surveyed were affected by chronic illnesses or were depressed, and needed specialised treatment and care. Others have studied specific categories of the aged such as widows addressing their special problems. The problems of widows seen from the dimension of aging are significant as more and more women outlive men. Questions are posed regarding support and care both from within the family and society, as well as the type of care and support they require and on whom the burden should fall in addressing them.

While all these studies have looked at women's lives in their later years, few studies have tried to specifically understand what women feel as they pass life through its mid years. One study, where women's subjective evaluation of the menopause has been explored, presented women's feelings about the menopause and their need to pursue their new interests in life in place of the role they had assumed till then. Changes within the family involving losses and separation from spouse and children affected women's self-esteem causing anxiety and worry. Many women did not feel interested in sexual activity. In term of health care women felt disappointed by the care from doctors who they felt did not understand their conditions completely.

In understanding the lives of women in India, it is more meaningful to view them through the process of the transitions that the family goes through in terms of marriage, childbirth, and deaths of its members, than the chronological ageing of women. Chronological age has little relevance for most Indian women, and the passage of years is realised more due to physical signs such as greying of hair, loss of teeth, cessation of menstruation. The life period of interest to us, referred by Vatuk as 'middle age', commences around early to mid-forties. It is the period when women, who are active workers in a public sphere as agricultural labour or seasonal workers, would have to decrease or even completely stop their involvement in wage earning activities due to age-related physical debility.

This reduced physical ability due to ageing, would mean an increase in dependence on sons or other members of the household for economic support despite changes in attitude and behaviour. Within the familial set-up, sons begin to marry and daughters-in-law join the household or even set up separate establishments. While there is record of benefits accruing and improvements bearing on the lives of women as they grow older, they also suffer some very real problems in terms of health and overall well-being. Changes also create considerable stress for women affecting their identity, self esteem, and social and familial relationships. Within this aura of change in a woman's roles, responsibilities, and relationships, occurs menopause.

The onset of menopause indicates a transition of another sort. Menopause is a reproductive milestone in a woman's life but it also is a critical juncture when women not only experience biological changes but concurring social and psychological changes. References to the menopause have existed through history; as early as the sixth century A.D. the average age at which menstruation ceases, was referred to being 50 years, which still remains to be so even today. Writing about the diseases of women in the late eighteenth century and the early nineteenth century, researchers have noted that the menopause was the phase when women were prone to chronic illnesses. In the twentieth century, psychoanalysts' attention was captured by the phenomenon of the menopause. Notable amongst them, Helene Deutsch and Therese Benedek writing in the mid-century made references to the psychological changes it caused in terms of negative reactions such as grief and disappointment, but also that it presented opportunities for growth.

In fact, today, one-third of women's adult years are spent beyond the menopause. Individual women vary in the beginning of pre-menopause and the time for the transition into menopause to be complete. Studies have also established that women experience changes in physical wellbeing which impact on their psychological states as well, and here too, some women may have severe symptoms, while others have few complaints.

While recent clinical studies have sought to indicate how the menopausal transition demonstrates the complex interplay of environmental, behavioural and biological factors, especially in midlife, earlier research in this area have brought out the descriptive aspects of menopause, as well as the clinical trials attempted to propose modes of treatment of the syndrome. Reviews however state that these descriptive aspects of the menopause are based mostly on insufficient data for scientific validity; surveys, estimating the age at menopause and the consideration of symptoms, pose methodological problems of the study design and problems of recall and reporting, while the methodological problems in the clinical trials of the treatment of the problems during menopause, concern the design and reliability in results.

Women's Health

Women's health is the effect of gender on disease and health that encompasses a broad range of biological and psychosocial issues. Women's health is the concept that examines gender differences in health and disease states. The average life expectancy has almost doubled for women (79 years for women and 73 years for men), when compared with averages during the turn of the century. Because of the gender gap in lifespan, women comprise approximately two thirds of the population older than 65 and three fourths of the population aged 85 years and older. Currently the fastest growing group in the United States is persons aged 85 years and older. Because of gender life expectancy differences, it is estimated that at the beginning of the twenty-first century, women will outnumber men in the 85 years and older category by 3:1. The reasons for this variance are primarily due to physiological differences among men and women.

During different phases of a women's life cycle there are complex interactions that exist between sex hormones, physiological changes, and emotional issues. Physiological changes occur as early as embryonic development when hormones program structural differences between male and female brains. During reproductive years, sex hormones profoundly influence reproduction and development, which creates a spectrum of gender specific health issues. With advancing age and onset of menopause, women's risk factors for disease are comparably similar to men's. Although the same disease may affect women as men, it is thought that biological mechanisms and psychosocial differences influence the clinical course of the disease (natural history) differently in women. The number of women working has doubled within the past 50 years.

The effect of work stress, new environmental exposures and multiple roles is expected to have health and social impact. The leading causes of death among women are cardiovascular disease, malignant cancer, cerebrovascular disease, chronic lung disease, pneumonia/influenza, and diabetes. Additionally, women can be prone to osteoporosis, alcohol abuse, psychological disorders, human immunod-eficiency virus infection, and violence. Heart Disease accounts for approximately a third of all deaths in women. About 250,000 women die annually of coronary heart disease or a one in three chance after age 40 years. The incidence of heart disease occurs about 10 years later in women than in men, since estrogens in premenopausal women have a protective effect. African American women are more prone to die from heart disease up to age 75.

Beyond 75 years of age the propensity is reversed. Native American and Hispanic women have lower death rates from heart disease. Malignant cancers are the most common cause of premature death among women. Breast cancer is the second leading cause of death in women and the most commonly diagnosed cancer. Lung cancer, secondary to cigarette smoking is the leading cause of cancer death among women. Cerebrovascular disease, or stroked related deaths account for approximately 6% of all deaths in women and it is the third leading cause of mortality. The least common form of stroke, subarachnoid hemorrhage, is the more common cause in women.

The prevalence of cigarette smoking has increased greatly in women and this is correlated with pulmonary disease. Death rates for pulmonary disease including cancer and infectious causes of death are expected to rise for women. Diabetes, a leading cause of death in women is more prevalent among Hispanic, African American, and Native American women. Past age 45, diabetes affects about one in six women.

Women can also develop:

- Osteoporosis or loss of the quantity of bone, common in postmenopausal women who have estrogen changes.
- Alcohol abuse, characterized by repeated usage of alcohol despite negative consequences. These women frequently

do not seek treatment because of fear of consequences (i.e., loss of child custody). This disease can also have adverse affects on fertility and in the developing fetus if the mother continues to consume alcohol (fetal alcohol syndrome).

- Psychological disorders, such as depression and eating disorders.
- Acquired immunodeficiency syndrome (AIDS), which represents the highest percent increase in death rates.
- Violence, a leading cause of death, primarily caused by a perpetrator who is or was a partner.

Women's Health and Complexity Science

At the turn of the 20th century, gross anatomy guided medical inquiry and discipline-bound specialties formed around organ systems. The microscope took the focus down to the cell; advances in imaging and biochemistry have reduced our focus further to the molecule and its biology. Medical education organized its curriculum with discrete basic science courses, and organ-system-based clinical clerkships, residencies, fellowships, and specialties. The explosion of knowledge fueled by faster and faster information technologies has shifted educational goals from knowledge acquisition to critical thinking and information management. In response, the basic sciences have begun to be integrated and new curricular topics, such as medical informatics and evidence-based medicine, have been added. Academic medicine has been slow, however, to create structures for true interdisciplinary learning, teaching, and research where discrete knowledge bases are brought into active connection. Interdisciplinary educational environments can prepare students and trainees not only to process information as it is added or changed but also to create new knowledge and to apply information in complex ways. Medical education in women's health is not just about incorporating new knowledge and improving clinical services, it is about new thinking. That is why faculty interested in growing the field of women's health have articulated the need for *inter* disciplinary approaches in addition to *multi* disciplinary ones, and content adjustments to existing specialties.

Interdisciplinary scholarship in women's health will not eliminate the continuing need for knowledge generated by existing specialties. It will, however, make a broader array of phenomena in women more understandable and lead to better diagnoses and more cost-effective treatments. Contact between and among a multiplicity of existing disciplines as experienced in the mind of the individual learner will lead to entirely new knowledge not currently predictable or expressed by the sum of all disciplinary scholarship. Ultimately, the knowledge that arises from all these venues, both discipline-bound and interdisciplinary, will become the scientific foundation upon which all clinicians will base their clinical decision making.

Complexity science, by nature interdisciplinary, is particularly well suited to women's health scholarship in both content and organization. Organizational theorists have shown that groups that explore possibilities by changing behaviour-learning by doing-evolve faster than groups that don't. Nontraditional approaches like those that are emerging in women's health are often the sources of innovation and creativity that lead to major transformations of the entire system. Instead of damping down these deviations from the norm, as occurs in linear systems, what if medical education took a nonlinear approach and acted as a CAS, attracting any and all disciplines to explore, create, and organize the areas between them? What if the emergent scholarship reflected the expertise and synergy of all participants rather than the predetermined funding streams and entrenched academic hierarchies?

What if the only rules governing the behaviours of the autonomous agents in this women's health CAS as they begin to learn together are that: (1) variability is the norm (health); (2) loss of variability indicates disease; (3) sex differences may exist at all levels of scale; (4) adaptations to the pregnant state reflect variability; (5) maladaptations to pregnancy represent a loss of variability; (6) gender differences exist in how men and women experience and respond to their environments; and (7) mind is connected to body through an integrated psycho- physiologic state. Medical knowledge has been limited by its partial perspectives, particularly when one perspective dominates the field. Medical education reform in women's health began as an awareness of how the 70-kg, white, middle-class, North American, heterosexual male perspective dominated normative standards in medicine.

Women have been outliers, deviant from the dominant norm. Even official definitions of women's health describe is as that which is different (implying a male-defined norm) Although developing and adding other perspectives to the dominant one creates a more complete picture, a more fundamental change in thinking is required. That change is to have variability as the norm. By shifting the norm to variability, education and research will automatically accommodate sex, race, age, ethnicity, etc. Nonlinear quantitative analysis of living systems is, in fact, showing that variability is normal and regularity (fixed response) indicates disease. Health and vitality are expressions of the system's plasticity in response to unpredictable environ-ments. In clinical medicine, a healthy heart is one that has a high degree of variability between successive beats.

The diseased heart has a regular beat-to-beat pattern, as seen in congestive heart failure and preceding sudden death. This seems counterintuitive given our grounding in homeostasis, where physiologic systems act to reduce variability and return perturbations to a normal steady state. The loss of variability and the appearance of pathologic periodicity have now been found to occur in several diseases such as epilepsy, Parkinson's disease, and bipolar disorder. Interestingly, women have higher rates of heart-rate variability than do men and maintain it longer as they age. Could a higher degree of complexity in physiologic systems be the reason women exhibit more heartiness at the extremes of life, as neonates and elders? As we move further away from measures that describe only the range, mean, and standard deviation toward nonlinear measures that appreciate the types of information present in a data set rather than collapsing them into a mean, our knowledge about variability as the norm in complex systems will dramatically increase.

Perhaps the ultimate example of complexity in biological systems is women's capacity for adaptation to the pregnant state. During pregnancy, every organ system within the woman must shift its interaction with every other organ and the fetoplacental unit to survive and maintain the woman's overall structural integrity. *What is invariant is the pattern of relationships between the elements.* Maladaptations to the pregnant state may represent failures in variability. For example, placental blood vessels in pre-eclamptic women show evidence of atherosis and a failure of remodeling. Educationally linking this vasculopathy to hypertension in general would stimulate learners to think about approaches to hypertension in both women and men that have not been evident as yet. Similarly, viewing a myocyte's failure to adapt to the pregnant state may be a way not only to explain the cardiomyopathy of pregnancy, but also to understand congestive heart failure.

Multiple interactions occur at the boundary of mother and fetus, as each adapts to the other. For example, maternal DNA expression interacts with the sex of the fetus. The female fetus of a mother carrying the gene for neural-tube defects will more often emerge with anencephaly; the male fetus with spina bifida. Low-birth-weight boy babies have, as adults, significantly higher cortisol levels, reflective of an altered hypothalamic-pituitary-adrenal axis and a higher risk of non-insulin-dependent diabetes later in life. Girl babies below the 10th percentile at birth have a 3.6-fold increased risk of manifesting gestational diabetes in their 20s. Pregnancy is also not a discrete and finite event for the mother. It can increase or decrease the mother's risk for subsequent disease (such as breast cancer, diabetes, hypertension), and persistence of fetal cells in the postpartum maternal circulation may lead to autoimmune disease. The uterine context and the dynamic interplay between fetus and mother may influence them both for future health and disease.

Reductionist models have further assumed that systems are closed or insulated from their contexts by impermeable boundaries, making predictions about the future possible. In contrast, complex systems are described as having permeable boundaries, with no way of knowing the future apart from the system's context. An example of the importance of context in complex systems is that of post-traumatic stress disorder (PTSD), which demonstrates the interdependencies between biology, cognition, relational contexts, and the larger environment in which women live. Although many individuals are exposed to trauma, only one in four will develop PTSD. Women, who are not at greater risk for exposure to trauma than men, are more likely to develop PTSD when exposed. Life-threatening physical injuries do not reliably predict PTSD or those psychiatric or somatic symptoms will subsequently emerge.

Instead, perceived threat, the sexual nature of the trauma, and age under 15 are more predictive. Girls and women suffering from sexual trauma may be more effectively understood and treated with a perspective that links social context with plasticity in the neural network, its neuro-chemical milieu, cognition, and subsequent behaviour. Psychotherapy based on relational theory could create a new relational context for altering connections in the neural network. The goal of such therapy would be the emergence of healthier psychic structures instead of the control of unhealthy behaviours, emotions, or thoughts. Imagine the understanding and treatment of other psycho- physiological states, be they depression in women or uncontrolled aggression in men, in an academic environ-ment that nudges the complex adaptive system of women's health into a place where it is at its most creative. In the language of complexity science, that place is at the edge of chaos-somewhere between order and disorder, a place of maximum possibilities.

Women's Nutrition

Women in general have disproportionately low social status and low economic power, which together with their reproductive role make them more vulnerable to life long health risks as compared to men.

While women can generally expect to live longer than men, this does not necessarily ensure a better quality of life since they are more sickly and disabled than men throughout the life cycle. In addition, with longer life spans, women face greater susceptibility to disease and disability as they age. Health status is influenced by complex biological, social, environmental and cultural factors that are highly interrelated. These factors affect men and women differently.

Biological and social factors affect women's health throughout their lives and have cumulative effects. It is therefore important to consider the entire life cycle when examining the causes and consequences of women's poor health. The cultural and socioeconomic environment can adversely affect women's life style, and in particular result in inadequate diet. In Israel, a part of the population is still in a state of "nutritional transition" with its attending risks and vulnerability. There are many nutrition-related health concerns which merit attention to improve women's health in Israel, including obesity, diabetes, hypertension, CHD, osteoporosis, anaemia and eating disorders.

Malnutrition in the Life-Cycle

Malnutrition is a major contributory factor to women's poor health and preventable mortality. Children of malnourished mothers are born with low birth weight, are disadvantaged from birth, fail to grow normally, and face a higher risk of disease and pre-maturity. Maternal iron deficiency anaemia is a known risk factor for the newborn. Preliminary data from the First National Health and Nutrition Survey in Israel (MABAT) reveals that 30% of Israeli women reported suffering from anaemia during their lifetime, compared with only 3.2% of men. This gap shows that a targeted approach to women is required.

Malnutrition and Cardiovascular Diseases

Although women are generally a decade older than men when they are first diagnosed with cardiovascular disease, it kills as many women as it does men throughout life. Moreover, women do not fare as well as men after suffering from the disease. Women are vulnerable to the same risk factors for cardiovascular disease as men but the risk factors carry different relative weights. Nutrition-related risk factors are powerful determinants of cardiovascular disease in women. For example, women with a body mass index (BMI) equal to or greater than 29 are three times more likely to suffer coronary heart disease. Women with a BMI between 25 and 28.9 are estimated to have an 80% higher risk of coronary heart disease than lean women with a BMI of less than 20.

Excess body weight also predisposes women to other risk factors, including hypertension, diabetes mellitus, and hyperlipidemia. The distribution of adipose tissue in the abdominal region, as measured by waist-to-hip ratio (WHR), is more predictive of cardiovascular disease risk than overall obesity. Clearly, nutrition plays a major role in relation to risk factors for cardiovascular disease in women. Preliminary data from MABAT reveal that 6.2% of women reported hypertriglyceridemia as compared with 5.7% of men. 12.6% of women reported hypercholesterolemia, compared with 12% of men. 12.2% of women and 8.3% of men reported hypertension. Waist to hip ratios may reveal the underlying risk in our population: 84% of men have waist to hip ratios under 1.0 while the ratio for 57% of women is higher than 0.8.

Cancer

It is assumed that sensible nutrition habits could prevent 30% to 70% of cancers, depending on type. Breast cancer is a result of a complex array of genetic, hormonal and environmental factors including diet. The role of dietary fat in the development of breast cancer is controversial. Ecological studies have shown that breast cancer rates are higher in countries with high fat per capita. Nevertheless, cohort and case-control studies are less consistent. Another theory suggests the role of a suppressed immune system that inhibits the body's natural defence system. Some researchers have suggested that fat intake must be below 25% of total energy to affect breast cancer rates. Researchers have also shown an inverse relationship between fibre intake and cancer. Studies of antioxidants found in fruits and vegetables are inconclusive in linking antioxidants to cancer prevention.

Excess body weight is believed to increase a woman's chance of breast cancer. There are data showing that gaining weight during the 30's substantially increases breast cancer risk later in life while other studies show that underweight pre-menopausal women and overweight postmenopausal women are at greatest risk. As with breast cancer, some ecological studies show an association between colourectal cancer rates and levels of fat consumption. Another hypothesis suggests that high calcium intake may have a protective role. Diets high in phytoestrogens are also reported to block the development of cancer-promoting substances invitro. Until more evidence based recommendations are established, it is suggested that professionals should advise women to reduce fat in their diets and increase intake of fruits, vegetables and whole grains while maintaining a healthy body weight.

Osteoporosis

According to the International Osteoporosis Foundation about one in three women and one in eight men over the age of 50 worldwide are at risk for an osteoporotic fracture during their lifetime. Osteoporosis cannot be cured. It can only be prevented or its progression delayed. The best way to prevent the disease is to build strong bones early in life primarily by consuming a well-balanced, calcium-rich diet and regular physical activity. Many nutrients influence bone formation, thus making the diet an important means to build healthy bones. Consumption of adequate dietary calcium starting from preadolescence through young adulthood until the early 30's is critical for building bone mass18. Bone mass remains unchanged between age 30 and the onset of menopause, after which women lose 2% to 5% each year until about 5 years after menopause, at which time bone loss becomes more gradual. High intakes of caffeine, alcohol, sodium, and protein increase the amount of calcium lost in urine.

Although most investigators agree that the rapid bone loss that follows early menopause cannot be prevented by calcium supplementation, total calcium intake in the range of 1,500 mg daily can reduce bone loss in later years. Vitamin D is important to bone health. Its active form, 1, 25-dihydroxycholecalciferol, stimulates intestinal absorption of calcium. Older women are especially at risk for vitamin D deficiency because of a lack of sunlight, poor diet, and decreased synthesis and absorption. Evidence suggests those women at high risk for osteoporosis benefit from vitamin D supplementation. It is essential that professionals become familiar with nutritional sources that are rich in calcium and stress the fact that milk products lows in fat have the same calcium content as high fat milk products. Moreover, in Israel, low fat milk has been fortified with vitamin D.

Eating Disorders

The media are an influential force in the socialization of women and men. They help create unrealistic expectations about weight and appearance and subtly encourage women to attach undue importance to them. Women and men respond differently to these pressures. Women, especially young women, tend to be more negatively affected by these messages, as evidenced by widespread preoccupation with weight loss and even more seriously, by rising rates of anorexia and bulimia. From the MABAT survey, it seems that more women are at the extreme of the BMI spectrum as compared with men. This may reflect the "trial and failure" cycle that women challenge through their life. Although not a disease, menopause brings many physiological changes for women and places them at risk of developing cardiovascular disease and osteoporosis. These risks, influenced by hereditary background, may be modified by diet, smoking and physical activity. Monitoring, research and analysis of the gender-sensitive consequences of malnutrition through the life cycle are important for policy reforms and setting program priorities, especially since data on these topics in Israel are scarce. The 1999-2000 MABAT attempts to enhance the capacity of health planners and providers to apply additional information in regard to risk factors and intervention programs. Physical inactivity in women is another problem. Women of all ages do not engage sufficiently in physical activity, despite its many positive effects on health. The health system must learn how to encourage healthy behaviours in women by developing approaches that take into account their values, lifestyles and roles.

The literature on human mating strategies emphasizes gender differences in the pursuit of short-term sexual strategies. In particular, women are believed to be most concerned with pursuing long-term sexual partners, because of the greater parental investment that women make in their offspring. We accept the premise of Parental Investment Theory, but take issue with the empirical studies that are used to support Buss and Schmitt's (1993) Sexual Strategies Theory (SST), and with the extent of the purported difference between the genders. All empirical studies of gender differences in preferences for casual sex have been conducted with college students. Even in the current era, young women reach sexual maturity under the backdrop of the sexual double standard, in which sex outside of a committed relationship is stigmatized.

For men, losing their virginity is often a positive event, but for women the initiation of sexual activity may be associated with loss, guilt, regret, and other negative affective experiences. College-aged may need to protect their reputation, and may be realistically concerned about the high prevalence of STDs within their cohort, to which women are more susceptible than men. They may therefore be more conservative in their actual or reported behaviour. Women are more at risk than men for childhood sexual abuse (CSA), sexual assault, and intimate partner violence, with estimates ranging between 15% and 34% for CSA alone. These events often have a detrimental impact on women's sexuality and mental health.

Evolutionary psychologists sometimes claim that society's preoccupation with female chastity and restriction of young women's sexual behaviour occurs because women's families needed to ensure their chastity to provide her husband with paternity certainty. But the facts that societies had to take drastic steps such as concealment, and excision of the clitoris indicates that women's natural behaviour would be less chaste were she not so controlled. SST ignores the trend towards more permissive sexual behaviours that has been observed through much of the twentieth century, which indicates a substantial influence of societal factors.

The narrow focus on college populations ignores the observation that for some women of childbearing age, sexual desire actually increases with age. There are some evidence women become less choosy as they age. It would be advantageous from an evolutionary perspective for women's sex drives to increase as they get closer to menopause. As they are older and thus less attractive to potential suitors and also beginning to be less capable of becoming pregnant, they may need to more aggressively pursue a mate than when they were younger, more fertile, and suitors were plentiful.

Evolutionary psychologists have ignored the possibility that women's sexual strategies may change over the lifespan. Being less choosy may be advantageous for older women; as there are fewer unpaired men around to choose from, they will be more likely to secure a mate if they relax their standards. In addition, younger women, because of less earning power and social status, must often acquire financial stability and resources through a mate. In contrast, because older women often have already accrued resources, their choice of mate is not as dependent on acquiring resources, and so they can afford to be less choosy. Short term sexual strategies may also be less costly for older women, as they are more experienced and thus there is less chance that they would make unwise choices in short- term mating that would put them in danger.

In the literature it is recognized that men often pursue both simultaneously, but there is less attention to the fact that women have much to gain from short-term mating. This is in contrast to the attention given to extra-pair copulation and the evolutionary advantages it may impart in the animal literature. We argue that observed differences represent what Wilson referred to as cultural hypertrophy of biological gender dimorphism, meaning that cultural influences exaggerates basic differences that evolved under adaptive pressure. While acknowledging the merit of the existing work on evolutionary approaches to sexual selection, the authors of this chapter propose that SST is at best a partially correct window into human sexual behaviour rather than being a completely accurate model. Researchers need to develop alternative models of sexual selection that pay more attention to the psychology of women's mating strategies.

Women's Victimization History and Surgical Intervention

Violence against women by an intimate partner is recognized widely as a significant health problem and is believed by many to have reached epidemic proportions in the United States today. An intimate partner is defined as a spouse, ex-spouse, boyfriend, ex-boyfriend, girlfriend, ex-girlfriend, or date. Intimate partner violence (IPV) is the reason an estimated 25% to 50% of all women present for treatment in emergency rooms. Women who have been battered or sexually assaulted use health care services at much higher rates than women who have not experienced abuse, and they have health care needs that go beyond the original trauma. Women who are abused are more likely to suffer from a range of chronic and acute illnesses than women who are not abused, yet few studies have considered the possibility of associations between victimization-related illnesses and surgery for abused women.

Recently, the trauma committee of the American College of Surgeons (ACS) issued a formal statement of its recognition that IPV is a major public health problem and acknowledged that victims frequently are in need of surgical care. According to the ACS, surgeons regularly treat women with injuries ranging from minor lacerations to severe blunt and penetrating wounds without an awareness of their patients' victimization status. The ACS statement suggests that IPV be viewed as causally related to these injuries. A practitioner who fails to diagnose IPV may be unsuccessful in the identification of a disease process that can be chronic.

The Relationship

One group of researchers found significant results in their study of the relationship between abuse in childhood and negative health outcomes in adults. Self-reporting female participants (n = 1,225) were selected randomly from a health maintenance organization in the northwest and grouped according to the amount and type of childhood maltreatment experienced. A history of abuse and neglect during childhood was acknowledged by nearly half (i.e., 43%) of these women.

History of childhood victimization was associated significantly with adverse physical health outcomes experienced as adults. The number of different types of maltreatment experienced was correlated significantly with the number of physical symptoms identified, diagnoses by physicians, increased functional disability, and health risks.

The physical symptoms included nausea, diarrhea, constipation, fatigue, insomnia, abdominal pain, back pain, and chest pain. There was no specific analysis of surgical intervention in this study, however.

The researchers suggest that knowledge of a possible connection between history of childhood maltreatment and poorer health status during adulthood should be taken into consideration when caring for women who may have survived such treatment as children. In addition to the acute physical trauma and injury, the consequences of victimization can include increased susceptibility to depression, post-traumatic stress disorder (PTSD), and other psychological symptoms in both children and adults, which may lead to greater use of health care services related to these disorders.

Few studies have taken into account the cumulative effect of multiple victimizations (i.e., abuse as a child and IPV experienced as an adult) on health care service use. Most studies to date have focused only on IPV, and little research has examined possible links between victimization and surgery. Consequently, the focus of this study is the cumulative effects of women's victimization and the need for surgical intervention throughout a lifetime.

Health Consequences of Victimization

Physical assault on women by intimate partners is recognized widely as a leading cause of injury to women in the United States. In addition, some studies suggest that many women who are victims of IPV report being sexually abused by their partners. Intimate partner violence may be part of a system of domination and control that includes emotional, verbal, and economic abuse, as well as sexual assault, coercion, or injury.

Acute Health Consequences

Intimate partner violence is a significant risk factor for many injuries and systemic disorders and diseases. Facial lacerations and skull, neck, and orbital trauma can occur as a result of direct force or assault to the head, neck, and face. Various types of fractures have been documented in women either from direct force or as the result of victims' attempts to defend themselves from physical assault. Direct force to the chest can produce pneumothorax. Internal injuries to the spleen, liver, and kidney occur when patients are punched or kicked in the abdomen or back. Forced sexual intercourse can cause vaginal bleeding and vaginal or anal tearing, or it may lead to development of hemorrhoids.

Chronic Health Symptoms

Chronic complaints, such as headaches, abdominal pain, fatigue, and musculoskeletal or soft tissue pain, and multiple admissions for undefined conditions could be indicative of ongoing violence in a relationship. The effects of victimization on gynecologic symptoms, such as pelvic pain, bladder infection, and dyspareunia, and gastrointestinal diseases, such as dyspepsia, abdominal pain, or irritable bowel syndrome, also have been examined. Studies examining the relationship between surgery and victimization have focused on acute care settings because of the frequency and severity of the acute trauma experienced by some victims of IPV. For example, two researchers reviewed data from 218 women who identified themselves as victims of IPV at an emergency department in the San Francisco area.

They found that more than 25% of these victims were admitted to the hospital for their injuries, and 13% required major surgical treatment. One study examined 1,952 women who were patients in one of four community-based primary care practices in an urban area in an effort to identify the presence or history of IPV and clinical symptoms associated with IPV. More than 600 of these women acknowledged experiencing abuse as a child, an adult, or both. Although patients who currently were experiencing abuse had more evidence of physical symptoms, depression, anxiety, and suicide attempts than those who had no ongoing abuse, no statistical significance was found between these two groups for number of lifetime surgeries.

Another researcher studied the impact that a history of rape or incest had on women who were recovering from a specific type of surgical intervention (ie, elective hysterectomies).In this cross-sectional study, 92 women were interviewed at four established times during the postoperative period, each several months apart. The results showed a significantly higher level of depression in the first year after hysterectomy among women who had experienced sexual assault compared to women who had not. The researcher suggests that undergoing a hysterectomy could serve as a trigger to past traumatic memories of abuse.

Depression might result when the victim is forced to deal not only with the surgical experience but also with the renewed memory of the abuse. Past abuse seems to leave people more vulnerable to depression and other forms of hyperarousal (i.e., state in which the body overreacts to subsequent new stressors by regularly producing excessive levels of stress hormones), which might further explain these findings. There is no indication that ongoing abuse was measured in this study. Studies of women seeking care from gastroenterology services also point to a link between victimization history and illness. In their study of 206 women seeking care in a gastroenterology practice, one group of researchers found that female patients who had experienced abuse either as adults or children (n = 89) underwent more surgeries throughout their lifetime than did patients who had not experienced abuse. A history of abuse was associated with more pelvic and abdominal pain and more surgeries throughout these patients' lifetimes.

In another study, researchers interviewed 239 women seeking care at a gastroenterology clinic and found that women with a history of physical and sexual abuse (66.5%) underwent more surgeries than those who had not been abused. Findings of this study indicate that assessment of abuse should be an essential component of medical histories and theoretical support for stress-illness link. Long-standing theoretical and empirical evidence suggests a relationship between stress and illness. For the most part, research has examined the association between social stress, life stress, and outcomes related to emotional health and well-being.

Adversity and victimization throughout one's lifetime, such as childhood maltreatment and adult trauma, including rape and psychological and physical abuse by intimate partners, also are associated with psychological distress and physical illness; however, the actual physiological mechanism underlying victimization and illness associations typically has not been examined by researchers in the field of IPV. Drawing on a body of research established by neuroscientists, one researcher speculated on the causal paths that link childhood victimization with chronic illness experienced by adults. For example, findings of higher levels of depression and PTSD are well established among adults who have experienced abuse as children.

According to this researcher, people who have experienced significant trauma in their lives are more vulnerable to the effects of subsequent stressors, resulting in a state of hyper arousal. Hyper arousal subsequently may manifest itself as a number of symptoms and conditions, including PTSD, depression, and irritable bowel syndrome, suggesting a common mechanism between pain and depression. Childhood abuse and adversity may exert independent effects on adult health status. Additionally, there may be cumulative effects of multiple forms of victimization on adult health status.

In the past, research on stress may have underestimated the contributions of cumulative adversities to emotional distress. Further elaboration on the biological effects of stress linked to victimization experiences is seen in studies of wound healing. For example, a group of researchers investigated the effect of stress or fear on surgical outcomes, such as wound healing. Citing research that psychological stress delays wound healing in their investigation of 36 women, researchers found that psychological stress can have marked adverse consequences for immunologic activity that must take place at wound sites for healing to occur.

Circumstances that upset the balance of immunologic competence, such as stress, can impair the local inflammatory response. These findings are consistent with the current medical literature on the relevance of psychological influences to postoperative recuperation. In a related study, another researcher described the nature of preoperative anxiety among a small group of women scheduled for abdominal and pelvic surgery. She found that the fear or anxiety in women related to upcoming surgery is related to previous experiences, as well as ongoing life events. A more inclusive preoperative interview with women facing surgery could reveal areas of anxiety or concern that otherwise may remain hidden and would have relevance to recovery.

Victimization of Women

The late 1940s were a volatile era for the Indian subcontinent both politically and religiously. The British Raj disbanded its colony because of economic turmoil and population decline in England caused by World War II. In addition, Hindus, Sikhs, and Muslims, once united against the imposing colonial power, were divided both religiously and geographically. The movement towards a divided India polarized these sects. Unfortunately, the women of these diverse groups were among the greatest victims of religious and cultural persecution. Religious, ethnic, or political conflict between men on the subcontinent was often performed through acts of violence on the bodies of women.

In the following study analyze how "the will of men"

subjugated Muslim, Sikh, and Hindu women during partition, resulting in a profound inequity in gender relations in the tense geographic area known as 1947 Pakistan – specifically the Punjab area also, to explore women's complex roles in this religiously fragmented society as dramatized in Bapsi Sidhwa's acclaimed novel *Cracking India*. In order to better understand the victimization of women during partition, it is pertinent for the student of women's studies to explore the gender's position in a patriarchal-colonial society prior to the annexation of Pakistan. By examining both the vulnerability of Muslim and Hindu women in the British Raj's Punjab in 1947, one can discern the gender roles for women in that era.

Purdah, or "the seclusion and segregation of women was a cultural norm of the Indian sub-continent amongst both Hindus and Muslims." Purdah, beginning at puberty controls the interaction between females and males. Many degrees of Purdah exist – from wearing a head scarf to living sequestered in the family home. Two basic types are practiced on the Indian sub-continent even today, according to Dushka Saiyid – one which allows women to move about encased in cloak-like garb disguising the entire body and face. Only a net over the eyes permits visibility. This covering is known as the burqa. The other form of Purdah physically confines women within the home. These forms of Purdah were enforced all over northern India during the nineteenth and early twentieth centuries – the Punjab being no exception. "Purdah, more than any other social institution, is an important indicator of the role women are expected to play in society."

Because the practice of Purdah at that time required women to be confined to the home, it is apparent that women's exclusive role in society was that of procreation and domestic chores. Saiyid suggests, the fact that it was felt necessary to keep them away from interaction with males who were outside the circle of immediate family meant that both sexes were not trusted to maintain the moral order of the society if allowed to mix freely. Because women were considered the more vulnerable of the two sexes, they were confined at home to prevent them from succumbing to desires of the flesh that would result from interaction with males. What is known as "purdah" on the Indian sub-continent is understood as "hijab" in the Muslim world. In Arabic, hijab means curtain. According to Saiyid, this term is used in the Koran both metaphorically and literally. One well-known location for instructions for hijab is located in sura 33, verse 59 of the Holy Koran. Saiyid asserts that "the instructions are for the women of the 'Believers' to distinguish themselves form the non-believers by observing hijab."

One translation explains: O Prophet! Tell thy wives and daughters and the women of the believers to draw their cloaks close round them (when they go abroad). That will be better, so that they may be recognized and not annoyed. Allah is ever Forgiving, Merciful. It is important in connection with the this passage to understand that for both Muslim and Hindu women, the practice of purdah or hijab restricted them to the home and forced them to cover their bodies in order to protect them from possible disgrace at the hands of strange men. As time went on, these practices were the subject of heated debate. For instance, the All-India Women's Conference in March 1918 in Bhopal conducted a serious debate on purdah. A resolution at the conference concluded that for the emancipation of women, purdah should be relaxed and that Muslim women should only have to observe it to the extent required by their religion. Saiyid asserts, "by the second and third decade of this century the observance of purdah was relaxed in its severity, at least in the cities of Punjab."

Even though the practice declined somewhat, it remained central to both cultures. Women's bodies were seen as the property of the men of their family and the religion they practiced. This concept proves quite significant in the context of the religious atrocities committed during partition. Women's bodies constituted a religious, geographic, and familial symbol. Defilement of the woman of a family would be the greatest dishonour the family unit could endure — and thus violence enacted on women during partition was tantamount to a sacrilege against one's religion, country, and family. In *Cracking India*, Ayah, Lenny's nanny, is a character Sidhwa develops to portray this sexual tension among Hindu women and "outside" men. Lenny describes Ayah's figure as having a "rolling bouncy walk that agitates the globules of her buttocks under her cheap colourful sari and the half-spheres beneath her short sari blouses".

Ayah's sexuality attracts men of varying occupations and religions including the Fallattis Hotel cook, the Government House gardener, the butcher, Masseur, the "Chinaman", the Pathan, and Ice-Candy-Man. According to Lenny, "Ayah's presence galvanizes men to mad sprints in the noon heat." As a lower caste servant for a Zoroastrian family, Ayah is not subject to the strict laws of Purdah required of the upper caste Brahmins. This position enables Sidhwa to portray in her novel more interaction between a Hindu woman and men of other beliefs. However, it also serves to register the extent of Ayah's decline in the final third of the novel. Once she was able to consolidate all religious groups, "Hindu, Muslim, Sikh, Parsee, are, as always, unified around her"; however, partition turns Ayah's sexuality against her. The men who once competed for her attention eventually reject her.

The victimization of this character will be explored subsequently. In contrast with Ayah's alluring nature, Lenny's godmother appears quite asexual. According to Lenny, "She wears only white khaddar saris and white khaddar blouses beneath which is her coarse bandage-tight bodice. In all the years I never saw the natural shape of her breasts". Practices like purdha and hijab desexualize women's bodies in order to shield them from sexual violence. In the novel, Lenny's godmother neutralizes her own sexuality by binding her breasts, which also shields her from physical harm but, along with her religion, age, and social status in the community, enhances her power. Although many Western thinkers believe these practices of veiling women to be repressive, Sidhwa suggests otherwise. Lenny's godmother suppresses her sexuality to become dominant over her husband and other men in the community like Ice-Candy- Man. Conversely, Ayah, who accentuates her sexuality, is kidnapped and defiled during partition.

The historical background leading up to and following the partition of India is quite intricate. However, a brief analysis of the events preceding partition will shed some light on the extreme religious tension that developed in this embroiled region. The Indian Mutiny or Sepoy Rebellion from 1857-1858 increased the domination of the British Raj under Empress Victoria (1877). Sidhwa personifies British colonialism with the statue of Queen Victoria in Queen's Park and the marching of British troops, which Lenny calls "a slick red and white caterpillar" throughout the city of Lahore. The British established a Victorian model of government which was socially and politically conservative. The Raj brought huge economic change to the subcontinent, including improvements in transportation and communica-tion, the opening of coal mines in Bihar and Bengal, and construction of irrigation canals in the Yamuna, Ganges, and Indus valleys. The expansion of irrigation in Punjab led to the development of canal colonies settled mainly by Sikhs and Muslims. While the British Raj stimulated economic growth to the Indian subcontinent, the Hindus, Muslims, and Sikhs largely detested colonial domination. Sidhwa recounts a dinner party hosted by Lenny's parents at which a guest, Mr. Singh, exclaims, "Hindu, Muslim, and Sikh: we all want the same thing! We want independence!" Indeed, political groups formed in India to ensure that each religious group was involved in British control. The Indian National Congress (1885) and the All-India Muslim League (1906) were both established in order to work with the British on political and social issues. Unfortunately, as partition became imminent, the groups simply could not agree.

The India National Congress, made up largely of Hindus, was founded to formulate proposals and demands to present to the British. Fearing Hindu domination in politics, Muslims created the All- India Muslim League to balance Hindu votes in the Congress. As conflict among the three groups ensued, the British began to feel the impact of World War II. The economic and human loss proved too great for the crown to continue maintaining its colonial holdings. In 1945, the Labour Party came to power in England and subsequently pushed Parliament to abandon the Indian sub-continent. Meanwhile, Gandhi launched the "Quit India Movement" (1942) in order to turn the native population against the British. Ali Jinnah, head of the All-Muslim League, was opposed to many of Gandhi's methods—especially the "Quit India Movement." Talks between Gandhi, Nehru, and Jinnah proved ever more difficult as the British planned to relinquish India to its native inhabitants.

The "Two Nations Theory", established during this politically volatile time, proposed that India be divided among Hindus and Muslims. Jinnah encouraged this theory propounded by a group of students at Cambridge University in England. These students issued a pamphlet in 1933 entitled "Now or Never," which opposed the idea of federation, denied that India was a single country, and demanded partition into regions, with the northwest receiving national status as a "Pakistan." The students explained that the term "Pakistan" is composed of letters taken from the names of their homelands: Punjab, Afghania, Kashmir, Iran, Sindh, Tukharistan, Afghanistan, and Balochistan. These students called this area the "land of the Paks."

The All-Muslim League supported a divided India, while Congress continually opposed it. On March 23, 1940, the All-Muslim League created the Lahore Resolution (or Pakistan Resolution) which advocated a religiously divided India. According to historian G. D. Khosla: the Muslim League demand for Pakistan was based on the idea that Hindus and Muslims constitute two separate nations, each entitled to a separate and exclusive homeland where they would be free to develop their culture, tradition, and religion and polity. On June 3, 1947, British Prime Minister Clement Attlee introduced a bill in the House of Commons calling for the independence and partition of India. By July 4, 1947, the House of Commons passed the India Independence Act, which created two independent dominions on the sub-continent. Throughout the summer of 1947, communal violence mounted, assets were divided, boundary commissions were established to demarcate frontiers, and British troops were evacuated.

On August 14, 1947, Pakistan and India achieved independence. Ali Jinnah subsequently became the first governor general of the Dominion of Pakistan. Power-playing and politics among this collection of political leaders is purposefully vague and confusing in Sidhwa's novel simply because it was confusing to the people of India at the time. Lenny complains of Ice-Candy-Man's political comments. Sometimes he quotes Gandhi, or Nehru, or Jinnah, but I'm fed up with hearing about them. Mother, Father and their friends are always saying: Gandhi said this, Nehru said that.

Gandhi did this, Jinnah did that. What's the point of talking so much about people we don't know? Because Lenny is a child during partition, the reader receives information filtered through an immature perspective. Although the politics of the novel are ambiguous, especially for Western readers not familiar with India's partition, her childishness also uncovers truths unseen by the adult world. For example, when Ghandi visits Lahore, Lenny's encounter with him reveals his true stance on partition and its effects on the people in the region.

Lenny asserts, It wasn't until some years later – when I realized the full scope and dimensions of the massacres – that comprehended the concealed nature of the ice lurking deep beneath the hypnotic and dynamic femininity of Gandhi's non-violent exterior. Lenny's direct encounter with one of the key figures in determining the fate of India's people reveals his evil – his responsibility for the thousands of deaths during partition. It is significant to mention, in conjunction with politics, that Lenny and her family are Zoroastrian and thus somewhat removed from the religious violence and tension that ensues. Colonel Bharucha exclaims at a community meeting of Zoroastrians, "Let whoever wishes rule! Hindu, Muslim, Sikh, Christian! We will abide by the rules of their land...We will cast our lot with whoever rules Lahore". This statement suggests that Zoroastrians, an extremely small religious community, accepted whatever ruling power dominated them.

Interestingly, no Zoroastrian women in Sidhwa's text are victimized because of religious persecution during partition. Thus, her book is a penetrating analysis of the atrocities that major religions of the world inflict upon one another. Historians have seen India's partition in the context of a horrific political upheaval between the British Raj, the Congress, and the All-India Muslim League. Unfortunately, the greatest victims of partition, women, have been left without a voice – largely ignored in light of political events leading to partition. According to scholars Ritu Menon and Kamla Bhasin, the story of 1947, while being one of the successful attainments of independence, is also a gendered narrative of displacement and dispossession, of large-scale and widespread communal violence, and of the realignment of family, community and national identities as a people were forced to accommodate the dramatically altered reality that now prevailed.

The division of India led to a great exodus of Hindus and Sikhs to India and Muslims to Pakistan. The end of British dominion and the creation of two separate, religiously identified states became a recipe for violence among the people. According to Khosla, the two-nation theory brought the problem of minorities into greater prominence than ever before, and partition, instead of offering a solution, made it even more difficult and more complicated. No matter where the line of demarcation was drawn, there would be Hindus, Muslims, and Sikhs on either side of it, in a majority or in a substantial minority; and, whatever the geographical boundaries of Pakistan, large numbers of Hindus and Sikhs would, overnight, become aliens and foreigners in their own homes. All over the now divided territory, people were in frantic flight in fear of religious violence and persecution.

Homes, crops, and animals were abandoned as people fled to the cities in search of safety in large numbers. Bapsi Sidhwa includes in her novel a section entitled "Ranna's Story," which effectively utilizes third-person omniscient narration in order to describe the invasion of a Sikh village. Lenny, the first-person narrator, is not able to describe such horrific events because she is confined to the city of Lahore. However, she is able to document widespread riots, arson, and looting which erupted throughout the cities of the Punjab by the first week of March 1947, starting with the central districts of Lahore, Amritsar, Ferozepur, Ludhiana, Sheikhupura, Gurdaspur, Sialkot, Montgomery, Lyallpur, Gujranwala, and the Jullundur Doab and spreading out into the countryside. One of Lenny's most profound coming-of-age experiences is watching the city of Lahore burn while a man is murdered.

Family businesses were singled out: Hindu and Sikh businesses were burned and looted in West Punjab, while Muslim property was destroyed in East Punjab. Because of the onslaught of religious fanaticism, many Hindu and Sikh families travelled by train or walked the distance to cross into India. Many Muslim families made the same journey into Pakistan. The partition itself and the days immediately following the actual decree are called the "August Anarchy," a phrase which emphasizes the chaos that ensued among native people. According to Menon and Bhasin, the Boundary Commission gave detailed accounts of the train massacres between August 9 and September 30. The authors assert, by August 13 it became impossible for passengers to reach Lahore station because they were attacked en route; between August 12-18, it became a veritable death trap, and in the rural areas, by August 15, nearly every east-bound train passing through Montgomery and Lahore was stopped and attacked.

Obviously, the Partition of India in 1947 amounted to

undeclared civil war, a dispute over borders, boundaries, culture and religion. Caravans of families were attacked simply because of their religious affiliation. When the exodus concluded, about eight to ten million people had crossed over from Punjab to Bengal. According to Menon and Bhasin, this was "the largest peace-time mass migration in history – about 500,000- 1,000,000 had perished." Sidhwa documents this mass exodus as well. Lenny says "wave upon wave of Muslim refugees flood Lahore – and the Punjab west of Lahore. Within three months seven million Muslims and five million Hindus and Sikhs are uprooted in the largest and most terrible exchange of population known to history". The countless rapes and kidnappings of women and young girls are perhaps among the most sordid tales of partition. These females, some with children in their arms, were reportedly abducted, raped and molested, passed from one man to another, bartered and sold like cheap chattel.

A young woman of twenty-two recounts her flight from Pakistan with a foot convoy from Lyallpur: When the convoy left Lyallpur we all joined it. The military had robbed us of everything before we left our house. First they took away our arms, then our valuables. On the way, I was separated from my people. Saw men being murdered and women being raped on the wayside. If someone protested he was killed. One woman was raped by many men. I was also raped by three men in succession. A man, at last, took me to his house and kept me there for eight days....He subjected me to physical torture, forced cow bones into my mouth so that I should be converted to Islam...He put my hands under the *charpoy* legs and sat down on it to say prayers while I suffered agonies of pain. This young woman recounted the acts of violence perpetuated against her because of her religion. Her being forced to eat cow bones signifies an obvious mocking of her Hindu beliefs.

Also, the rape itself represents a perverse form of conversion. By these actions alone, one can see that this undeclared civil war was rooted in religious hatred. Only when the British evacuated did Hindus, Muslims, and Sikhs turn on each other and women's bodies became the battleground on which these factions clashed. This woman's account of the atrocities committed against her is quite similar to Ayah's sordid tale. Ayah is also kidnapped and forced to marry Ice-Candy-Man, a Muslim, while she is Hindu. The fact that Ayah is forced to prostitute her body and coerced into having sex with Ice-Candy-Man indicates that women's bodies have historically become territory in which men act out their aggression and whatever love Ice-Candy-Man has for Ayah is smothered by his complete subjugation of her. He changes her name from Shanta to Mumtaz, a Muslim name.

Also, Ice-Candy-Man and Ayah continue to live in a *kotha* (brothel) even after their marriage. She is adorned completely in the attire of a Muslim woman. Ice-Candy-Man successfully strips Ayah of her identity as a woman and as a Hindu. Although she eventually escapes her maniacal abductor and partially regains her identity and power as a woman, the reader is left with the idea that, even with her family in Amritsar Ayah will be marked by her defilement during partition if not physically then clearly emotionally. Perhaps Ice-Candy-Man's abduction and defilement of Ayah may be seen as a gesture of contempt against India, Hindu men, and Hindu property. Menon and Bhasin suggest, the most predictable form of violence experienced by women, as women, is when the women of one community are sexually assaulted by the men of the other, in an overt assertion of their identity and a simultaneous humiliation of the other by "dishonoring" their women. In this respect, the rape and molestation of Hindu, Sikh and Muslim women before and after Partition probably followed the familiar pattern of sexual violence, and of attack, retaliation and reprisal.

By dishonouring another's wife, daughter, or sister, one ridicules his religion, cultural, and personal honour. In many written accounts, women were forced to strip and parade naked through the marketplace. Other accounts tell of women being forced to dance naked in gurudwaras (Sikh hostels) and being raped in front of the men of their family. One doctor at a refugee camp in Jhang testified: One of the cases that I treated was of a woman from village Chund Bharwana who was the wife of a railway porter. One of her hands was chopped off above her wrist and then she was thrown into the fire, as a result of which her lower portion got burnt. Perhaps one of the most gruesome injuries cited by doctors was the amputation of breasts of women. One doctor in particular said that "six such cases of chopped-off breasts were brought to the refugee camp and all of them proved fatal." This macabre act of disfigurement is sordidly depicted in *Cracking India.* Ice-Candy-Man reports to his friends that a train from Gurdaspur has arrived in Lahore filled with murdered Muslims.

Ice-Candy-Man shouts, "Everyone is dead. Butchered. They are all Muslim. There are no young women among the dead! Only two gunny-bags full of women's breasts!" However, this act of violence against Islamic women only spurs him to perpetrate violence on Hindu and Sikh women. He exclaims, "I want to kill someone for each of the breasts they cut off the Muslim women". And, of course, Ice-Candy-Man satiates his appetite for revenge by kidnapping Ayah and forcing her to marry him, while also prostituting her body. Perhaps, as he claims, Ice-Candy-Man truly loves Ayah, but his mercurial identity and con-artist habits suggest otherwise. His ability to change from popsicle salesman to prophet to poet persuades the reader to believe that truth is a very shifting quality for this character. Many women died trying to avoid sexual violation, preserve their chastity, and protect their religious and family honour. Scholars of India's partition have noted numerous ways in which women took their lives. Some jumped into the nearest well or set themselves ablaze.

Sometimes the act was accomplished alone, sometimes all the women in a family committed mass suicide. Menon and Bhasin assert, "many women and girls saved their honor by self-immolation. They collected their beddings and cots in a heap and when the heap caught fire they jumped onto it, raising cries of `Sat Sri Akal'!" There is also a story of ninety women of Thoa Khalsa who jumped into a well on March 15, 1947, in order to preserve their chastity and the religious honor of their families. In Sidhwa's novel, acts of violence against women are not limited to acts of religious hatred and xenophobia. Lenny's mother, a Zoroastrian, is a victim of the "will of men" as well. Lenny states, "Although Father has never raised his hands to us, one day surprise Mother at her bath and see the bruises on her body". Thus Sidhwa reminds the reader that victimization and abuse of women does is not always occur in the context of warfare and religious hatred but in the daily course of domestic life. The forgoing depictions of violence against women are shockingly savage. These acts of brutality indicate what women's bodies symbolize for these religiously diversified groups.

The appalling physical injuries inflicted on these women suggest that in this time and place the female body became territory to be fought over, conquered, and subsequently "branded" by the assailant through rape or disfigurement. According to Menon and Bhasin, acts of raping women in public in full view of their relatives, or "tattooing and branding the body with 'Pakistan, Zindabad!' or 'Hindustan, Zindabad!' not only marked the woman for life, they never permitted her [or her family and community] the possibility of forgetting her humiliation." In the context of Partition, "it engraved the division of India into India and Pakistan on the women of both religious communities in a way that they *became* the respective countries, indelibly imprinted by the other."

By marking a half moon on the breasts or genitalia of a woman, the male assailant extended the violation of her body to future generations. The amputation of a woman's breasts desexualized her – in effect denying her the role of wife and mother. In fact, amputation literally denied her the ability to nurse and thus be a nurturer. She was transformed into a freakish figure, an outcast, a barren woman. Sudir Kakar, in his studies of civil unrest, states that the amputation of breasts "incorporates the (more or less conscious) wish to wipe the enemy off the face of the earth." According to Stasa Zajovic, in analyzing the recent mass rape of women in Bosnia Herzegovina, "the female womb becomes occupied territory."

The violence against women cannot be separated from the larger hostilities that erupted among Muslims, Hindus, and Sikhs. Violence between these sects extended to defiling religious symbols and artifacts. Pigs and cows were slain in front of mosques and temples, non-Muslim men were circumcised, and Hindus were forced to consume beef. Because consumption of beef is proscribed for Hindus, as is pork for Muslims, these acts of religious hatred were, indeed, horrifying. Sidhwa's character, Hari, is forced to change his religion. Lenny remarks, "Hari has had his *bodhi* shaved. He has become a Muslim. He has also had his penis circumcised". All these acts of sacrilege extended to raping and physically disfiguring another's women. Menon and Bhasin assert, "The preoccupation with women's sexuality formed part of the contract of war between the three communities."

The attempt to preserve the chastity of one's own women became so great that a new form of terror erupted among the religious groups. Men turned against their own wives, daughters, and sisters, murdering them before they could be dishonoured through rape and disfigurement. The practice of sati, the immolation of widows on their husbands' funeral pyres, is well known among those who study Hindu religion. Because dishonour and defilement was such a great fear among women and their families, many women committed suicide or were murdered by their own kin. A Sikh woman, Taran, recounts her story: We would listen stealthily and overheard them saying that all of us should be locked up in a room and burnt alive. Our own families were saying this—they had seen what some Muslims had done to the women, raped and killed them. The ones who escaped and came back were in such bad shape—disfigurement, mistreated. They felt it was better to kill their women than have them go through this. Sidhwa alludes to the horrifying practice of female self immolation in "Ranna's Story." Prior to an invasion of a Sikh village, it is planned that the women will set themselves ablaze. The narrator details the scheme: "The women and girls will gather at the *chaudhry's.*

Rather than face the brutality of the mob they will pour kerosene around the house and burn themselves". Ironically, the attempt fails, resulting in even greater carnage. One Sikh father, Charanjit Singh Bhatia, tells the story of his uncle who murdered his own daughters and he to avoid their being married off to Muslim neighbours. Bhatia comments, "That was a terrible time, people were made to do terrible things." Interestingly, this story illuminates the notion prevalent at this time that death was actually a better fate than conversion through marriage. Menon and Bhasin affirm, "This response that chose real, but honourable, death over the symbolic death that marriage and conversion entailed seemed not just preferable, but almost prescribed for Hindus and Sikhs." One Sikh man, Dr. Virsa Singh, was known in Amritsar for murdering many women during Partition in order to preserve their honour. Miridula Sarabhai recounts his tale: Virsa Singh claimed he had shot 50 women personally.

First he shot his own wife because the Muslims came to get them. Once he had done this, all the women in the neighbourhood gathered around saying 'Viran, pehle mannu maar, pehle mannu maar' (Brother, kill me first). Because Dr. Virsa Singh could not bear to see his wife and daughters fall into the hands of the Muslims, he saw himself as their saviour from Muslim domination even if death was the only means of escape. This ideology seems inherent in Sikh concepts of bravery and warfare. Women are the silent victims during civil war, religious unrest, and political violence. Fortunately, both Pakistan and India eventually established an Abducted Persons (Recovery and Restoration) Bill which required that abducted women and children be returned to their families.

Refugee camps were established in both countries to secure safe transfer of the women back into their native culture. Sidhwa places one of these refugee camps near Lenny's home, where, at night, she hears the cries of these abused women. Hamida, herself a recovered woman, consoles Lenny and states, "poor fate-smitten woman...what can a sorrowing woman do but wail?" Lenny is tormented by the cries of this woman. The narrator cries, "My heart is wrung with pity and horror. I want to leap out of my bed and soothe the wailing woman and slay her tormentors. I've seen Ayah carried away – and it had less to do with fate than with the will of men". In this passage, the narrator supports Menon and Bhasin's argument that men, with their savage. y, were responsible for the abject plight of women during partition. One social worker commented on the predicament of women in the camps: They looked like human skeletons -- the women and children! They looked as if they belonged to another time. Those who were young had also become old by being used. I feel like crying when I remember the sight. They had been completely ruined. These women were cleaned and fed but some were forced to have abortions because the government did not want them giving birth to children who were a product of religious hatred and civil violence.

When cultural and religious brutality subsided, women continued to suffer nevertheless. Because of their defilement, some women were rejected by their families. Hamida, Lenny's new ayah, depicts a woman who has been besmirched and subsequently discarded by her family. Lenny's godmother informs Lenny that Hamida was kidnapped by the Sikhs. Godmother states, "she was taken away to Amritsar. Once that happens, sometimes, the husband or his family won't take her back....Some folk feel that way they can't stand their women being touched by other men". In *Cracking India,* one is able to observe the artistry with which a gifted novelist interlaces the drama played out on the vast scale of history with the drama enacted in ordinary human lives. Memories of the horrors of Partition have faded, but the boundaries of Pakistan and India continue to be disputed even today. Hindu, Muslim and Sikh women will never totally recover from the atrocities committed against them in 1947.

Near the conclusion of the novel, Lenny's godmother consoles Ayah for the horrors she has been forced to endure: "That was fated daughter. It can't be undone. But it can be forgiven...Worse things are forgiven. Life goes on and the business of living buries the debris of our pasts. Hurt, happiness...all fade impartially...to make way for fresh joy and new sorrow. That's the way of life". Godmother's words resonate with the inherent pain and transcendent hope of woman. Perhaps her message constitutes Bapsi Sidhwa's consolation to the women of India and Pakistan who, like Ayah, lost their spirits because of the "will of men."

Special Challenges of Women

The cycle of violence permeates the lives of women living on or near the streets. Most women living on or near the streets are victims of domestic, physical or sexual abuse at home. They seek refuge at shelters and secondarily on the streets only to experience more victimization. There are no official statistics of homelessness in Canada. However, in 2006, an attempt was made by the City of Toronto to conduct a Street Needs Assessment, counting people that were homeless on the night of April 19 to gain a better understanding of what services were necessary for these individuals. The Assessment found that approximately 5,052 individuals living in Toronto were homeless. Noted was the fact that 3% of these individuals were currently residing in violence against women shelters, however an overall count of homeless women was not conducted.

The count of 5,052 homeless individuals is likely an underestimate, as the "hidden homeless" (those not living in the city's shelters but temporarily "couch-surfing" - staying with family or friends or trading sex for a place to sleep) were not counted. Michael Shapcott, Senior Fellow of the Wellesley Institute refers to the hidden homeless as "the single biggest group of homeless people." Women undeniably form a substantial proportion of the city's "hidden homeless." Carolyn Whitzman, who conducted a study on homelessness and health of Canadian women living outside of Ontario's major cities, noted that, "while men are more likely to be visibly homeless, sleeping rough or in shelters, women's homelessness is largely hidden from public view".

Since many women are "living in households where they are subject to family conflict or violence" and/or spend most of their meager income on purchasing basic necessities such as food, they face the possibility of eviction or living in overcrowded and unsafe residences. The Street Health Report 2007 found that "women become homeless and remain homeless due to poverty and because there is a lack of safe, affordable and supportive housing". Women who were surveyed said that they became homeless for a number of reasons: 33% cited not being able to afford rent or eviction, 12% pointed to poor housing conditions, and 18% mentioned lack of safety as the main reason for becoming homeless. The other 24% cited family or relationship breakdown as the cause of homelessness.

In terms of visibly homeless females, the recent Street Health Report 2007, which surveyed 97 homeless women in Toronto, described homelessness as having a "life threatening impact on women's health" (2008: 1). The Report also noted that for homeless women in Toronto, "homelessness is not a short term crisis, women in the study had been homeless an average of 3 years." An investigation of the factors that make certain women more vulnerable to being homeless than others is pertinent if we want to create greater awareness of the distinct obstacles faced by homeless women in Toronto and propose meaningful solutions to ease the burdens currently endured by women living on or near the streets.

Risk Factors

Carolyn Whitzman describes homeless women as women "of every age and socio-economic background [with] certain risk factors" that act to form "interlocking 'structures of constraint' that limit access to social goods and choices".

The following are well-documented risk factors that have repeatedly surfaced in the literature as key determinants of female homelessness in Canada and elsewhere. It must be noted that any one factor in and of itself will not determine homelessness; rather it is the interplay of these factors that predispose some women to homelessness.

Age

The likelihood of experiencing ongoing or repeated instances of homelessness as opposed to one-time homelessness is correlated with the age at which one first becomes homeless. A study conducted in the United States by Lehmann et al, found that "women under the age of 35 appear to face unique risks for homelessness. This variable may reflect instability in the support network...young women may be more likely to have young children, which has been previously reported as a risk factor for homelessness". In Canada, homelessness has been found to affect thousands of girls and young women.

History of Family Violence

Violence has been noted as a leading cause of homelessness. Many homeless women have experienced a history of abuse (physical, sexual and/or emotional) that began in childhood at the hands of people they trusted and continued into their adult lives in their domestic relationships, making home life intolerable. It is estimated that "about half of all homeless women and children have become homeless while trying to escape abusive situations".

Alcohol and/or Drug Abuse

Many women turn to alcohol and/or drugs as a means of

coping with their victimization. This can set the scene for a downward spiral into homelessness. However, the misuse and/or abuse of drugs may be a more potent precursor to homelessness than alcohol. As one American study found, "by the late 20th century, drugs may have begun to displace alcohol as an important precursor of homelessness for some individuals".

Mental Health Problems

According to a study conducted by the Canadian Institute for Health Information (CIHI) "people with severe mental illness may experience limited housing, employment and income options" increasing their risk of being homeless. Most homeless women with a mental health diagnosis suffer from depression and anxiety. The Street Health Report 2007 noted that "this does not support the stereotype of the mentally ill homeless person who suffers from psychosis and wants to live on the street".

Feminization of Poverty: Many women find themselves at the lower rungs of the socio-economic ladder; they barely make an adequate income and lack affordable and safe housing. These problems are frequently exacerbated when there is a breakdown in marital relations. As Lyne Casavant stated: "While men's income increases slightly women's household income after divorce drops over 40%, and the poverty rate increases almost threefold". The Street Health Report 2007 found that 42% of respondents reported living on $2,400 or less per year. Lack of Female Shelters: The feminization of poverty, coupled with a lack of shelters for abused women, increase the potential for homelessness. According to the Street Health Report 2007, "of approximately 2,500 single adult shelter beds in the City [Toronto], only about 725 are for women. It is evident...that there is a connection between lack of access to shelter and the victimization of women". Aboriginal Women: Aboriginal women are more likely to be single mothers and to live on social assistance or on a below poverty-line income, factors that make homelessness more likely. As Whitzman noted:

"Aboriginal women are more likely than other women to be sleeping rough in the centres of big cities".

The Street Health Report 2007 found that, out of the 97 homeless females surveyed, 21% were Aboriginal when, according to the 2001 census, Aboriginal women only make up 0.5% of Toronto's population. This showcases the painful fact that "Aboriginal people are vastly overrepresented among the homeless".

Sexual Orientation: Women who identify as queer (lesbian, bisexual, transsexual, transgendered, two-spirited, or inter-sexed) are overrepresented among the homeless population in comparison to their numbers in the general population. For instance, a recent study that sampled 150 street-involved youth found that 36% of females reported a sexual orientation falling under the umbrella term queer. The Street Health Report 2007 found that 16% of homeless adult females identified as queer (2008:1). Reasons for this overrepresentation include conflicts at home over sexual orientation and instances of abuse and neglect.

Victimization on the Streets

Women who leave their homes in search for a safer haven quickly find that life on the streets is also marked by violence. As Reid et al, remarked "Violence is the most important issue facing homeless women, more so than mental health or addiction problems". In 2007, the Wellesley Institute characterized the lives of the homeless in Hobbesian terms as "nasty, brutish and short". Citing the results of a study on family homelessness and poverty in Massachusetts, the Institute notes that "violence is pervasive in the lives of homeless women. A staggering 92% of homeless women experience severe physical and/or sexual assault at some point in their lives".

In Toronto, homeless women face a similar fate with 37% reporting being physically assaulted and 21% reporting one or more sexual assaults in the past year. Homeless women in the Street Health Survey 2007 were found to be 10 times more likely to be sexually assaulted compared to homeless men. Homeless women also face a greater risk of illness and premature death. Toronto-based doctor Stephen Hwang, "a leading authority on morbidity and mortality among the homeless," notes that "homeless women 18-44 years of age were 10 times more likely to die than women in the general population of Toronto...in the homeless population...the mortality rate among younger women was similar to that among their male counterparts, which indicates that the adverse health effects of the social environment and health behaviours of younger homeless women must be particularly severe".

The Challenge of Leaving the Streets

A number of interrelated factors work to prevent women from transitioning off the streets. One of these factors is the attractiveness of the street as an illusory symbol of freedom. Reid et al, reported that although homeless women routinely experience violence on the streets many of them expressed that "homelessness provided a welcome respite from oppressive conditions at home. As several of the girls and young women explained, from their perspective homelessness was preferable to their family environments, which typically included exposure to violence and substance abuse". Substance abuse remains a reality for many homeless women, a lifestyle choice that either preceded or followed initial homelessness, making it increasingly more difficult to leave the streets without effective treatment plans and community support.

The same can be said about women who are suffering from mental health issues such as depression, often correlated to their drug and substance abuse. Other factors include a lack of resources available to help women transition off the streets, a shortage of marketable skills and low employability, and the fact that, while on the street, women's socio-economic status has remained the same or worsened, putting the most basic housing options out of reach.

Pregnancy as a Potential "Turning Point"

While there are a number of obstacles to leaving the streets, a recent study conducted by researchers at the Centre for Addiction and Mental Health and the University of Toronto, found that pregnancy could serve as a protective factor, or as they called it a "turning point," in the lives of young homeless women wanting to leave the streets in order to provide themselves and their child or children with a better life and future.

Further, researchers for the National Online Resource Centre on Violence Against Women in the United States found that "women who do not have children with them are at particularly high risk for sexual violence after the age of 18, in part because they are more likely to sleep outside than are women with children, who might fear for their children's well being or worry about the intervention of child protective services". Thus, what might at first appear to be an additional challenge can, for some women, be the push that motivates them to get off the streets and into a more stable and protective environment for themselves and their children.

Embracing Empowerment over Victimization

Throughout the world, there are over 175 million migrants – people who have left their countries of birth to search for employment, to escape war or internal strife, or for countless other reasons. The number of migrants is at an all-time high, comprising three percent of the world's population. This is a dramatic increase in the sheer numbers of migrants during the middle half of the twentieth century, when in 1960, there were 75 million international migrants.

Migration affects all parts of the world, developed or developing. Sixty percent of migrants reside in developed nations, while 40 percent live in developing nations. Almost one out of every ten persons in the developed world is a migrant, while one out of every 70 in the developing world is a migrant. Countries with the largest numbers of migrants include the United States, with almost 35 million migrants, followed by the Russian Federation, with 13 million. The top four countries with the largest percentage of their total population being migrants, in contrast, are all in the Middle East. The United Arab Emirates, the leader of this category, has a migrant population that is over 73 percent of its total population. Migrants make up at least one-quarter of the populations of all of the top ten countries in this category.

Migrant workers are present throughout the developed and the developing world. There are 30 million migrant workers and their families in Europe, 20 million in Africa, 18 million in North America, 12 million in Central and South America, 9 million in the Middle East (West Asia), and 7 million in South and East Asia. The largest number of migrant workers comes from Mexico, followed by the Philippines. Workers from the Philippines are more geographically dispersed than those from other countries, prompting some scholars to label Filipinos as the most globalized workforce in the world. Over the past 30 years, several trends in labour migration have emerged. The first is a growing restrictiveness in the admission of labour migrants, particularly in developed countries. Many countries have attempted to curb migration levels in recent years. In 2001, 44 per cent of developed nations had policies aimed at lowering migration into their countries. Thirty-nine percent of developing countries had policies with similar goals. Second, there has been a sharp increase in the number of countries, particularly developing countries that host migrant workers.

The dominant demographic pattern in labour migration is south to north migration, as Western Europe and Gulf states become major labour recruiters. Poverty is a major factor for migrant workers who leave their home countries. Migrants travel not only from developing nations to developed nations, however, but from one developing nation to another, where employment prospects appear better.

Next, there has been a growing recognition of the need to protect the human rights of migrant workers. In addition to significant attention paid to the plight of migrant workers, a major breakthrough in this area is the International Convention on the Protection of the Rights of All Migrant Workers and Members of Their Families (Convention on Migrant Workers), discussed in Part V in detail, which entered into force in 2003.

Finally, increasing numbers of countries and regions have adopted agreements on labour migration. Bilateral and multilateral agreements allow countries with labour needs to recruit labourers from abroad with a minimum of procedural difficulty, and provide for government involve-ment in the employment process.

Under such agreements, migrant workers may be recruited in groups tied to a project, or may be recruited individually. Agreements typically include the aims of the treaty, the definition of the labour concerned, admission criteria, the legal status of migrants, the terms of migration, and annual quotas. These agreements can allow both host and home countries to share the burden of ensuring adequate living standards and working conditions, monitoring the agreement, and more actively managing the labour migration process, including the periods prior to and following migration.

The Feminization of Migration

Until recently, women were neglected in the study of international migration. As many commentators have observed, women are often invisible in national statistics. Furthermore, significant barriers exist for social scientists interested in women and migration, including linguistic, geographic, disciplinary, and other barriers. These barriers, combined with a lack of awareness of women's role in international migration, often result in women migrant workers being studied only on a national or regional basis, if at all. When not ignored, women have been depicted either as non-migrants who remain in their home countries waiting for male family members to return, or as passive reactors who accompany male migrant workers.

However, this treatment of women belies the fact that women have comprised a large percentage of migrant workers for decades, and their numbers continue to climb. Almost as many women as men have migrated since 1960, where 47 per cent of migrants were women. In 1990, 48 percent of migrants were female, and in 2000, 49 percent of migrants were women. Furthermore, in 2000, 51 percent of all migrants in developed countries were women. In contrast to the significant attention paid to undocumented workers, that paid to migrant women workers is minimal. Significant differences in the percentage of women migrant workers exist country by country. In the United States, a receiving country, documented migrants have been predominantly female since 1930. In the Philippines, a sending country, women make up 46 percent of all workers who migrate internationally.

In Indonesia, 68 per cent of migrants are women, and in Sri Lanka, 75 per cent of migrants are women. Major destination countries for women migrant workers include the Middle East and Pacific Rim nations in Southeast Asia.

In Southeast Asia in 2000, the majority of migrant workers were women, with women migrant workers outnumbering male migrant workers by 100,000 workers. In many countries, the large numbers or percentages of women migrant workers do not occur by accident. Indeed, many countries engage in bilateral or multilateral agreements so that their citizens may more easily engage in migration for work.

The Victimization Perspective

As a result of decades of effort at the international and national levels - including work by the International Labour Organization and workers' initiatives around the world - human rights standards involving the right to work are highly developed. This stands in sharp contrast to the labour rights of women migrant workers, which largely have been ignored. Although women make up an increasingly large percentage of all migrant workers, and in some nations vastly eclipse the number of male migrant workers, much of the discourse on women migrant workers has centered on victimization. When international organizations discuss women migrant workers at all, their discussions are usually limited to violence and human trafficking.

The years 1976 to 1985 marked the United Nations' Decade for Women, "the most comprehensive global undertaking" devoted to improving the status of women. Despite the significant attention brought to women and the struggle for equality, the special circumstances faced by women migrant workers remained largely invisible. In its brief discussion of women migrant workers in a fact sheet on migration, the UN focuses on issues of violence and sexual exploitation. "The plight of women migrant workers is also of concern to the United Nations, as they have been victims of violence and sexual exploitation." The UN also points to a preliminary report of the Special Rapporteur of the Commission on Human Rights on violence against women. In that report, the Special Rapporteur makes several recommendations for States to protect women migrant workers.

These recommendations while important safeguards for women, nonetheless promote a view of women migrant workers as victims. Later attention to women migrant workers also centers on the women as victims.

The UN's 2002 report on migration fails to mention women migrants or gender-related issues in its discussion of the focus of the UN Secretariat on international migration, and in its overview of the attention paid to migration throughout the UN system. The role of women in migration is only specifically addressed in the report's section on undocumented migration, where the report notes the importance of information campaigns in deterring the trafficking of women for sexual exploitation.

A 2002 UN resolution, one that specifically addresses women migrant workers, focuses solely on violence against women. The Violence Resolution was written out of concern over the large numbers of abuse and acts of violence against women migrant workers. Unfortunately, the Resolution emphasizes criminalization and victimization.

The Resolution calls for States to enact penal sanctions against perpetrators of violence against women migrant workers, provide victims with assistance, and enact legal measures against smugglers who exploit women migrant workers. It further encourages States to consider ratifying the Convention on the Protection of the Rights of All Migrant Workers and Members of Their Families; the Convention against Transnational Organized Crime; the Protocol against the Smuggling of Migrants by Land, Sea, and Air; the Protocol to Prevent, Suppress, and Punish Trafficking in Persons, Especially Women and Children; and the Slavery Convention of 1926. With the exception of the Convention on Migrant Workers, these instruments tend to focus on the criminalization of trafficking and smuggling, with women cast as victims.

Even the Fourth World Conference on Women, which paid considerable attention to women migrant workers, called on states in its Platform for Action to recognize the vulnerability of women migrant workers to violence. Although the Conference engaged in a more even-handed treatment of women migrant workers than other international efforts have demonstrated, it is nonetheless telling that women migrant workers were cast in a role of victimization. Violence against women migrant workers and the trafficking of women is a serious worldwide problem, and the international community must address it. However, at issue is the extent to which the world focuses on violence and victimization to the exclusion of all other aspects of women's migration. As stated, women migrant workers face discrimination, the denial of basic workers' rights, and other forms of exploitation. The international community must address all types of human rights violations faced by women migrant workers, and not simply address human rights when the women's lives are at risk. The problem of a victimization perspective is not just a deficiency in rhetoric. The focus on the criminalization of trafficking and violence against women migrant workers often does little to prevent abuses.

Often, the "victims" of such abuses, when rescued, face quick deportation because of their immigration status. This creates a revolving door, where women and girls return to their homes and are likely to be re-trafficked because little has changed in their home countries. Additionally, overemphasizing trafficking and taking it out of the migration context is counterproductive to the fulfillment of women's human rights. Rather than focusing on migrants' human rights first, trafficking puts migration in a crime control and prevention context. Further, trafficking is sometimes used by governments as a reason to develop more restrictive laws and regulations dealing with migration.

Violence Against Women

Violence against women is a technical term used to collectively refer to violent acts that are primarily or exclusively committed against women. Similar to a hate crime, this type of violence targets a specific group with the victim's gender as a primary motive. The United Nations General Assembly defines "violence against women" as "any act of gender-based violence that results in, or is likely to result in, physical, sexual or mental harm or suffering to women, including threats of such acts, coercion or arbitrary deprivation of liberty, whether occurring in public or in private life."

The 1993 Declaration on the Elimination of Violence against Women noted that this violence could be perpetrated by assailants of gender, family members and even the "State" itself. Worldwide governments and organizations actively work to combat violence against women through a variety of programs. A UN resolution designated November 25th as International Day for the Elimination of Violence against Women. Some historians believe that the history of violence against women is tied to the history of women being viewed as property and a gender role assigned to be subservient to men and also other women

Domestic Violence

Women are more likely to be victimized by someone that they are intimate with, commonly called "Intimate Partner Violence" or (IPV). The impact of domestic violence in the sphere of total violence against women can be understood through the example that 40-70% of murders of women are committed by their husband or boyfriend. Studies have shown that violence is not always perpetrated as a form of physical violence but can also be psychological and verbal. In unmarried relationships this is commonly called dating violence, whereas in the context of marriage it is called domestic violence.

Instances of IPV tend not to be reported to police and thus many experts believe that the true magnitude of the problem is hard to estimate. Though this form of violence is often portrayed as an issue within the context of heterosexual relationships, it also occurs in lesbian relationships, daughter-mother relationships, roommate relationships and other domestic relationships involving two women. Violence against women in lesbian relationships is about as common as violence against women in heterosexual relationships. Violence against women by women also exists outside the sphere of relationship violence, probably even less research has been done on this subject.

Diagnosis Planning

The American Psychiatric Association planning and research committees for the forthcoming DSM-V (2012) have canvassed a series of new Relational disorders which include Marital Conflict Disorder without Violence or Marital Abuse Disorder (Marital Conflict Disorder with Violence). Couples with marital disorders sometimes come to clinical attention because the couple recognizes long-standing dissatisfaction with their marriage and come to the clinician on their own initiative or are referred by an astute health care professional. Secondly, there is serious violence in the marriage which is -"usually the husband battering the wife". In these cases the emergency room or a legal authority often is the first to notify the clinician. Most importantly, marital violence "is a major risk factor for serious injury and even death and women in violent marriages are at much greater risk of being seriously injured or killed (National Advisory Council on Violence Against Women 2000)."

The authors of this study add that "There is current considerable controversy over whether male-to-female marital violence is best regarded as a reflection of male psychopathology and control or whether there is an empirical base and clinical utility for conceptualizing these patterns as relational." Recommendations for clinicians making a diagnosis of Marital Relational Disorder should include the assessment of actual or "potential" male violence as regularly as they assess the potential for suicide in depressed patients. Further, "clinicians should not relax their vigilance after a battered wife leaves her husband, because some data suggest that the period immediately following a marital separation is the period of greatest risk for the women.

Many men will stalk and batter their wives in an effort to get them to return or punish them for leaving. Initial assessments of the potential for violence in a marriage can be supplemented by standardized interviews and questionnaires, which have been reliable and valid aids in exploring marital violence more systematically." The authors conclude with what they call "very recent information" on the course of violent marriages which suggests that "over time a husband's battering may abate somewhat, but perhaps because he has successfully intimidated his wife. The risk of violence remains strong in a marriage in which it has been a feature in the past. Thus, treatment is essential here; the clinician cannot just wait and watch." The most urgent clinical priority is the protection of the wife because she is the one most frequently at risk, and clinicians must be aware that supporting assertiveness by a battered wife may lead to more beatings or even death.

State Violence

Labour Camps

Many women underwent extrajudicial punishment in labour camps of Nazi Germany and the Soviet Union. Their suffering was described in memories of former Gulag women prisoners Yevgenia Ginzburg, Eufrosinia Kersnovskaya and others. Militarism produces special environments that allow for increased violence against women. For example, during World War II, the Japanese military established brothels for soldiers exploiting women for the purpose of creating access and entitlement for men. Another example of violence against women incited by militarism during war took place in the Kovno Ghetto. Jewish male prisoners had access to (and used) Jewish women forced into camp brothels by the Nazis, who also used them. The 1998 United Nations International Criminal Tribunal for Rwanda recognized rape as a war crime.

Violence in Empowerment Systems

Shelter workers are often reduced them to contributing to violence against women by exploiting their vulnerability in exchange for a paying job.

Violence Against Women Act

The Violence Against Women Act of 1994 (VAWA) is a United States federal law. It was passed as Title IV, sec. 40001-40703 of the Violent Crime Control and Law Enforcement Act of 1994 HR 3355 and signed as Public Law 103-322 by President Bill Clinton on September 13, 1994. It provided $1.6 billion to enhance investigation and prosecution of the violent crime perpetrated against women, increased pre-trial detention of the accused, imposed automatic and mandatory restitution on those convicted, and allowed civil redress in cases prosecutors chose to leave unprosecuted.

VAWA was drafted by Senator Joe Biden's office with support from a number of advocacy organizations including Legal Momentum and The National Organization for Women, which described the bill as "the greatest breakthrough in civil rights for women in nearly two decades." VAWA was reauthorized by Congress in 2000, and again in December 2005. The bill was signed into law by President George W. Bush on January 5, 2006.

International Violence Against Women Act of 2007

In 2007 Senator Biden proposed the International Violence Against Women Act. The bill did not pass either the Senate or the House. The bill is far-reaching in its scope and controversial in many of its provisions:

- Amends the Foreign Assistance Act of 1961 to establish in the Department of State the Office of Women's Global Initiatives (which shall replace the Office of International Women's Issues) to coordinate U.S. government efforts respecting international women's issues. Establishes within the Department an Advisory Commission on International Violence Against Women.
- Directs the President to develop a comprehensive strategy to prevent violence against women and girls. Directs the Coordinator of the Women's Global Initiatives to ensure that foreign assistance programs incorporate measures to prevent and respond to violence against women and girls. Provides that U.S. training of foreign military and police forces incorporates training on prevention of violence against women and girls.
- Directs the Department and the United States Agency for International Development (USAID) to assist programs that prevent and respond to violence against women and girls in all humanitarian relief, conflict, and post-conflict operations. Directs the Secretary of State to:

1. Encourage U.N. member states to expand the number of female members of U.N. peacekeeping missions; and

2. Take emergency measures to respond to violence against women and girls during conflict or post-conflict operations.

Expresses the sense of Congress that the United Nations should strengthen its ability to prevent violence against women and girls by U.N. military and civilian personnel. Provides that Foreign Service training include instruction on prevention of violence against women and girls. Authorizes appropriations to support the United Nations Development Fund for Women Trust Fund in Support of Actions to Eliminate Violence Against Women.

The World Conference on Human Rights, held in Vienna in 1993, and the Declaration on the Elimination of Violence against Women in the same year, concluded that civil society and governments have acknowledged that domestic violence is a public health policy and human rights concern. The World Health Organization conducted an extensive study on world-wide domestic violence. Released in 2005, the study analyzed data from 10 countries and sheds new light on the prevalence of violence against women. It seeks to look at domestic violence from a public health policy perspective. The survey is viewed as controversial by many because it did not assess the extent of partner violence against men, and its failure to use a validated survey instrument.

The findings from this and other studies can be used to inform a more effective response from government, including the health, justice and social service sectors, as a step towards fulfilling the state's obligation to curtail domestic violence under international human rights laws. The American Civil Liberties Union had originally expressed concerns about the Act, saying that the increased penalties were rash, the increased pretrial detention was "repugnant" to the US Constitution, the mandatory HIV testing of those only charged but not convicted is an infringement of a citizen's right to privacy and the edict for automatic payment of full restitution was non-judicious.

However, the ACLU has supported reauthorization of VAWA on the condition that the "unconstitutional DNA provision" be removed. The ACLU, in their July 27, 2005 'Letter to the Senate Judiciary Committee Regarding the Violence Against Women Act of 2005, S. 1197' stated that "VAWA is one of the most effective pieces of legislation enacted to end domestic violence, dating violence, sexual assault, and stalking. It has dramatically improved the law enforcement response to violence against women and has provided critical services necessary to support women and children in their struggle to overcome abusive situations." In 2000, in a controversial 5-4 vote, the Supreme Court of the United States held part of VAWA unconstitutional in United States v. Morrison on federalism grounds. Only the civil rights remedy of VAWA was struck down. The provisions providing program funding were unaffected.

In the last two decades violence against women, (gender-based violence) has emerged as the most pressing and intractable social problem across regional, social and cultural boundaries. Violence against women is recognized as a serious human rights violation and a pervasive public health problem that concerns all sectors of society. Irrespective of a nation's level of development, women are susceptible to exploitation, oppression and other types of demeaning violence from men in all societies where cultural norms, tradition and the legal system endorse women's subordination to men. In the South Asian Region, violence against women begins long before they are born and continues throughout their lives. The lives of unborn girls are terminated through sex selective abortions.

Every sixth death of a female infant in India, Banglad-esh and Pakistan is due to neglect and discrimination. In the Region, females face restrictions in mobility, usually have less to eat than their male counterparts, are denied proper education and health care, are often forced into early arranged marriages, have few opportunities of employment and are underrepresented in the governments. All too frequently women are targets of extreme forms of aggression such as incest, rape, public humiliation, trafficking, acid attacks and dowry deaths. Bangladesh is no exception. Violence against women is a common and insidious phenomenon in Bangladesh. Newspaper reports in the country clearly indicate that the prevalence of violence against women is very high. Evidence from research supports the above conviction.

It is against this background that we have reviewed published literature on violence against women, primarily focusing on domestic violence, to assess and explore the prevalence, causes and consequences of the problem and to understand the strategies undertaken by the women victims themselves in order to plan effective prevention and intervention strategies. Furthermore, the knowledge of effective attitudes and practices among health service providers and law enforcers to support victims of violence is crucial for the formulation of appropriate policies and programmes.

Prevalence and forms of violence

Gender violence, namely violence against women, is now defined very broadly to include anything "involving use of force/coercion with intent of perpetuation/ promotion of hierarchical gender-relationship all social structures: family, community, workplace and society". United Nations Commission of the Status of Women defined violence against women as "any act that results in, or is likely to result in physical, sexual or psychological harm or suffering to women". The types of violence commonly committed against women in Bangladesh are, domestic violence, acid throwing and burning, sexual harassment and indecent assault, rape, kidnapping and abduction, trafficking and importation for immoral purposes and forced prostitution.

In every country where reliable large-scale studies have taken place, domestic violence has been found to be by far the most common, widespread and far-reaching form of gender based violence. Violent behaviours such as beating, pushing, slapping or throwing things by family members are considered domestic violence. Domestic and intimate partner violence involves physical, sexual and emotional abuse against women in the home, within the family or within an intimate relationship. Several studies have indicated that domestic violence against women, especially violence perpetrated by a woman's husband, is a serious problem in Bangladesh.

Although domestic violence includes child abuse, parent abuse and in-law abuse committed by male aggressors on female victims, available information from research indicated that the "most common type of violence in Bangladesh against women is domestic violence perpetrated by intimate partners or ex partners". Many Bangladeshi women endure daily beatings, harassment for dowry, verbal abuse and acid attacks for refusing to comply with male demands.

For many, home is not a haven but a place of pain and humiliation, where violence is an integral part of everyday life hidden behind closed doors and avoided in public discussion. The estimated prevalence of physical violence against women by husbands in Bangladesh varies between 30 and 50 per cent. In earlier research the estimates on the magnitude of physical violence against women in Bangladesh were either focused on a particular socio-economic group or did not relate exclusively to intimate partner violence.

The study by Schuler *et al* addressed the prevalence of violence amongst economically disadvantaged women in rural Bangladesh. The study reported that 47 per cent of the women were beaten by their husbands in their lifetime and the prevalence of current abuse of women was 19 per cent in 1994. A different study by Steele and colleagues found the rate to be 32 per cent in another rural area of Bangladesh. Koenig *et al* included women from all socio-economic strata but explored factors associated with abuse of women by the husband and in laws. However, the time period for abuse was not explicitly specified in this study. They reported that 42 per cent of the violence was perpetrated by the husband or the in laws.

Azim observed the rate of violence to be 61 per cent in the urban areas of Bangladesh. However, the questions used in the earlier studies, with the exception of the study by Azim, did not have a direct and behaviourally explicit definition of physical violence, thus leaving the meaning of violence open for interpretation. As there were methodological differences among the earlier studies, the estimates of the magnitude of spousal physical violence were incomparable. Using data from the most comprehensive population based survey of 2,702 women conducted in 2000-2001, collected in collaboration of ICDDR, B and Naripokkho, Naved *et al* have shown a high prevalence of lifetime spousal physical violence against women, 40 per cent in the urban and 42 per cent in the rural areas of Bangladesh. About 19 per cent of urban and 16 per cent of rural women reported experiencing current physical abuse, defined as abuse during the twelve months prior to the interview.

In both the urban and rural sites, 19 per cent of the women had experienced severe physical violence defined as hit with fist or something else or kicked, dragged or beaten up or choked or burnt or threatened or actually injured by a weapon or some other tool. For most of these women physical violence was not a one-time event. This was true regardless of the type of assault, ranging from slapping to burning. About 10 per cent of the ever-pregnant women in the urban and 12 per cent of such women in the rural area reported being physically abused during pregnancy. This suggests that physical violence does not escalate during pregnancy. In another analysis using the ICDDR, B-Naripokkho survey data, Naved *et al* observed that of the abused pregnant women, 37 per cent in Dhaka and 28 per cent in Matlab were punched or kicked in the abdomen. In a study by Bhuiya and colleagues, it was reported that 50.8 per cent of the women were battered by their husbands, 2.1 per cent by other family members, and a small proportion (5.2%) by both their husbands and other family members.

Hitting was mostly done with the use of hand (85.4%), followed by stick (63.5%), and kicking (51%) alone or in combination. The study reported that 20 per cent of women were physically abused by their husbands during pregnancy and 2.6 per cent by other family members as well. About, 13.7 per cent were throttled by their husbands and 2.1 per cent by other family members. In a recent study, Ahmed explored the effect of micro credit based development programmes of Bangladesh Rural Advancement Committee (BRAC) on domestic violence. The study reported that 17.5 per cent of women had experienced spousal violence during the study period of 4 months in 1999 and the proportion of abused women was greater among BRAC households (P=0.05). The study also demonstrated that violence decreased with age, more so for the poor non-member households.

In addition, irrespective of BRAC membership status of the household, women with some schooling had reported less violence, while women with children had reported more. Furthermore, it was observed that, women above 35 yrs of age, schooling of the household head, and the non-deficit economic status of the household were associated with a lower level of reported violence. Nevertheless, the study concluded that the higher level of domestic violence reported during the initial stages/phase of BRAC membership declined over time with the introduction of skill development or training among the women participants.

In a recent WHO multi-country study, based on the ICDDR, B-Naripokkho survey data, it was reported that more than 50 per cent of the women in Bangladesh were subjected to physical or sexual violence by intimate partners. The lifetime prevalence of partner violence (either physical or sexual) was observed to be 53.4 per cent in the urban and 61.7 per cent in the rural areas of Bangladesh. The magnitude of lifetime prevalence of physical violence, alone, against women was estimated to be 39.7 per cent in the urban and 41.7 per cent in the rural areas. The percentage of ever-partnered women, who had experienced severe physical violence, was 18.7 per cent for the urban and 19.4 per cent in the rural areas of Bangladesh. The most common act of violence reported by women was being slapped or having something thrown at them. In general, as the severity of the act of violence increased; the percentage of women having experienced that particular act decreased. Further analysis of the ICDDR, B-Naripokkho sample survey of women in reproductive age group women revealed that the majority of women in Dhaka (60%) and Matlab (61%) had reported sexual or physical abuse or both by their husbands.

Emotional Abuse

Emotional or psychological violence includes intimidation and humiliation where the victim is made to feel bad about oneself and is subjected to excessive controlling, curtailing and/or disruption of routine activities such as sleeping or eating habits, social relationship, access to money; verbal insults and so on. In the study by Bhuiya and colleagues a higher prevalence for verbal abuse than physical abuse against women was observed. The study reported that 66.8 per cent of women in the survey were verbally abused by their husbands and 23.7 per cent by other members of the family. In verbal abuse demeaning words were used only against the women in 70.9 per cent of the cases, and in 17.9 per cent of the cases the abusive words were used against only the parents of the women. About 6.8 per cent of the women in the study area were abused verbally on a daily basis, and for 37.8 per cent the abuse was occasional. Infrequent verbal abuse was suffered by 16.8 per cent of the women. In addition, it was observed that, during pregnancy, 37.9 per cent of the women endured verbal abuse from husbands and 11.6 per cent from other members of the family.

Analyzing data from the ICDDR, B-Naripokkho survey, the WHO multi-country study findings reported that two thirds or more of the women had experienced repeated emotional abuse for either a few or many times. Usually, the acts most frequently mentioned by women were insults, belittling and intimidation. In general, physical abuse in intimate relationships was almost always accompanied by severe psychological and verbal abuse. In addition, the findings from the study suggest that a woman who suffered violence, physical or sexual, from an intimate partner was significantly more likely to experience severe constraints on her physical and social mobility or, in other words, highly controlling behaviours by the intimate partner. Qualitative research has consistently revealed that women often consider emotional abuse to be more devastating than acts of physical violence.

From the analysis of the ICDDR-B Naripokkho survey data, Naved *et al* reported that 37 per cent of the ever-married, reproductive age group women in Dhaka and 50 per cent in Matlab had experienced sexual violence within marriage. From the ICDDR-B-Naripokkho survey data the WHO multi - country study reported that the percentage of women who had experienced sexual abuse by an intimate partner during their lifetime was 37.4 per cent in the urban area and 49.7 per cent in the rural areas of Bangladesh. Substantial overlap between sexual and physical violence was observed. Out of four victims of domestic violence, one was also observed to have experienced sexual abuse. In the rural areas of Bangladesh, women reported more sexual violence than physical violence and a high proportion of the women (33%) in the rural areas reported sexual violence only by an intimate partner.

Bhuiya *et al* reported that the most frequently mentioned reasons for verbal abuse included wife's questioning of the husband on day to day affairs (29.1%) followed by failure of the wife to perform household work satisfactorily (17.6%), economic hardship of the family (11.5%), failure of the wife to take proper care of the children (10%), not wearing the veil or conforming to other expected behaviour (5.5%),inability to bring money from the natal home (3%), not taking good care of in-laws and relatives (2%). The rest of the reasons included supporting the natal home, failure to have children, having too many children, dark complexion of children, family feud between the husband's family and natal family and suspected relation with others. Similarly, the most frequently mentioned reasons for physical abuse included questioning of the husband (29.9%), failure to perform household work satisfactorily (18.8%), economic problems (9.4%), failure to take care of children properly (5.1%), stealing (3.4%), refusal to bring dowry from natal home (2.6%). Jahan reported that family quarrel was the reason given by most of the women as the cause of violence.

Family quarrel was referred to as a value term that included many specific reasons such as husband's dissatisfaction over wife's management of expenses, house keeping and child care, jealousy and suspicious nature, exaggerated sense of superiority over a wife as reflected in household decision making, sexual maladjustment and such. The reasons for discord were found to be exacerbated by stress resulting from prolonged illness in the family, sudden financial loss, loss of job and aggravation by in-laws. Non-payment of dowry was the next most important cause mentioned for violence.

Factors Associated with Domestic Violence

Bhuiya *et al* reported that the age of women, age of husband and membership of women in micro credit organizations had significant relationship with husbands beating of wives in univariate analysis. In the multivariate analysis, age of the husband and membership of micro-credit organizations showed statistically significant relationship with battering. Further, the study revealed that the odds of being beaten were lowest for women with husbands aged 50 yrs or more and highest for women with husbands less than 30 yrs of age (6 times more than the former). Moreover, women who were members of micro credit organizations were two times more likely to be abused by their husbands than those who were non-members. Conversely, results of a BRAC study, by Hadi reported that the prevalence of physical violence against participating women was 19 per cent compared to 40 per cent among non participating eligible non members.

The risk was also lower for sexual violence among members. However, some studies contest this argument. Chowdhury and Bhuiya studied data from 2,038 currently married women aged 15-55 yrs and reported a higher level of physical violence among BRAC members than among non members. Nonetheless, it was observed that the prevalence of violence tended to decrease as the duration of membership with the micro credit organization increased. Violence peaked when membership was initiated but tapered off when other inputs such as training were offered. The logic behind the assumption was that greater economic opportunities for women, ensured through access to credit, awareness increasing activities and skill training, would enhance the self esteem and status of women within households, improve spousal relationships and therefore reduce domestic violence.

Despite the lack of effect of women's contribution to family support on domestic violence in a multivariate analysis, an ethnographic study by Schuler *et al* showed that group based credit programmes could reduce men's violence against women. These programmes could reduce women's vulnerability to violence by strengthening their economic roles and making their lives more public. However, women's role as wage earners was capable of provoking hostility and violence in the husband when and if the traditional gender norms were challenged by the women. Further, in the rural area it was observed that earning an income increased the risk of being abused. Khan reported similar findings explaining that it may undermine the power relations between the couple and provoke violence in husbands.

Naved and Persson, from the previously mentioned ICDDR, B-Naripokkho population based survey data and in depth interviews of 28 abused women investigated the factors associated with domestic violence in urban and rural

Bangladesh. Multilevel analysis revealed that in both areas, the strongest factor associated with husband's violence against the spouse was the history of abuse of the husband's mother by his father. The study reported that men witnessing physical violence in the family during childhood were 2.29 times more likely to physically abuse the wife. Past exposure to familial violence probably endorses poor emotional development in the perpetrator, or may result in adoption of physical strategies as a means of coping with conflict. Lack of spousal communication was the second most important factor associated with domestic violence. Nonpayment or partial payment of dowry also, increased the likelihood of the wife experiencing abuse. Educational attainment of the husband, and the age of the woman were the other two important variables associated with violence, however, the influence was observed to vary by region. In the urban area, husband's education above the sixth grade had a protective effect but in the rural areas educational attainment only had such an effect when the husband had a very high level of education probably because conventional gender norms are stronger in the rural areas. In the urban area participation in savings and credit groups created tensions and increased the risk of abuse. Further, women being younger than the husband had a negative effect on violence for urban women but not for the rural women.

In the urban areas those in the younger age group of 15-19 yrs were more likely than older women to be abused. Previous studies have shown similar findings, that a woman's relative youth was an important risk factor for violence within marriage. The explanation put forward is that women who are married at a young age usually start their marital lives in their husband's family home and as young wives their status is quite low. The findings from the study by Naved *et al* also indicated that the presence of in-laws in the household was not associated with spousal abuse. Koenig *et al* found that extended family structure was negatively related to violence in Bangladesh. Further, Naved *et al* observed that once other factors were controlled for, household income was found to have no effect on physical violence. Amin *et al* assessed the impact of female education and mobility on the extent of female abuse in the rural areas of Bangladesh.

The study reported that 78 per cent of the women had encountered verbal abuse, 42 per cent physical abuse and 18 per cent were threatened with divorce. Women were found to be more likely to be abused if they were older, not educated or less mobile and if their husbands were less educated and less wealthy. Women's ownership of land and husband's occupation were also statistically significant predictors of abuse.

The WHO multi-country study18 reported, from the data collected by ICDDR, B-Naripokkho survey, that 53.3 per cent in the urban and 79.3 per cent of women in the rural area believed that a man had a right to beat his wife under certain circumstances. The various circumstances included were not completing housework adequately, refusing sex, disobeying the husband, or being unfaithful. The most commonly agreed upon reason for which beating was accepted as justified by women, was when the wife was unfaithful.

The proportion of women who agreed that wife beating was justified under certain conditions was higher among women who had experienced partner violence than among those who had not. This may be an indication that women learn to accept or rationalize violence in circumstances in which they are victims themselves, or that women are at a greater risk of violence when it is accepted as the norm by a significant number of people. The circumstances under which wives have the right to refuse unwanted sexual demands from their husbands were also explored, *e.g.*, situations including if she was sick, if she did not want to, if the husband was drunk, or if he mistreated her. Fewer women felt that a wife had the right to refuse sex because she did not want to than when her husband was drunk or abusive. About 45 per cent of urban and 35.8 per cent of rural women agreed that a wife had a right to refuse sex under all circumstances mentioned and 5.3 per cent urban and 11.3 per cent rural women agreed to none.

The Reasons for Silence

The underreporting of violence is of serious concern and the major reasons for silence in abusive relationships are (*i*) the universal acceptance of gender inequality reinforced by social and religious beliefs in favour of male dominance; (*ii*) the deep seated reverence for family as an institution for continuing the existing social order and values related to regulating sexual behaviour, particularly female sexuality within the bounds of marriage; (*iii*) the prevalent bias amongst the middle class, who form the bulk of lawmakers, law enforcers, social norm setters and opinion makers, in regarding domestic violence as inconsequential; and (*iv*) the fear of social censure and loss of face. The nature of family relationship forces women to struggle alone against violence where society encourages the husband to exercise his right to dominate and control the wife.

In general, women are socialized to accept physical and mental abuses as part of a husband's marital prerogatives. Entrenched social attitudes define violence against women as normal practice and not as a punishable crime. Underlying the acceptance of violence against women is the deep rooted social belief that women are fundamentally of less value than men. Violence against women is typically enmeshed in a complex web of institutionalized social relations that make women particularly vulnerable to it. Violence against women is rooted in the patriarchal ideology, which to a large extent is responsible for the internalization of female inferiority through a process of socialization, customs, religious laws and rituals. The legitimization and promotion of rigid gender roles, masculinity, toughness and male honour within the society perpetuates gender violence.

The social forces that perpetuate gender based violence

can be viewed from various approaches *viz.*, cultural values that tend to rationalize violence, legal systems that are not sensitive to the rights of women, economic systems that subordinate women and political systems that marginalize women's need. The shame associated with domestic violence, rape and other forms of abuse may contribute to the fact that women are afraid of repercussions and stigma and consequently never tell anyone and often suffer the abuse in silence. Women with lowered self-esteem, severe depressive symptoms with minimal personal resources and least institutional support are more vulnerable to be abused by her spouse.

From the population based cross-sectional survey data of ICDDR-B- Naripokkho, Naved *et al* reported that most of the abused women (66%) were silent about their experience. In addition, 75 per cent of the moderately abused women in the urban area and 86 per cent of them in the rural area never talked about their experience to anybody. The main reasons behind this silence was the fear of tarnishing family honour, stigma of ruining the woman's own reputation, securing the children's future, fear of repercussion from the husband, hopelessness, expectation that things would change, threat of murder, and belief that violence was the husband's prerogative. A high percentage of women (30% urban and 40% rural) reported that they had remained silent because of the shame they had felt, the fear they had of not being believed or being blamed for the violence. Moreover, 26 per cent of urban and 34 per cent of rural women felt that such disclosure would detract from family honour. Fear of repercussion was present particularly in cases where the violence experienced was severe.

Coping strategies of abused women

The findings from the analysis indicated that a third of the women did disclose or talk about their experience of violence. Severely abused women were more likely to disclose violence, almost 3 times as much as moderately abused women in the urban area and 8 times more than those in the rural area. Women who had frequent verbal disputes with their husbands were more likely to disclose violence in both urban and rural (5 times) areas. In the rural area, women with education above 10th grade were 3 times more likely to disclose their experience compared to women with no education. The study reported that only 2 per cent ever sought help from any institutional sources. The women who sought help from formal sources generally did so because they could not endure anymore (79% in urban and 84% in rural areas), husband threatened to do something to the children or actually hit children (32% in urban and 37% in the rural area), or because she was badly injured or afraid of being killed (21% urban and 31% rural women).

The study revealed that about 60 per cent of urban and 51 per cent of rural abused women never received any help from others. Moreover, those who could count on their natal homes for support were more likely to report violence. Women experiencing both physical and sexual assault were more likely to disclose their sufferings. Unlike other studies the survey found that age, income earning by the women or history of violence in the woman's family was not associated with disclosure of violence in any sites. Naved *et al* reported that women in both urban and rural areas were more likely to talk to their parents (18% in urban and 19% in rural area) and siblings (16% in urban and 14% in the rural area).

The abused women mentioned in-laws, parents and siblings as those from whom they received help most often. In the rural area, as women generally married outside their villages and lived away from their natal family, a high proportion of the rural women talked to their in-laws about the abuse (16%). In addition, 10 per cent of urban and 11.5 per cent of rural women disclosed violence to their neighbours. It was revealed that disclosure was not always a means of stopping violence but simply a coping strategy of the abused women to get some relief from mental stress. Urban women were less likely to use formal sources of support such as a local leader than the rural women, probably because they did not feel connected to a local leader in a high-density area.

Bhuiya *et al* found that in 23.9 per cent of the abuse cases, the family members undertook a direct mediating role and appealed to the husband to not to abuse the wife. Younger children would cry (16.7%) when witnessing verbal and physical abuse and in 12.3 per cent of the cases would remain quiet. Grown up children would normally be on the mother's side and would confront the father. In 25 per cent of the cases, neighbours would advise the husband not to abuse the wife, in 30.8 per cent of the cases would remain indifferent and in 5 per cent of the cases would be unsympathetic to the woman. In 36 per cent of the cases the neighbours would intervene and take initiatives to stop the abuse. The neighbours in 43.2 per cent of the cases arranged arbitration to mitigate the problem.

Men's violence against women compromises women's health and well-being in a wide variety of social settings. A growing body of evidence documents the consequences of violence on women's health and well-being, ranging from fatal outcomes such as homicide, suicide, and AIDS related deaths to non fatal outcomes such as physical injuries, chronic pain syndrome, gastrointestinal disorders, unintended pregnancies, pregnancy complications and sexually transmitted infections.

Psychiatric morbidity, such as depression, stress related symptoms, chemical dependency and substance abuse and suicide are consequences observed in the context of violence in women's lives over time. Abused women are more likely than others to suffer from depression, anxiety, psychosomatic symptoms, eating problems, sexual dysfunction and many reproductive health problems, including miscarriage and still birth, premature delivery, HIV and other sexually transmitted infections, unwanted pregnancies and unsafe abortions. Consequences of abuse, such as HIV/AIDS or unplanned pregnancies, may in themselves act as risk factors for further aggression, forming a cycle of abuse.

Further, adolescents who had experienced sexual abuse were more likely to experience it again later in life. At a global level, the health burden from violence against women aged 15-44 yrs is comparable to that posed, in the age group, by HIV, tuberculosis, sepsis during child birth, cancer or cardiovascular diseases. Violence against women is a major cause of death and disability for women 16 to 44 yrs of age. The World Bank estimates that rape and domestic violence together account for 5 per cent of the healthy years of life lost to a woman of reproductive age in developing countries. The economic cost of violence against women is substantial involving direct medical and health care services, productivity loss leave alone the pain and anguish involved. Violence against women impoverishes individuals, families, communities and governments and reduces the economic development of each nation.

Bhuiya *et al* found that nearly half (47.9%) of the women who were physically abused by husbands suffered injuries from the assault. In 78.3 per cent of the cases it was necessary to consult a health care provider. Approximately 57.1 per cent of the women who suffered from beatings by other family members sustained injuries and for nearly half of the cases, a health care provider was consulted. About 25 per cent of physically abused women reported having lost children after they were born alive compared to 18 per cent women who were never abused. In Bangladesh, 13.8 per cent of maternal deaths in pregnancy were reported as resulting from injury/violence. In addition, children who witnessed violence were at a higher risk for a whole range of emotional and behavioural problems including anxiety, depression, poor school performance, low self-esteem, disobedience, nightmares and physical health complaints.

Paltiel found that severe beatings usually perpetrated by the husband accounted for 49 per cent of household deaths in Bangladesh. The WHO multi-country study, from the ICDDR, B-Naripokkho survey, reported that among the physically abused, 26.7 per cent in the urban and 24.8 per cent in the rural area reported that they had been injured as a consequence of an assault by an intimate partner. The majority of ever-injured women reported minor injuries (bruises, abrasions, cuts, punctures and bites), however, in some areas more serious injuries were relatively common. Data from the WHO study demonstrated that far from being an isolated event, most acts of physical violence by an intimate partner were part of a pattern of continuing abuse.

About 16 per cent of ever abused women in the urban area and 11.6 per cent in the rural area reported that they had been injured more than 5 times as a consequence of an assault. In Bangladesh, at least 50 per cent of ever injured women reported that they had lost consciousness because of a violent incident. Of those who had ever been injured by an intimate partner, 80.4 per cent in the rural area and 68.5 per cent in the urban area reported having needed healthcare for an injury (whether healthcare was actually received or not). In the WHO multi-country report18, based on the ICDDR, B- Naripokkho survey data it was revealed that 27 per cent of the urban and 25 per cent of the rural physically-abused women were injured as a consequence of violence. The injuries ranged from cuts and bruises and bites to broken limbs, broken teeth and burns. Married women who reported physical or sexual abuse by their husbands were 1.5 times (95% CI:1.2-1.7) more likely to report problems in walking, 1.7 times (95% CI 1.4-2.0) more likely to report pain and 1.7 times (95% CI 1.5-2.1) more likely to report dizziness and 1.4 times (95% CI 1.2-1.6) more likely to report problems with memory. Naved *et al* observed from the ICDDR, B Naripokkho survey that approximately 13.8 per cent of maternal deaths in pregnancy resulted from injury and violence. The 15-19 yrs old women who were pregnant, or had recently given birth were nearly 3 times more likely to die from violence inflicted by others than the women of the same age who were not abused.

Mental Health

Using a self-reporting questionnaire of 20 questions (SRQ-20) developed by the WHO as a screening tool for emotional distress, the mean score for women who had experienced abuse was found to be significantly higher than that for non abused women in both areas (7.9 as compared to 5.4 in the urban areas and 7.4 compared to 5.2 in rural areas). Women who reported violence by an intimate partner were significantly more likely than women who had not experienced violence to report their general health to be poor. From the survey data by ICDDR, B-Naripokkho, Naved *et al* reported that 16 per cent of only physically abused ever married women, 12 per cent of only sexually abused and 28 per cent of those who had experienced both forms of violence reported suicidal thoughts in comparison to 7 per cent of those ever married women who never experienced any violence.

In addition, it was reported that women who were physically or sexually abused by their husbands did much worse on a scale of mental health compared to those who had not experienced any forms of violence. However, 20 per cent of only physically abused women, 22 per cent of sexually abused and 35 per cent of those abused both ways reported attempting suicide compared to only 14 per cent of non-abused women.

Acid Attacks

Every week more than ten women in Bangladesh suffer from an acid attack that leaves them brutally disfigured and disabled. In 1999, there were 178 such instances reported and 101 in 1998. In 2000, Odhikar, a human rights organization, recorded from reports of 8 daily national newspapers 186 incidences of acid attacks. Many of the victims were children between the ages of 6-15 yrs. In a majority of the cases the main reasons cited were jealousy, refusal of sexual advances and revenge after an argument and dowry disputes.

Rape

Early sexual abuse is a highly sensitive issue that is difficult to explore in survey situations. The WHO survey reported that levels of sexual abuse before the age of fifteen years ranged from 1 per cent or less in rural Bangladesh to 7.4 per cent in Bangladesh city. Strangers were the most frequently mentioned perpetrators in the urban areas of Bangladesh. However, very low level of sexual violence by non-partners for women over 15 yrs was reported (0.5% in rural and 7.6% in urban areas) in Bangladesh. Higher level of non partner violence was reported in the urban than in the rural areas. More than a fifth of the respondents in the urban area reported being physically or sexually abused by a non partner in Bangladesh.

Generally the most frequently mentioned perpetrators were acquaintances or strangers. In the rural areas of Bangladesh, more than a fifth of the respondents who had experienced non partner physical violence reported that two or more perpetrators had assaulted them. The extremely low level of violence by non partners reported in Bangladesh may be a function of the great stigma associated with sexual violence in these rural settings. The early age of marriage prevailing in the society offers protection from the risk of sexual violence, through the guardianship of the husband. In 2002, a total of 1434 cases of rape were reported and 35 per cent were gang rapes and 10 per cent were rapes followed by murder.

Rape is the worst form of intimidation, the taboo surrounding sexuality and the "shame" and loss of honour generally prevent women from seeking justice in cases of rape. Moreover, the burden of proving the assault rests on the victim and the focus is more on the victim's character, possible provocation and temptation rather than the offence perpetrated by the assailant. The extent of this violence may be seen from the official figure of the rape victims (5,738 in 1991-1996) as quoted in the Parliament by the Home Minister. Taking into account the reasons for non reporting cited above, this might be a reflection of only the tip of the iceberg. The most shocking part is that 16.26 per cent, were minors. This is the manifestation of society's failure to protect female children from such devastating violation.

Sexual abuse among young girls and adolescents is a violation of a young girl's basic rights and bodily integrity and may have profound health consequences such as behavioural and psychological problems, sexual dysfunction, relationship problems, low self-esteem, depression, thoughts of suicide, deliberate self harm, alcohol and substance abuse and sexual risk taking. In addition, women who are abused in childhood are at a greater risk of being physically and sexually abused as adults. Sexual abuse in childhood has also been linked to a range of negative reproductive health outcomes such as unwanted pregnancy and sexually transmitted infections, including HIV. A study in Bangladesh showed that 32 per cent of women working outside their homes experienced disruption of work due to incidents of domestic violence.

A distressing development in this area is the increased reports of incidents of violence against women committed by members of State agencies entrusted with the enactment of law and order in the country and the security of the people and the State. Instances of rape, sexual harassment, torture and other types of abuses, including physical and psychological violence and violation of basic human rights of women by members of the police, civil defense force and armed forces, including custodial rape, have given rise to apprehension and mistrust about the State's will and commitment towards protection of women against violence.

Early Marriages

In Bangladesh where early marriages are arranged for a majority of girls, it was found that maternal mortality among teenage mothers was double the national figures. The trend of early marriages limits educational opportuni-ties among adolescent girls and deprives them of opportunities in life.

Labour Migration and Trafficking

Trafficking in women and young girls includes all acts involved in capture and acquisition of girls and women for trade and transport with the intent to sell, exchange or use for such purpose as prostitution, sexual abuse, forced labour, bonded labour, slavery, *etc.* Three hundred thousand children from Bangladesh have been trafficked to brothels in India and 4500 women and children are trafficked to Pakistan annually. Sometimes the family are themselves responsible for trafficking of women and girl children. This problem though not new has increased tremendously in recent years. It is extremely difficult to assess the number of prostitutes in Dhaka but according to police sources their number in Dhaka and the adjacent port town of Narayangonj is nearly 50,000.

Some work in brothels and some are street prostitutes and some hotel call girls and the increasing poverty in the rural areas force young girls to come to the cities in search of work, which causes them to be vulnerable to the lure of false promises of pimps. The conservative attitude of the society which regards prostitutes as fallen makes rehabilitation of the prostitutes harder. A study in Bangladesh on female labour migration and trafficking revealed that 82 per cent of the women went to the Gulf States with domestic visas and the rest went with company visas to work as cleaners in schools and hospitals. A majority of them admitted that sex work was an integrated part of their job and 10 per cent said that it was their only occupation.

In addition, in population policy and programme implementation, poor rural women in many areas have been subjected to accepting methods of family planning, without proper counselling about side effects, inadequate follow up and referrals. Instances of provision of obsolete or experimental methods also exist. On the other hand, many women have faced hostility from family members and community elders for accepting these methods. Instead of safeguarding poor rural women's health and welfare, the programme has, in effect, caused harm and violated women's rights to health and well-being.

Violence Against Women at the Work Place

At the work place two major forms of violence take place (*i*) sexual violence, and (*ii*) violation of basic human rights of workers. Human rights violation include deliberate exploitation such as unequal and low wages, forced overtime work, harassment, deprivation of benefits such as maternity leave and locking the workers in during factory shifts.

The informal sector especially the export oriented industries such as garments and shrimp farming offer alarming examples of this violation of basic rights. In the study by Naved *et al*, 32 per cent of working women in Dhaka and 23 per cent in Matlab reported work disruption as a consequence of physical violence by husband, about 50 per cent of working women reported that they frequently suffered ill health because of violence and were frequently on leave. A study in Bangladesh showed that 32 per cent of women working outside their homes experienced disruption of work due to incidents of domestic violence.

Litigation

So far, the Bangladeshi legal system, based mainly on the British Penal Code and common law, has done little to diminish women's vulnerability to violence. The interventions undertaken by the government and non governmental organizations (NGOs) include the following: constitutional provisions, legislative actions, support services, shelter homes, advocacy, legal aid and counselling services. The Dowry Prohibition Act (1980), Cruelty to Women (Deterrent Punishment) Ordinance (1983), Family Court Ordinance (1985), and the Women and Children Repression (Special Provision) Act (1995) have all been very inadequately formulated and implemented, therefore the actual impact has been very marginal. However, it is worth mentioning that in Bangladesh, the Women and Children Repression (Special

Provision) Act 1995, Section 8 provides a maximum penalty of life imprisonment and also, provides deterrent punishment for committing rape, murder and acid throwing.

However, in many instances of rape, molestation, abduction, and sexual harassment, technicalities and legal loopholes deprive women of justice, especially where the aggressors are in a dominant socio-economic position. Moreover, women's socio-economic powerlessness and ignorance of legal rights limit the scope of legal protection. In addition, litigation does not always guarantee that the desired judgment will be received. So far, imperfect understanding and inadequate knowledge of this multidimensional problem has produced limited success in this area. In many cases full enforcement and implementation of existing laws have not been achieved due to various factors, including the lack of awareness of women's rights among law enforcement agents. The scarcity of effective agencies offering supportive intervention and the excessive expenses and the time-consuming process involved in litigation also prevent many women, especially the poor and uneducated ones (who are the worst sufferers), from seeking redress through criminal proceedings.

A review of interventions shows that the success of the attempts designed to reduce violence has been limited and the implications of the limited success very grave. However, interventions by NGOs and government have generated knowledge about the causes and consequences and the need to prevent violence against women. A review of successful methods of prevention and elimination of violence and effective legislative and policy intervention is absolutely necessary. Existence of variations in definition and recognition of violence against women among the various agencies engaged in actions designed to resist/reduce violence against women prevails. The conventional categorization of abuse by the police is based on a very narrow definition. For instance, marital rape is not recognized in law and culture. Incest is a taboo topic.

There are laws regarding rape and acid attacks but there are no clear law defining domestic violence. In Bangladesh, psychological violence and emotional abuse and deprivation and denial of basic rights, especially among married couples, is not given serious consideration either by family or police and therefore remains unreported. Wife-abuse (battering) is widely condoned and tolerated. These particular problems due to variations in definition and recognition make it extremely difficult to motivate people to contest violence against women and to formulate appropriate strategies.

Tacit support by State agencies, especially in cases of custodial rape and State violence renders implementation of laws quite difficult. Of all the cases of rape in police custody brought to light so far, very few have been held accountable or chastised. Moreover, suppression of evidence by colleagues and foot dragging over procedures by officials frequently helped the suspects in such cases. Collusion between local elites and religious leaders who abuse the traditional local arbitration procedure is one of the main factors that makes redress of abuse difficult.

Policies and Programmes

Interventions to alleviate the problem of domestic violence have mostly been directed towards reducing the harm after the occurrence of the incident through medical treatment and counseling. Preventive efforts on the other hand have been limited to enactment of punitive legislative measures against the aggressor for abusing women. Although the occurrence of domestic violence directly involves husband, wife and other family members and is possibly perpetuated by the social context, a family and/or community approach to alleviate the problem has been largely absent so far.

Many of the contributing risk factors for sexual and physical assault have been identified in childhood and adolescence and these need to be incorporated into prevention goals. Peer attitudes, past experiences of child maltreatment and substance abuse in adolescence have all been linked to greater risk of domestic violence and sexual assault. Changing the norms and custom about relationships and providing the future generation with skills needed to foster healthy relationships is the only viable way to shift from a society where violence against women is widely condoned. Much of children's social learning takes place in schools and influences the development of behaviours and attitudes supportive of interpersonal violence in its many forms. Schools are an ideal place where primary prevention programmes can be introduced to a wide range of children.

Discussion of personal safety and injury prevention in the classroom and integration of such discussion within the context of trusting relationships is necessary. Early and mid adolescence is another important phase of life when awareness of violence in relationships can be built and healthy ways of forming intimate relationships can be taught. As such some researchers agree that institutions should provide universal programmes to address and challenge violence against women. Public awareness campaigns such as public service announcements and advertisements are common approaches to primary prevention providing information regarding the warning signs of violence and community resources for victims and perpetrators. Developing community-based networks for coordinating services and programmes are important in raising awareness for prevention of violence. Community-based educational activities should be used to raise awareness and knowledge about women's legal and social rights, and hence, empowering them to seek help for abuse. Effective implementation of legislation is constantly impaired by the lack of support from dominant interests in the community who legitimize violence as normal. Despite punitive legislation most women have to abide by the rules of a patriarchal social system, which reinforces gender inequalities.

Health providers are typically reluctant to ask women

about experiences of abuse in fear of either offending the victims or getting involved into issues deeper than what they can handle. Providers often feel that they do not have the knowledge or skill to address the problem. They lack knowledge of national legislation as well as available services to which women may be referred. Poor co-ordination among and across agencies and institutions makes the process of negotiation complex, inefficient and confusing. In addition, there are only a few counsellors in Bangladesh with relevant training, thus capacity building should be prioritized.m.

Objectification Theory in adolescent girls

Objectification Theory, recently proposed by Fredrickson and Roberts (1997), attempts to understand the consequences of being female in a society that sexually objectifies the female body. Sexual objectification occurs when a woman's body is treated as an object (especially as an object that exists for the pleasure and use of others), and is illustrated interpersonally through gaze or "checking out," and in the representation of women in the media. As such sexual objectification is not within a woman's control; very few women are completely able to avoid contexts that may be potentially objectifying.

Of central importance to Objectification Theory, however, is the proposal that the pervasiveness of sexual objectification in our society influences girls and women to internalise the views present in society and to begin viewing themselves in the same way. That is, girls and women gradually learn to adopt an observer's perspective on their physical selves and to treat themselves as an object to be looked at and evaluated on the basis of appearance. Fredrickson and Roberts term this particular perspective "self-objectification," and describe it as a form of self-consciousness that is characterised by habitual and constant self-monitoring of one's outward appearance. Fredrickson and Roberts propose that the constant monitoring of appearance accompanying self-objectification has a number of negative behavioural and experiential consequences. In particular, internalising an observer's objectifying perspective leads to increased levels of shame about one's body and increased levels of appearance anxiety. These experiences arise partly because it is virtually impossible for women to match the current culturally prescribed ideal image of beauty. Further, habitual self-monitoring of outward appearance reduces the perceptual resources available for attending to inner body experiences, and therefore results in a diminished awareness of internal body states. Finally, self objectification is thought to limit women's opportunities for peak motivational states or "flow," identified by Csikszentmihalyi as a prime source of optimal experience.

In turn, these negative consequences are argued to contribute to three particular psychological disorders that are experienced pre dominantly by women: unipolar depression, sexual dysfunction, and eating disorders. Since the formal proposal of Objectification Theory, certain aspects of the model have received empirical support. In samples of undergraduate students, links have been found between self-objectification or body surveillance and body shame or disordered eating. More specifically, Noll and Fredrickson and Tiggemann and Slater found body shame to mediate the relationship between self-objectification and disordered eating. Only a few studies have investigated the proposed model in older samples than undergraduate students, but to date, no study has examined Objectification Theory in younger people.

Thus the present study aims to extend the existing research by examining the components of Objectification Theory in a sample of adolescent girls. With its greater focus on the self, adolescence may be a critical period for the development of self-objectification. Adolescence is not only a time of establishing one's identity, but also of increased self-awareness, self-consciousness, preoccupation with image, and concern with social acceptance. Thus the self-monitoring and concern with external appearance intrinsic to self-objectification may be particularly salient. A number of studies have shown that the majority of adolescent girls suffer dissatisfaction with their bodies and wish to be thinner, with many engaging in dieting or other unhealthy weight loss behaviours. The eating disorders of anorexia and bulimia nervosa also typically have their onset during late adolescence.

The present study also included a sample of girls who currently participate in classical ballet. Although Objectification Theory assumes that all women exist in a culture in which their bodies are always potentially objectified, objectification will not affect all individuals equally. Certain situations that accentuate women's awareness of observers' perspectives on their bodies are likely to enhance self-objectification. One group that might be expected to be particularly high in self-objectification is female ballet dancers. Dancers not only perform on stage where their bodies are looked at by others, but also spend several hours a day practising in front of mirrors scrutinising their own bodies. Further, it has been suggested that women who are identified as "at-risk" for eating disorders may objectify their bodies more than other groups of women.

A high incidence of eating disorders has been shown among both professional dancers, and ballet students. Recently, Tiggemann and Slater reported that adult former students of classical ballet scored more highly on measures of self-objectification, self-monitoring, and disordered eating than women who had never studied classical ballet. As yet, however, there has been no examination of self-objectification within a current "at risk" group.

5

Humanistic Psychology and Women

Career Theory for Women

Theories that inform current practice in the UK were primarily formulated to explain the career development of men. Women's career development is, however, generally different from men. It is often more complex (e.g. conflict between work and family) and is often characterised by different career stages or patterns (e.g. intervals away from full time employment to assume care responsibilities). Various pieces of research (e.g. EOC, 1999) indicate that:

- Women's labour market participation is more restricted than men i.e. they are under-represented in a variety of fields and professions, and enter low paying and low status jobs;
- Women abilities and talents are underused i.e. they are less likely to advance to higher levels in their occupational fields.

Betz (1994) presents an overview of issues relating to women of particular relevance to careers counseling. Citing numerous research studies, she establishes the importance of employment for the psychological (as well as economic) well-being of women. She charts the nature of women's participation in the labour market in North America (similar to the UK) which has increased dramatically over the past four to five decades, discusses occupational segregation (horizontal and vertical) and highlights the particular implications for career theories.

Since the majority of women are employed in restricted occupational areas and at lower status levels, Betz questions whether career theories which are based on the assumption that occupational choice involves either matching jobs to abilities or 'self-actualising' as part of career development apply to women at all. In response to the perceived inadequacies of current theories underpinning the practice of careers counselling and guidance, approaches specifically designed to respond to the needs of women are being evolved.

Approaches to Careers Counseling For Women

Gottfredson's Theory of Circumscription and Compromise

Gottfredson's developmental theory of occupational aspirations (1981) is applicable to both women and men. She set out to explain 'how the well-documented differences in aspirations by social group (e.g. race, sex, social class) develop'. Strongly influenced by John Holland (she was a student in his research centre), and a sociologist by professional training, Gottfredson's theory represents an attempt to reconcile the different perspectives of psychology and sociology.

The theory is concerned with both the content of career aspirations and how they develop. Gottfredson acknowledges the influence of the theories of both John Holland and Donald Super. It is similar to these earlier theories in that it proposes that career choice reflects the process of attempting to implement an individual's preferred self concept and because it argues that career satisfaction depends on the match or fit with the self-concept. It is different from psychological theories since:

- It views career development as an attempt to implement primarily a social self and secondarily a psychological self;
- It focuses on how cognitions of self and occupations develop;
- It treats vocational choice largely as a process of eliminating options and narrowing choices;
- It considers how individual compromise their goals in coming to terms with reality as they try to implement their aspirations.

The model contains several basic tenets, summarised by Brooks as:

- People differentiate occupations along dimensions of sex type, level of work and field of work.
- People assess the suitability of occupations according to their self-concepts (i.e. their images of who they would like to be) and the amount of effort they are willing to expend to enter the occupations. Occupations that are compatible with the self-concept will be highly desirable; those that are not will be highly undesirable.
- Elements of the self-concept that are vocationally relevant are gender, social class, intelligence, interests, values and abilities. Occupational aspirations are circumscribed according to these elements of the self-concept.
- Vocationally relevant elements of the self-concept are developed during four stages of cognitive development

These stages are:

- *1st stage:* Orientation to size and power

The child develops 'the concept of being an adult. Ages 3-5.

- *2nd stage:* Orientation to sex role

The child develops a gender self-concept. Ages 6-8.

- *3rd stage:* Orientation to social evaluation

Is concerned with developing abstract concepts of one's

social class and intelligence. Ages 9-13.

- *4th stage:* Orientation to Internal Unique Self

  Involves a refinement of one's distinctive values, traits, attitudes and interests. Age 14+.

As people progress through these 4 developmental stages, they successively reject occupations:

- As unsuitable for their gender;
- Then as inappropriate for their social class and ability level; and
- Finally on the basis of personal interests and values.

The result is a zone of acceptable alternatives, or a 'set or range of occupations that the person considers as acceptable alternatives'. It is only under unusual circumstances that a person will reconsider an occupation rejected as outside this range.

- People's occupational preferences are the product of job-self compatibility (i.e. with the zone) and judgments about the accessibility of jobs. 'Accessibility refers to obstacles or opportunities in the social or economic environment that affect one's chances of getting into a particular occupation'.
- Perceptions of accessibility are based on such factors as availability of a job in the preferred geographical area, perceptions of discrimination or favouritism, etc.
- Because the jobs people view as suitable for themselves are not always available, they must compromise. The typical pattern of compromise is the following: people first sacrifice interests, then prestige, and finally sex type. In other words, given two choices - one that fits one's interests but not one's sex type, and one that does not fit one's interests but is viewed as sex-appropriate - the latter will be chosen.

Gottfredson's explanation of why women are in lower-status, lower-level positions is that these occupations are compatible with their self-concepts and views about accessibility. Her 1996 formulation of the theory is 'the same in most respects as the 1981 version'. It differs 'in providing a clearer definition and account of compromise, more discussion of cultural change and/or race and gender differences, and more guidance on counseling applications'.

Implications for Practice

i. Individual career counselling should encourage both exploration and realism. In particular:
   - Why certain options seem to be out of the question or why some compromises are more acceptable or accessible than others;
   - By encouraging clients to re-examine the full range of occupations in the economy (challenging circumscription);
   - Helping clients develop strategies for enhancing the individual's competitiveness in obtaining the preferred option and succeeding at it.

ii. Careers education programmes should span stages 2 (ages 6-8) through to 4 (ages 14+) and should:
   - Be sensitive to the mental capabilities of the age group;
   - Introduce students to the full breadth of options in a manageable way;
   - Display for youngsters their circumscription of alternatives so that its rationale can be explored;
   - Be sensitive to the dimensions of self and occupations along which circumscription and compromise take place (sex type, social class, ability, and vocational interests) so that their role, positive or not, can be explored where appropriate.

iii. Exploration and constructive realism can do much to free individuals from unnecessary circumscription and compromise. Caution should be exercised in assuming the role of change agent on behalf of the client.

Gottfredson and Lapin discuss the results of field testing an instrument referred to as 'Mapping Vocational Challenges which is based on the premises of the Gottfredson's theory of circumscription and compromise. It is described as an example of 'theory-based assessments and interventions to counteract inappropriate circumscription' which aims to increase awareness of choices which have been rejected by clients as unacceptable, since circumscription is a question of 'deciding what one wants to avoid'. Findings include that high school and middles girls and boys agreed in their ratings of gender difference for different types of work, that 'one group of seventh grade girls linked their avoidance of careers currently dominated by men to their fears about encountering sexual harassment on the job and 'assessed and expressed interests are often discrepant.

Need-Based Sociopsychological Model

Astin's primary intent was to construct a theory that would describe more adequately the career-choice process of women, as well as explain recent changes in women's career aspirations. It is also applicable to men. She attempted to develop a model of career choice and work behaviour that attempted to combine both personal (psychological) and social forces as well as their interaction. Her need-based sociopsychological model contains four key constructs:

- Motivation;
- Expectations;
- Sex-role socialization;
- Structure of opportunity.

Thus - both psychological and sociological variables are included in the model.

Motivation

All humans are motivated to expend energy to satisfy 3 primary needs - survival (primarily physiological survival), pleasure (intrinsic satisfactions from work) and contribution (need to be useful to society and be recognised for one's contributions). These 3 needs are the same for men and women - though they can be satisfied in different ways.

Expectations

Concerned with the individual's perceptions of kind of work that will satisfy needs and the types of work that are accessible and that the person is capable of performing. They differ for men and women because of the sex-role socialization process and the structure of opportunity (e.g. distribution of jobs, sex typing of jobs, discrimination). During the sex-role socialization process, a person is rewarded and reinforced for gender-differentiated behaviour. The result is that the individual internalizes social norms and values regarding appropriate sex-role behaviours and choices.

Sex-role Socialisation and Structure of Opportunity

Interacting with the sex-role socialization process is the opportunity structure, which is different for men and women, and is not static. Social changes modify the opportunity structure for all. Thus, the interactive relationship between sex-role socialization and the opportunity structure is what accounts for the changes in women's aspirations and choices in recent years. The socialization process probably sets limits to changes win the structure of opportunity, whereas the structure of opportunity ultimately influences the values that are transmitted through the socialization process.

Astin's contribution represents the first invited theoretical statement on women's career development, yet it has had limited impact on practice to date. Fitzgerald et al suggest that it may be 'best thought of as a general conceptual framework rather than an articulated theoretical statement', since its value lay in the way in which it directs our attention to important factors influencing women's career development Astin's most important contribution, they contend, is the attention she focused on the structure of opportunity.

Implications for Practice

Astin's model suggests some general diagnostic directions that can be pursued by counsellors. For example, women's indecision may result from lack of clarity about which of the three needs is the more important to satisfy, or about which occupations would satisfy these needs. A client may feel conflict between internalized views of sex-role appropriate occupations and changes in the occupational structure (for example, one woman may feel restricted by the occupational structure; another may feel changes are placing pressure on her to expand her view of sex-role appropriate occupations).

Career Self-efficacy Theory

One notable example of an attempt to develop theoretical approaches that are more relevant for women and girls is Hackett and Betz's career self-efficacy theory (1981). They argued for a need to move beyond 'listings of barriers' to women's choices and achievements to an investigation of the mechanisms which are effective in embedding society's beliefs and expectations in women's vocational behaviour and achievement. A study of twenty occupations was designed to 'investigate the usefulness of self-efficacy theory to the understanding of vocational behaviour and, in particular, to the understanding of women's career development'.

The results of this study indicated that there exists 'significant and consistent sex differences in self-efficacy with regard to traditional and nontraditional occupations'. So, women demonstrated more career self-efficacy in relation to jobs that are traditionally female (like dental hygienist, social worker, secretary) and men were more efficacious in relation to traditionally male jobs (like accountant, mathematician and engineer). Betz and Hackett found from this research that the self-efficacy approach to career development for women (and men) provides a potentially useful framework for further study, and could have important implications for practice.

Humanistic Psychology

The role of women in humanistic psychology is a complex one. On the one hand, much of humanistic thought, especially in regard to the centrality of personal experience and holistic and tacit ways of knowing, has much in common with feminist theories of inter-subjectivity, personal knowledge, and the importance of finding one's own voice. On the other hand, existential, humanistic and transpersonal psychologies have all been subject to feminist critiques that these perspectives privilege the sole self-evolving individual on a solitary and heroic journey of self- discovery. This journey is characterized by subduing nature, overcoming matter, transcending the body, promoting individuation, differentiation, and abstraction, and is filled with masculine terms of agency, control, and self-sufficiency. Humanistic psychology, these critics charged, had forgotten the body and nature.

In fact, existential humanism was based on the experience of the modern, alienated, urban white European male, which left out relevant experiences of women, children and indigenous peoples. Even the postmodern trend in humanistic psychology can also be critiqued as sharing "modernity's groundlessness", being disembodied, and lacking a sense of place and body. A truly radical feminist postmodernist humanistic psychology, therefore, would have to be grounded in an "eco-social matrix" which restored elements of earth, body and community. Finally, a feminist perspective on humanistic psychology can itself be critiqued as being insensitive to issues of power and social context. "Womanist" philosophy extends the themes of feminist psychology by focusing on the centrality of community, mutual caring, and family, and it challenges us to move beyond experience to liberation and transformation. Although these criticisms are true for only part of humanistic psychology, as challenges they are important reminders for the field.

The Role of Women in Humanistic Psychology

While the 'third force" or humanistic orientation to psychology was fathered by such men as Abraham Maslow, Carl Rogers, Rollo May, Sidney Jourard, and others, many women served as the mothers of humanistic psychology. Humanistic psychologists believed that all human beings are basically creative and behave with intentionality and values. Their focus was on the experiencing person and the meaning of experience to the person; they emphasized the human qualities of choice, and self-realization; they were concerned with problems that are meaningful to humans; and their ultimate concern was with the dignity and worth of humans and an interest in the development of the potential inherent in every person. During the late 1960s and 1970s, many women were attracted to humanistic psychology because of its philosophy, practices, and promises of self-fulfillment. At approximately the same time, parallel social movements were beginning. For example, in the late 1950s the women's liberation movement led by Betty Freidan championed similar humanistic principles and rights. The world of humanistic psychology was a favorable environment for women. Many women attended workshops in growth centers throughout the country, which continue to be characterized by a great deal of exploration, experimentation, and creativity. The Humanistic Psychology Institute (now Saybrook Graduate School and Research Center) was founded by Eleanor Criswell from the Association for Humanistic Psychology (AHP) in 1970 as its academic arm, as a place for training humanistic psychologists, both men and women.

The humanistic psychology movement and the human potential movement were not identical, but were mutually supportive. Many women answered the call to human potential events. Their spirit of coming closer with others, the hallmark of women's ways of being and knowing, was therefore significant in the zeitgeist of humanistic psychology. In the 1970s the second contemporary wave of the women's movement came in, led by Gloria Steinem and others. Women in AHP began to assert their feelings about not having enough of a voice, and were encouraged to move into leadership positions in the organization and were given more program time devoted to women's issues.

Up to 1976 there were three women AHP presidents: Charlotte Buhler, Norma Lyman (the first organizational secretary of AHP), and Eleanor Criswell, in contrast to the 11 male presidents. After 1976, there were 13 female presidents and 12 male presidents. Twice there were male and female co-presidents. Women presidents after 1976 include: Jean Houston, Jacquelin L. Doyle, Virginia Satir, Peggy Taylor, Lonnie Barbach, Frances Vaughan, Elizabeth Campbell, Maureen O'Hara, Sandy Friedman, Ann Weiser Cornell, MA Bjarkman, Jocelyn Olivier, and Katy Brant. The AHP conventions were always highly experiential and featured women's issues, community issues, relationship concerns, somatic practices, and environmental concerns.

Both inside and outside AHP and APA, there have been other outstanding women humanistic psychologists and therapists. For example, Laura Perls, who with Fritz Perls "brought individual responsibility into an active experiential process" and Virginia Satir, founder of conjoint family therapy, were both well-known in their day. Stella Resnick, Ilana Rubenfeld, and Natalie Rogers were active in AHP conventions. Charlotte Buhler, a personality theorist, met with the others at Old Saybrook, Connecticut, a seminal gathering for the founding of the humanistic psychology field. Carol Guinn was the long-time editor of The *AHP Newsletter*, an important voice in the field. Some women were active in their humanistic institutions of higher education, such as Anne Richards (State University of West Georgia), Nina Menrath, Norma Lyman, and Eleanor Criswell.

There have been many unsung women in humanistic psychology. Some of them are the wives of the founding fathers Carl Rogers, Abraham Maslow, and Sidney Jourard;

for example, Helen Rogers, Bertha Maslow, and Antoinette Jourard. It is interesting that they are/were all artists. Helen Rogers was a painter; Bertha Maslow was a sculptor; and Antoinette (Toni) Jourard is a photographer. All were deeply self-actualizing persons, who were fully functioning, and inspiring to their husbands and to others.

While the leadership of AHP had many women, the leadership of Division 32 (Humanistic Psychology) of the American Psychological Association (APA) did not. Division 32 was founded to bring humanistic psychology specifically into academic and professional psychology organizations: "The perspective of humanistic psychology was officially born in APA with the establishment of Division 32 in 1971.

Its credo was to apply 'the concepts, theories and philosophy of humanistic psychology to research, education, and professional applications of scientific psychology,' and to ensure 'that humanistically oriented ideas and activities operate within APA and some of its divisions'". A number of women participated in the founding of Division 32.

Joyce Howard, Louise Riscalla, and Constance Moerman, for example, attended the founding meeting of Division 32 and Gloria Gottsegen was named its Acting Secretary. During the first Division 32 election, Elizabeth Mintz, Joen Fagen, and Janette Rainwater were elected members-at-large of the Executive Board. Karen Goodman and Marta Vargo helped run the Hospitality Suite during the APA conventions, which started the general APA tradition that hospitality suites host the more experiential programs at APA. Zaraleya was named newsletter editor, and Nora Weckler, a California psychologist, was also active in the governance of Division 32.

Past-Presidents include Gloria Gottsegan and Mary Jo Meadow. Contemporary women humanistic psychologists active in the division are Eleanor Criswell, (President), Constance Fischer (President-elect), Ilene Serlin (Past-president and APA Council Representative),, Ruth Heber (Past-president), Mary Anne Siderits, Maureen O'Hara (Member-at-large), and others.

Despite the involvement of women members, however, the leadership has been predominantly male. Compared to 38.5 per cent women among all members of APA, Division 32 is close to average with 30.1 per cent female membership. Statistics on the percentage of women officers in divisions, however, shows Division 32 to have only 16.6 per cent women officers, as compared with 42.8 per cent women officers of the division of Theoretical and Philosophical Psychology (24), 46.6 per cent in the division of Psychotherapy (29), 33.3 per cent in the Psychology of Religion division (36), and 38.8 per cent in the division of Psychoanalysis (39) (APA, 1999). That trend may be changing with four women elected president in recent years: Ruth Heber (1993-1994), Ilene Serlin (1996-1997), Eleanor Criswell (1999-2000), and Constance Fischer (2000-2001).

Women's ways of Knowing

In a recent sequel to the now well-known *Women's Ways of Knowing* (Belenki et. al, 1986), this same group of women extended their epistemological analysis to Knowledge, Difference and Power. The position that they lay out echoes core values of humanistic psychology. In their opening chapter to *Knowledge, Difference and Power*, Goldberger et. al framed their argument with a statement that the discussion would be in terms of gender roles and the archetypally feminine, not in terms of real, complex women and men. In the same way, the distinctions we make here about women's versus men's ways of knowing, and experiential versus cognitive approaches to humanistic psychology, are simply helpful conceptual tools.

Since society has always "genderized" knowledge, understanding women's ways of knowing can raise our consciousness to include "the situational and cultural determinants of knowing" and "the relationship between power and knowledge", "standpoint epistemologies" and "social positionality and situated knowledge".

The key concepts, therefore, of those women's ways of knowing are:

1. Connectedness. In contrast to the separate, male way of knowing that emphasizes separation and individuation, critical analysis, rational debate and detachment, whose mode of discourse is the argument, and is hostile to new ideas, connected knowing draws on empathy and intuition, is receptive to new ideas, and seeks collaboration with others. Women's epistemo-logy of connected knowing is supported by their physiology of connected knowing. Brain research shows that women tend to be less lateralised, less biased in one cerebral hemisphere.

Women have larger corpara callosa than most men-especially the posterior part of the corpus callosum-which connects the two occipital lobes. Since the corpus callosum is the bridge of neuron axons that connects the two brain hemispheres, women have more integrated cerebral functions as a biological condition. Connected knowing is also closely related to the humanistic psychology concept of empathy. Carl Rogers, the main theorist on empathy, described empathy as a way of knowing another through connection, through taking his or her frame of reference in order to fully experience that him or her. Humanistic psychotherapists sense their client's worlds by being open to them, transparent to themselves, and lying "aside all perceptions from the external frame of reference".

2. Social construction of methodologies. Whereas separate knowing is concerned with the discovery of truth, connected knowing is concerned with the discovery of meaning. While separate knowing uses rational debate to validate truth, connected knowing, as it informs humanistic research methods, looks for validity in the empathetic resonance and the meaning it awakens in the other. Qualitative research is concerned with quality rather than numbers, and is descriptive rather than prescriptive. Feminist research, as a form of qualitative research, is "passionate; it is communal rather than

hierarchical. It seeks meaningful patterns in experience, not for prediction or control.

3. The Self. In connected knowing, the Self is not experienced in isolation, but is known through interaction with others and "self-insertion" into experience Feminist psychology shares, with humanistic psychology, a view that the self is not a solitary entity, but is known only in relationship. The self, itself, is the instrument in psychotherapy and in research. It is used as an instrument of knowing both in the experience of everyday life, and in participatory research methodologies. In contrast to the more rigid boundaries of separate knowing, its boundaries are flexible and sometimes permeable, demonstrating the "paradox of separateness within connection". Finally, not a static object, the self is a "self-in-process", collaboratively created and re-recreated in the context of relationships.
4. Dialogical knowing. In connected knowing, the "I" transforms an "It" into a "Thou". Meaning is found in the inter-subjective space between the two, so that the act of interpretation is dialogical). Dialogical knowing characterizes humanistic theory, therapy and research, and happens between speaker and listener, reader and text, researcher and co-researcher.
5. Feeling. In connected knowing, thinking is inseparable from feeling. It is feeling which allows one to feel oneself into the world of the other, to differentiate the particularities of his or her unique experience, in contrast to the abstract, categorical and generalized thinking of separate knowing. Psychological research shows women to be emotionally expressive, while brain research shows that women have greater metabolic activity in the emotional areas of the brain than men, are more empathic, and more concerned with communication and relationships. It could be said that there is a masculine version of humanistic psychology and a feminine version. The masculine version deals mainly with intellectual conceptions, perhaps explaining why Division 32 is male oriented.

The more feminine version is concerned with the experiential aspects of relationship and nurturing the development of the person, perhaps explaining the fact that AHP is more female-oriented. Both masculine and feminine approaches to humanistic psychology are important. The theoretical understandings are important for the foundations of the field; the experiential aspects are important for the implementation of humanistic perspectives in life. On the one hand, categories of feminist epistemologies are close to humanistic values of holism, subjectivity, and the centrality of the experiencing human being, and "experiential humanism".

Feminist values can bring humanistic psychology back down to earth, to matter and flesh, to connection with other humans, other species and nature. On the other hand, humanistic psychology can give women an opportunity to fully develop their potentials and leadership skills. Their contributions to society need to be valued, such as their sense of relationship, communication, and nurturance. Humanistic psychologists have a concern for all persons and their basic human rights: their right to be treated as individuals with worth and dignity; the right to the primacy of their experiences; the right to the holistic development of their various talents and capacities, and the rights of society to receive the contributions of all individuals toward the cultural evolution of humankind. This is a fertile ground for the continued development of all toward global and environmental wellbeing.

Centered leadership

Women start careers in business and other professions with the same level of intelligence, education, and commitment as men. Yet comparatively few reach the top echelons. This gap matters not only because the familiar glass ceiling is unfair, but also because the world has an increasingly urgent need for more leaders. All men and women with the brains, the desire, and the perseverance to lead should be encouraged to fulfill their potential and leave their mark.

With all this in mind, the McKinsey Leadership Project an initiative to help professional women at McKinsey and elsewhere set out four years ago to learn what drives and sustains successful female leaders. We wanted to help younger women navigate the paths to leadership and, at the same time, to learn how organizations could get the best out of this talented group. To that end, we have interviewed more than 85 women around the world (and a few good men) who are successful in diverse fields. Some lead 10,000 people or more and others 5 or even fewer. While the specifics of their lives vary, each one shares the goal of making a difference in the wider world.

All were willing to discuss their personal experiences and to provide insights into what it takes to stay the leadership course. We have also studied the academic literature; consulted experts in leadership, psychology, organizational behaviour, and biology; and sifted through the experiences of hundreds of colleagues at McKinsey. From the interviews and other research, we have distilled a leadership model comprising five broad and interrelated dimensions (exhibit): meaning, or finding your strengths and putting them to work in the service of an inspiring purpose; managing energy, or knowing where your energy comes from, where it goes, and what you can do to manage it; positive framing, or adopting a more constructive way to view your world, expand your horizons, and gain the resilience to move ahead even when bad things happen; connecting, or identifying who can help you grow, building stronger relationships, and increasing your sense of belonging; and engaging, or finding your voice, becoming self-reliant and confident by accepting opportunities and the inherent risks they bring, and collaborating with others.

We call this model centered leadership. As the name implies, it's about having a well of physical, intellectual, emotional, and spiritual strength that drives personal achievement and, in turn, inspires others to follow. What's particularly exciting is that we are starting to discover ways women can actively build the skills to become more self-confident and effective leaders. Centered leadership also works for men, though we have found that the model resonates particularly well with women because we have built it on a foundation of research into their specific needs and experiences.

Centered leadership emphasizes the role of positive emotions. A few characteristics particularly distinguish women from their male counterparts in the workplace. First, women can more often opt out of it than men can. Second, their double burden – motherhood and management drains energy in a particularly challenging way. Third, they tend to experience emotional ups and downs more often and more intensely than most men do. Given these potentially negative emotions, centered leadership consciously draws on positive psychology, a discipline that seeks to identify what makes healthy people thrive. Although none of the women we interviewed articulated her ideas in precisely those terms, when we dived into the literature and interviewed leading academics, we found strong echoes of what our female leaders had been telling us.

Women Make Better Leaders

Searching for better leaders? Don't overlook the women in the office. An analysis of 45 leadership studies found that the best bosses are inspirational mentors who encourage underlings to develop their abilities and creatively change their organizations. Women, on average, are more likely than men to enact this "transformational" style. In this "transformational" management style, managers are more like good teachers than traditional bosses. But the analysis, conducted at Northwestern University, revealed that men are more likely to use a "transactional" management style doling out punishments for poor performance and rewards for good behaviour—or a laissez-faire style, characterized by a basic lack of management. Previous research has shown the transformational style to be most effective, particularly when companies rely on innovation to stay competitive.

"CEOs should level the playing field, and make sure women are given equal opportunities to be managers," says lead author Alice Eagly, a professor of psychology at Northwestern. "The study shows they are not only doing just as well as men, but they are doing better."

Eagly speculates that the transformational leadership style may suit women because it includes nurturing aspects, and women are traditionally socialized to be nurturers. Women who instead use a tough "command and control" leadership style meet with resistance and suspicion from employees, other studies have found. Women striving for leadership roles may also have to meet a higher standard than men. They may therefore adapt their leadership tactics along the way to fit the more effective transformational style, Eagly says.

Asian Women

Asian women will play a vital role in safeguarding their families' and nations' financial welfare as three economic trends affect the lives of people around the globe, a top U.S. Treasury official said. Speaking at the 18th Global Summit of Women in Hanoi, Vietnam, June 6, U.S. Treasurer Anna Escobedo Cabral identified microfinance practices, changes in Asia's demographics and financial literacy rates as the top reasons for the growing role Asian women are taking in economic matters. The first major trend – microfinance – allows the poor to deposit small savings with reputable financial institutions and receive small loans or low-cost insurance to help them expand small businesses.

"Women achieve great success when given access to resources through microfinance," Cabral said. "There is overwhelming evidence from developing regions of the world that women's investments help families, help the economy, and reduce poverty in the developing world." She said women were key to the reconstruction of Rwanda's economy and plays an important role in India, a country that over the past 15 years has had a high percentage of working women and has enjoyed the rapid economic development and large reductions in poverty.

Microfinance's role in alleviating poverty is of particular importance to Asian women, Cabral said, because two-thirds of the world's poor live in Asia and women are often disproportionately affected by poverty. The second major trend affecting Asian women is the aging of Asia's population. While places such as Laos, Cambodia and Vietnam have relatively young populations, Thailand, Singapore, South Korea and south India are beginning to see increases in the number of older citizens. Japan already has one of the oldest populations in the world. U.S. Treasurer Anna Escobedo Cabral, who frequently speaks to international audiences, addressed the 18th Global Summit of Women.

When a large percentage of a country's citizens are older, that nation's economy faces certain challenges and opportunities. Countries will need strong national pension systems and health care systems to support the elderly, Cabral said. As long-time workers retire, female workers will become instrumental in their nations' continued economic growth and in their families' financial well-being, she said. "In many economies, fewer traditional workers will be in the work force, and more nontraditional wage-earners, including more women, will have to play an even greater role in the work forces throughout Asia in order to support growth," she said.

"Also, families will bear an increasing financial burden of taking care of older individuals. Caring for aging family members, educating their children, and saving for their own retirement will create an increasing financial burden for women in Asia," Cabral said. The third major trend is an increase in women's financial literacy. Cabral defined financial literacy as "knowing how to save, plan for retirement, understanding credit, and understanding the importance of using banks and financial institutions."

"By educating people about these issues, we can make a positive impact on the world economy," she said. "If we figure out how to help families before they get into trouble – maybe by taking simple steps such as making a daily budget, or educating young people about savings – we can improve lives."

Asian women should learn more about saving and investing, since inefficient saving is the biggest challenge for many Asian countries, Cabral said. "As retirement and education costs increase, it becomes more and more important that households have access to more and better investment options, so that they can meet their future financial needs while also being able to consume more now."

Women start careers in business and other professions with the same level of intelligence, education and commitment as men. Yet comparatively few reach the top echelons. This gap matters not only because the familiar glass ceiling is unfair, but also because the world has an increasingly urgent need for more leaders. All men and women with the brains, the desire and the perseverance to lead should be encouraged to fulfill their potential and leave their mark.

With all this in mind, the McKinsey Leadership Project—an initiative to help professional women at McKinsey and elsewhere—set out four years ago to learn what drives and sustains successful female leaders. We wanted to help younger women navigate the paths to leadership and, at the same time, learn how organizations could get the best out of this talented group.

To that end, we have interviewed more than 85 women around the world (and a few good men) who are successful in diverse fields. Some lead 10,000 people or more others five or even fewer. While the specifics of their lives vary, each one shares the goal of making a difference in the wider world. All were willing to discuss their personal experiences and provide insights into what it takes to stay the leadership course. We have also studied the academic literature; consulted experts in leadership, psychology, organizational behaviour and biology; and sifted through the experiences of hundreds of colleagues at McKinsey.

From the interviews and other research, we have distilled a leadership model comprising five broad and interrelated dimensions:

- Meaning, or finding your strengths and putting them to work in the service of an inspiring purpose.
- Managing energy, or knowing where your energy comes from, where it goes and what you can do to manage it.
- Positive framing, or adopting a more constructive way to view your world, expand your horizons and gain the resilience to move ahead even when bad things happen.
- Connecting, or identifying who can help you grow, building stronger relationships and increasing your sense of belonging.
- Engaging, or finding your voice, becoming self-reliant and confident by accepting opportunities and the inherent risks they bring and collaborating with others.

We call this model centered leadership. As the name implies, it's about having a well of physical, intellectual, emotional and spiritual strength that drives personal achievement and, in turn, inspires others to follow. What's particularly exciting is that we are starting to discover ways women can actively build the skills to become more self-confident and effective leaders. Centered leadership also works for men, though we have found that the model resonates particularly well with women because we have built it on a foundation of research into their specific needs and experiences. Centered leadership emphasizes the role of positive emotions. A few characteristics particularly distinguish women from their male counterparts in the workplace.

First, women can more often opt out of it than men can. Second, their double burden—motherhood and management—drains energy in a particularly challenging way. Third, they tend to experience emotional ups and downs more often and more intensely than most men do.

Given these potentially negative emotions, centered leadership consciously draws on positive psychology, a discipline that seeks to identify what makes healthy people thrive. Although none of the women we interviewed articulated her ideas in precisely those terms, when we dove into the literature and interviewed leading academics, we found strong echoes of what our female leaders had been telling us.

Modern Women Today Revealed

Modern women today see balancing their work and home lives as their biggest challenge in today's world. They also see Nelson Mandela and Margaret Thatcher as their greatest role models. Almost two out of five women now see themselves as feminists. Nearly three out of four women would rather have a man, than a woman, as their boss. Nearly half of women (46%) think a couple should live together before they marry.

This figure rises to more than three quarters (77%) among women aged 18-24, but falls to nearly one in four (27%) among women aged 55 and over. These figures come from research compiled for *Stella* magazine by YouGov, a research agency who interviewed more than 1,000 women of all ages and backgrounds on everything from family values to their eating habits, and from their views on plastic surgery to those on sex and shopping. Health and weight are clearly major issues for the modern woman. Four in five (80%) say losing their health is their greatest concern, followed by putting on weight (52%) and losing their job (24%).

Nearly one woman in four (23%) is currently on a diet and nearly three women in five (58%) has dieted in the past. Exercise however is lower down on the priorities of many women. More than one in five women (21%) take no exercise during the week and less than one woman in twenty (4%) takes seven hours or more of exercise a week (an average of an hour a day or more). Women have high expectations of a partner.

Two thirds would rather hold out for the perfect romantic partner than settle for a man who's "good enough". One in five women (20%) smokes but nearly one in three (31%) does not drink. 50% of women are "very unhappy" or "fairly unhappy" with their body. Less than one woman in 200 has had Botox. When questioned about family values the women interviewed were asked to choose from a list of the biggest challenges faced by women today. Balancing work and home life was the main challenge followed by raising happy children (56%) and finding time for yourself (52%).

Almost half of women (49%) think that between 25 and 29 is the best age to get married. An identical amount think between 25 and 29 is also the best age to have children. Nearly three out of five women (59%) think fathers should take more responsibility for their children and two thirds of women (66%) think it is better to divorce than to stay in an unhappy marriage for the sake of the children. More than half of women (51%) think it is best for a couple to marry before having children, while nearly two out of five women (38%) think a woman should stay at home until her child goes to school. More than half of women with partners (51%) say they currently do three quarters of household chores.

It is known that 18 is the average age for women to lose their virginity, yet the survey shows that one woman in 50 (2%) remains a virgin and 7% of women lost their virginity aged 14 or younger. Yet, those women now aged 18 to 24, 30% lost their virginity aged 15 or less – below the age of consent.

The average number of sexual partners for a woman is seven. However the survey shows 17% of those aged 18-24 have already had ten partners! The average number of women who have cheated on their husbands is 10%. The average for all women prepared to forgive their partners is 16%. Nearly two women in five (38%) regards herself as a feminist. This rises to 41% in the age group 55 and over. The issue of role models throws up some interesting names from Prime Ministers to pop singers and from actors to models. The most admired women are Margaret Thatcher (7%), the Queen (5.5%) and Katie Price/'Jordan (4.6%). The most admired men are Nelson Mandela (5.6%), Winston Churchill (4.2%) and David Beckham (5.5%). The most attractive men are George Clooney (8.9%) followed by Brad Pitt (6.1%) and Johnny Depp (5.5%). Actress Angelina Jolie (9.4%) tops the list of famous women that fellow females find attractive followed by Cheryl Cole (3.9%) and actress Catherine Zeta Jones (2.6%).

Role Models of Modern Women

Almost two out of five women now see themselves as feminists, research for *Stella* magazine has revealed. However, nearly three out of four women would rather have a man, than a woman, as their boss. Nearly half of women (46 per cent) think a couple should live together before they marry. This figure rises to more than three quarters (77 per cent) among women aged 18 to 24, but falls to nearly one in four (27 per cent) among women aged 55 and over. YouGov, the research agency, to interview more than 1,000 women of all ages and backgrounds on everything from family values to their eating habits, and from their views on plastic surgery to those on sex and shopping. Health and weight are clearly major issues for the modern woman. Four in five (80 per cent) say losing their health is their greatest concern, followed by putting on weight (52 per cent) and losing their job (24 per cent).

Nearly one woman in four (23 per cent) is currently on a diet and nearly three women in five (58 per cent) has dieted in the past. Yet exercise seems low down on the priorities of many women: more than one in five women

(21 per cent) take no exercise during a week and less than one woman in 20 (4 per cent) takes seven hours or more of exercise a week (an average of an hour a day or more). Women have high expectations from a partner: two thirds (67 per cent) would rather hold out for the perfect, romantic partner than settle for a man whose "good enough". One in five women (20 per cent) smokes, but nearly one in three (31 per cent) does not drink. Fifty per cent of women are "very unhappy" or "fairly unhappy" with their body: virtually the same number (49 per cent) is either "very happy" or "fairly happy" with it. Less than one woman in 200 (0.3 per cent) has had Botox.

Those interviewed were questioned about family values and asked to choose three from a list of the biggest challenges faced by women today. Balancing work and home life was the main challenge (82 per cent) followed by raising happy children (56 per cent) and finding time for yourself (52 per cent). Almost half of women (49 per cent) think that between 25 and 29 is the best age to get married, and an identical per cent believe that between 25 and 29 is also the best age to have children. Nearly three out of five women (59 per cent) think fathers should take more responsibility for their children and two thirds of women (66 per cent) think it is better to divorce than to stay in an unhappy marriage for the sake of the children. More than half of women (51 per cent) think it is best for a couple to marry before having children, while nearly two out of five women (38 per cent) think a woman should stay at home until her child goes to school. More than half of women with partners (51 per cent) say they currently do three quarters of household chores. It is known that 18 is the average age for women to lose their virginity, yet the survey shows that one woman in 50 (2 per cent) remains a virgin and 7 per cent of women lost their virginity aged 14 or younger. Yet, of those women now aged 18 to 24, 30 per cent lost their virginity aged 15 or less - below the age of legal consent.

The average number of sexual partners for a woman is

seven, but the surveys shows that at least 17 per cent of those aged 18 to 24 have already had more than ten sexual partners. Labour supporting women are more likely to cheat on their partners - and also more likely to forgive their partners for being unfaithful. More than one in five (22 per cent) of Labour supporting women have cheated on their partners compared with less than one in ten (8 per cent) of Conservative supporters. The average for all women who have cheated is 10 per cent.

A quarter of Labour supporting women (25 per cent) would forgive their partners for cheating, but only 16 per cent of Conservative supporters would do the same. The average for all women prepared to forgive is also 16 per cent. Nearly two women in five (38 per cent) regards herself as a feminist and, surprisingly perhaps, the highest figure (41 per cent) is in the age group of 55 or more. The figure falls to 34 per cent for those aged 18 to 24. Of all women, 73 per cent would rather have a male boss than a female boss, although this figure rises to 81 per cent for women aged 55 and over.

The issue of famous role models throws up a range of names from Prime Ministers to pop singers and from actors to models. Baroness Thatcher is the most admired women (7 per cent) followed by the Queen (5.5 per cent) and Jordan/ Katie Price (4.6 per cent). The most admired man is Nelson Mandela (5.6 per cent) followed by Winston Churchill (4.2 per cent) and David Beckham (3.1 per cent). The famous man that women find most attractive is George Clooney (8.9 per cent) followed by fellow actors Brad Pitt (6.1 per cent) and Johnny Depp (5.5 per cent). Actress Angelina Jolie (9.4 per cent) tops the list of famous women that fellow females find attractive, followed by singer Cheryl Cole (3.9 per cent) and actress Catherine Zeta Jones (2.6 per cent).

6

Family Values

The family as we know it is a social unit that goes back to a time before our remote ancestors became fully human. But does it go much farther back than that? Perhaps not, judging from the behaviour of our nearest relatives, the chimpanzees which are genetically more similar to our ancestors of four or five million years ago than any other species, and studies of their behaviour in their undisturbed, natural state probably give us as good a picture as we are likely to get of how our own forebears behaved at that time. Carl Sagan graphically describes chimp social behaviour in various works, notably Shadows of Forgotten Ancestors, which he coauthored with Ann Druyan. The picture we see is a troop of perhaps twenty-odd individuals loosely connected by blood ties.

The males dominate, with an alpha male enjoying priority in the business of inseminating females, a business that engages almost everyone's attention most of the time. Basically all males fornicate with all available females, with the big alpha male customarily getting first whack. A somewhat different picture emerges from another study which describes how raiding parties of young males from one troop poach on the territory of another troop, and kill when they find an isolated individual. Are we descended from a bunch of homicidal sex maniacs? If so, we've come a long way...haven't we? How did the ethical constraints on our behaviour evolve that enabled us to follow the evolutionary path we did?

All of us, humans and chimps and other primates, share the instinct to avoid incest. This must have evolved earlier, through biological selection, because inbreeding over generations will almost always produce less fit individuals. The incest taboo militates against the basic primate social unit being limited to a nuclear family that doesn't breed outside, since there has to be at least some genetic diversity. The Biblical account that we are all descended from two individuals, Adam and Eve, is a biological impossibility. A kin-based group of say, twenty or so individuals may have enough genetic diversity to get by, but just barely. In "Mother Nature," Sarah Blaffer Hrdy cites a study based on DNA analysis of a band of chimps that lived in a tight little community whose boundaries were patrolled by males, dedicated among other things to "protecting" their females from outsiders. "Just over half the infants born in this community (seven out of thirteen births) were sired by outside males."

Evidently the females of this troop sometimes got bored with the readily available males and were willing to take very real risks to slip off and have a fling. That's enough about the chimps. Let's turn to our own remote, proto-human ancestors. They lived in the African savannah several million years ago, and at first they were probably grouped, like the chimps, in small, kin-based bands. Was their social behaviour more like ours, or more like modern chimps, or what? We'll never know for sure, but research in recent decades has given us some clues. The fossil evidence shows that early lines of the genus homo were slowly developing erect posture and a larger brain. These two features must have had a fairly direct impact on social behaviour, because eventually females had more trouble in giving birth than before, because of the infant's larger brain and changes in the configuration of the birth canal. The evolutionary answer to this problem was that the gestation period became reduced. It didn't get shorter in a chronological sense, but in the sense that birth occurred sooner in the total period between conception and the child's ability to fend for itself.

A baby chimp matures much faster than a human; the period when it still needs parental care, feeding, and protection ends much earlier in its life cycle. But with humans, the infant requires many years of parental coddling, or its survival chances are sharply reduced. The mother cannot do the whole job unassisted without risking her own survival prospects, let alone her chances of reproducing again in a reasonable period. The first and most obvious source of help is the father. After all, his genes are implicated just as much as the mother's are, so his biological interest also lies in ensuring that his offspring survive. Ergo, the principle known as Male Paternal Investment, which comes down to much the same thing as monogamy, was reinvented, replacing the sexual free-for-all of the chimps. (I say "reinvented" because other species, unlike the chimps, had already become monogamous in response to a variety of different environmental pressures).

For both males and females, male paternal investment changed the fitness equations governing biological evolution. The selfish genes in the female favored her developing an acute ability to determine which male suitor was most likely to settle down and devote the rest of his active years to helping raise the family. No deadbeat dads, if you please. If her kids are to survive, dad must be there to help shelter, feed, and protect them. Meanwhile, selfish genes propelled the egoistic male toward perfecting an equal and opposite adeptness at persuading his targeted female that he really did mean to stay the course, even if he didn't mean it. In fact, the strategy that most favored his genetic fitness was the "love 'em and leave 'em" one where he ended up inseminating a lot of females, and leaving it to the losers among his sex to cope with the diapers.

But wait, the little woman had an evolutionary trick up her sleeve as well: she not only wanted a male that would stay the course, she also wanted her offspring to have the best chance of success and that might not happen if she limited herself to her intended hubby's sperm. Hence her ideal strategy, from a purely egoistic point of view, involved picking a man who would be a good husband, while engaging in a certain amount of hanky-panky on the side, like the lady chimps we have just cited. Philandering husbands and cheating wives: it sounds like the material for a series of bad soap operas, and most likely this kind of scenario was already beginning to show up many hundreds of thousand years ago when our homo erectus ancestors were first beginning to become monogamous. If human nature was based exclusively on our selfish genes, we'd be in deep trouble, (even worse than we actually are).

But group selection based on individual altruism, fortunately, stepped in and took the rough edges off what the evolutionary psychologists insist is our basic "human nature." For no social group can survive very long if the games their genes incline them to play are not tempered and held in check by social pressures. One of the first ethical principles ever invented, after the incest taboo, may well have involved some variant on not sleeping with your neighbor's wife. After all, if you did, and if the husband caught you, there would be a row, and the group as a whole would suffer. A close reading of the applicable injunction in the Ten Commandments suggests that this taboo extended only to married women within the group, not to the wives of outsiders, usually enemies, or to unmarried women generally. Never mind, it was a beginning. The rules have been expanded in many ways and at many times since those early days, but the game's intrinsic nature remains the same. Let's face it, men have had a major hang up throughout the ages about being cuckolded. This obsession has taken many forms, but it has always been a cause of conflict between men, and the basic factor underlying male oppression of women. Whether it's a question of female genital mutilation in Africa, or eunuchs guarding harems in Baghdad, or the burka in Afghanistan, or denying women the vote in earlier days in America, our male preoccupation with "faithfulness" derives quite directly from the simple biological fact that everyone knows who the mŏther is, but the identity of the father can never be fixed with absolute assurance.

So the poor beleaguered male, as long as his gender is dominant, imposes whatever cultural rules he can devise to keep the little woman in a closet and ensure that the child he cares for is really his. The themes of philandering men and cheating women have been at the hard core of fables, poetry, and literature through the ages. Poor Othello, who was gulled into thinking his beloved Desdemona had been unfaithful, expressed the anguish men have felt forever and beyond when he uttered these words:

- Then must you speak,
- Of one that loved not wisely but too well;
- Of one not easily jealous, but being wrought,
- Perplexed in the extreme; of one whose hand,
- Like the base Indian, threw a pearl away,
- Richer than all his tribe.

But this raises another point: according to some theories, the eternal game between philandering men and conniving women has also been at least indirectly responsible for much of the cultural evolution that has marked our meteoric rise as a species. I'm referring to a basic principle of evolution, running parallel to fitness selection, which Darwin himself noted but which has received relatively little attention until recently: sexual selection. Males and females may have different reproductive strategies but they are united in the instinctive desire that any children that bear their genes should be as fit as possible, and as likely as possible to transmit their own genes on to further generations. How does a male judge this kind of fitness in a female?

Well, the psychologists have studied this issue ad nauseam, and determined that males go for youth plus certain secondary sex characteristics that can be explained as constituting indicators of fecundity—breasts, hip/waist ratio, and so forth. How does a female judge the males, though? If you are a lady chimp you presumably find the alpha male most attractive because he has the biggest biceps and roars loudest and has the biggest testicles. But human females must have developed more elaborate criteria early on. And this implicates the evolution of language. Exactly how and when did language evolve? We cannot tell for sure, but we can be fairly certain that once it appeared on the scene it proved highly functional for the development and maintenance of group cooperation.

A capacity for sweet talk and flattery and general persuasiveness took over from mere brawn as a general fitness indicator. Sexual selection favored it and we soon became distinguished as the animal chatterbox. It fitted right in with the male strategy of picking the right woman, and even better with the female strategy of finding a husband who would stay the course. This quintessentially state of uneasy equilibrium between the sexes has dominated the human scene forever, as far as our species is concerned but no longer. In our lifetimes, a new factor has come on stage that threatens to louse up the whole drama, the playhouse, and even the institution of the theater. The underlying sexual basis of male-female relations is threatened as never before. Why? Contemporary moves for gender equality combined with scientific advances are changing the basic ground rules that have dominated family structures since the birth of our species. The liberated modern woman simply will not put up with the harassment and confinement imposed on her grandmother by a passle of dominant, domineering males. Enough already! Trust me or get out! To which the male can now give a brand new and conclusive reply: I don't have to trust you, my dear. I don't have to confine you and supervise you to make sure you don't run around with another man when my back is turned. All I have to do is take the baby down to the lab and run a DNA test!

We cannot say that male domination has always been the social pattern for all of our species at all times in the past, though it has been the majority route most cultures have followed as far as we know. We can, however, say with some confidence that never in the past history of our species has hubby been able to run a DNA test to get a definite answer to the question as to whether he really did father that child he is stuck with bringing up. What next, said the tadpole? I for one don't know how this eternal battle of the sexes is going to take this new factor. But pretty soon, the world will be a very different place. Count on it.

Mister Right for Today's Modern Woman

In the modern age, the woman has become something socially that the sex has not been in recent generations. Today's woman is more accomplished, educated highly, and has more goals, dreams, and ambitions than ever. As a result, the typical woman is now slowly becoming more selective in the man that they choose for a romantic interlude or to start a family with than ever before. The average woman in the modern age is now a college educated woman seeking a career in a field that she has been well educated in and is well suited for, all while trying to establish for herself a good, healthy lifestyle with little stress and all of the comforts she is seeking. At this point, a woman usually feels well equipped to seek out a long term relationship, although she is still going to be discriminating about the men she chooses to date.

This woman is looking for a man who meshes well with the values that have been instilled in the woman through her upbringing. Many successful women want a man who is somewhat of an equal to themselves, but status isn't as much of a concern as it once was. The woman will also be careful to hold the man up to the standards of her mother and father and comparatively reference their influences when seeking a man. Ultimately, the woman is looking for a man who can inject some excitement into her life while also being grounded and realistic in many facets.

The different desires of different women today can result

in the options being available to be plentiful for the woman seeking a mate. Finding a mirror image of her own values may be ideal, but cannot be the only measure that the woman seeks out. Often, a woman will put some emphasis on the man making sure he has some value of himself as well as of the woman in the relationship.

Many women want a relationship that mirrors that of her parents, specifically if that relationship went well and had a positive influence on her upbringing. In this case, the biggest characteristics that a woman may be seeking out lie in faithfulness and loyalty to her and family values. However, if the family life of the woman wasn't as ideal as she would have liked, the measuring stick of a man for her may be how different the man is from her father in certain areas of character.

Many women are seeking a man to provide them some stimulation and excitement, and to this end looks for a man whose life is filled with activity. A woman seeking a man who is daring, adventurous, and not afraid to act out against society would fall certainly into this category. The woman likely would be seeking a man who can meet her own desires to be rebellious and outgoing as well, and wants a man to help foster this desire within her. Ultimately, a woman may still be, even at the stage of life where she may be ready to find a mate, unable to describe what she is exactly seeking in a man. She may need time to date around and determine exactly what she's looking for. Lastly, women want some sort of attractiveness in looks or personality that can lure them in and entice them to want to find out more about the man. Plain vanilla personalities may not appeal as much even if a man is handsome, but the man who isn't necessarily the best looking can exude enough personality to lure in a woman to his charm. Ultimately, this is just one more complex piece of the puzzle of what women are looking for in a modern man.

Woman and Family

Looking at all the topics picking words from the main theme as above, one has no doubt that the women embrace all the words on the theme because they are the ones who carry the babies in their wombs for nine months. They will bear the babies and take care of them up to teenage level. They take care of the whole family from young, old men and women, that is Human Development. They perform all duties with love at heart and go on without any reward. Women are community leaders, teachers, and counselors, managers, also used as shape tools to cut through bearer for personal gains by those who oppress. They are the producers and processors of food just to mention a few.

They continue until they get to a stage where they no longer be able to look after all the people and themselves. They will find themselves without security because they have been working with not remuneration. They are not able to plan for their last days or serve for the future because all will not be there for any action plan. They die destitute yet during their women-hood they had shown that they had certain reasonable status in the community. Women have grown following family structures and even for the different religions. The family duties should be responsibility of both the father and all family members and the society at large. There is need for the systems to change with times in different families and religious so that we equally participate on issues affecting our lives.

What should we do as NGO policy makers? We should have ways of protecting, educating by lobbying our law makers, and governments to come out with law acts which are people centered. All leaders of any nature must be seen to be vehicles of change by playing a pivotal role that is transparènt in building peace, love and development of the body, mind, and spirit. These can be measured through the homes, societies, communities, nations and states. Family can be successful, peaceful if all of us live in peaceful states, put all our development efforts together, people work as family globally. We should critically look at what each one of us has been doing in building strong sustainable life for human development. We should trust each other and treat each other as equals in life in good faith.

Human development is a process in which co-ordinated and systematic efforts are being carried out for development of the material and spiritual dimensions of human life. A mere emphasis on the conventional indexes of human development cannot, by itself, be indicative of the meaning of real human development. Therefore, while there are indexes such as literacy, health and nutritional status and level of income to evaluate the current status of human development, experts in this field should present additional parameters to evaluate the spiritual dimension of human development based on moral and ethical values.

In fact, only the establishment of such values will make possible the realization of equality, justice, human rights and fundamental freedom as well as true peace. This will allow women to develop their potentials to the fullest and to give their maximum contribution to human develop-ment. This will also allow women and men to work together in harmonious partnership both as agents and beneficiaries of development to ensure a more secure and humane world.

The ultimate objective of human development is the attainment of the highest quality of human being and human life. In this light, the following objectives must be taken into consideration.

1. Enhancement of the status and human dignity of women as a basic factor of sustainable development.
2. Enhancement of the role of women both as agents and beneficiaries in all fields and all levels of development.
3. Enhancement of the full participation of women in strategic decision making processes particularly in those related to security and peace as well as social justice.

4. Enhancement of the recognition, respect, protection and support for the proper exercise of the woman's reproductive function as a basic requirement for human development.

Obstacles

1. Alarming disparities of cultural, social, economic and political opportunities among and within nations, particularly for women.
2. Cultural encroachments and increasing tendency toward including religion as one of the main causes of cultural and historical backwardness including the disadvantaged and subordinated position of women who follow divine religions.
3. Increasing social humiliation, commercialization, sexual exploitation and violence against women.
4. Continuing traditional practices based on superstitions in the name of religions seriously hamper role of women in human development.
5. Women's limited participation in strategic decision-making at all levels, from family to global, and in cultural, political, economic, and social fields.
6. Unawareness of nations of women's divine rights and worth. Lack of comprehensive mechanisms and organizations with specified responsibilities and recognition to promote the advancement of women.
7. Women's lack of participation in the mass media particularly at the decision making level and increasing use of women as means of amusement and commercial advertisement and continuing negative portrayal of women by the media.
8. Continuous discrimination against the girl-child in many parts of the world, and lack of equitable investment in girl-children as the future mothers who are also half of the active human potential of their communities.

9. Gender discrimination in the world of work.

Strategies

Governments, NGOs, communities' at large as well international organizations and institutions should take the following actions as appropriate:

1. Promote international co-operation in order to prevent political, economic and cultural exploitation among and within nations and to ensure fair distribution of economic opportunities, equal share of political power and wide dissemination of information particularly for women.
2. Enhance better understanding of and promote respect for the strategic role of religion in cultural development particularly for the recognition of the status of women in divine religions.
3. Combat the different types of humiliation of women such as harassment and exploitation for sexual and economic purposes.
4. Conduct necessary studies and research to identify negative traditional practices based on superstition in the name of religion and to support the formulation and implementation of policies and programs for the elimination.
5. Enable women to actively participate in strategic decision making processes at all levels, from family to international, in political, economic, social and cultural fields.
6. Formulate and implement legal literacy programs to raise social awareness about women's rights, also ensure school curricula include lessons about human rights, particularly for the girl-child.
7. Establish and/or strengthen existing national machinery for the advancement of women including the strengthening of their capabilities to develop new indicators for spiritual dimensions of human development.

8. Promote higher participation of women in the mass media particularly at decision-making levels, enhance the elimination of the use of women as a means for amusement and commercial advertisement, eliminate the negative and increase the positive portrayal of women in the media.
9. Eliminate discrimination against the girl-child, ensure their access to basic education and primary health care and eliminate negative traditional practices against the girl-child.
10. Eliminate gender discrimination in occupations considering the specific mental, spiritual and biological aspects of women.
11. Support non-governmental organizations for women and provide grounds for government co-operation in order to carry out projects specializing in women's development.

Marriage and establishing a family are fundamental natural needs of human beings which originate from their creation and nature. The wife and husband make up the heart of the family, the smallest, most basic social institution and provide the means for transmission of culture. The family is considered responsible for the procreating of human beings, their socialization and the molding of their personalities. This institution has always been venerated by all the divine religions and schools of thought which are based on morality. It is a center in which natural necessities such as sexual and emotional needs are met. A healthy, stable family can serve as the main source of physical and spiritual well-being for its members and present a healthy, balanced and fruitful resource for the society.

Respecting the human dignity of woman in the family structure and meeting her true needs as woman, wife, mother or daughter of the family are the most fundamental elements in consolidating the family institution. Such a family has the potential to create the circumstances for personal and dynamic growth for all members of the family. There has always been a positive correlation between psychological health and a fruitful marriage. In addition to such indicators as health, education and income, which are important in terms of human development, the stability of the family should also be taken into consideration as a very tangible index of human development. Therefore, some criteria to evaluate the authentic moral values significant in the consolidation of the family like loyalty, affection, chastity, faith and self-sacrifice should be presented. Providing the necessary environment to consolidate the family and bring about profound and immense development in the stability of society. Such measures can lead us to a practical solution for elimination problems such as cruelty, crime and rebellion of the younger generation which has taken the shape of a serious and severe problem in many countries. The following goals should be considered so that the family can play its institutional role in human development.

1. Providing at least the basic standards of living which afford physical and spiritual health and convenience for all families in such a way that parents have the needed time and energy for spending time with their families and working out family problems.

2. Preserving and supporting the family institution and maintaining its stability thus preventing it from disintegration and healing the damage arising from the dissipation of family ties.

3. Providing fundamental cultural planning to educate teenagers and help them recognize the benefits of forming families through marriage at the appropriate time and inform them about the disadvantages of irresponsible sexual behaviour which could lead to illegitimate children, sexually related diseases and psychological trauma.

Obstacles

1. Insufficient information, knowledge, commitment and

caring efforts by policy makers, implementers, community leaders and the relevant institutions to support and consolidate the family unit.

2. Misinterpretation of personal freedoms without considering the consequences and responsibilities (particularly in some societies where a man and woman are free to have children outside of marriage).

3. Lack of needed counselling and guidance in selecting a spouse, considering improper, forced and non-fruitful marriages as well as parental indifference often lead to the collapse of the family or even to various physical, psychological and social problems.

4. The existence of social-economic problems and negative cultural and traditional practices very often are detrimental factors toward marriage and establishment of family.

5. Insufficient access to health education, counselling and related services for mothers and families, malnutrition and drug and substance abuse which can lead to mental and physical disabilities in present and future generations.

6. Cultural encroachment through the misuse of mass media particularly via satellite which exposes the family, including children to crime, acts of violence, disrespect, improper sexual behaviour and lifestyles which are often negative to one's culture.

7. Lack of international recognition of family stability and contentment as one of the main indicators for social stability required for sustained economic growth and sustainable development.

8. Lack of awareness of the impact of global issues on family stability such as structural adjustment policies, militarisation and armed conflicts, refugees, displaced persons/families, environmental degradation and natural disasters.

Strategies

1. To inform and advocate with and mobilize leaders and relevant institutions to support and consolidate the family unit.
2. To provide the youth with essential religious, moral and responsible sexual education within the family and providing healthy environments full of love and affection inside the family.
3. To combat through information, education and public awareness campaigns negative traditional and cultural practices and address the economic impediments that act as limiting factors toward marriage.
4. To provide the appropriate training, education and traditional family counselling to women and men so that their families enjoy the necessary physical, psychological and sound moral values as well as harmonious intra-family relationships characterized by mutual care, respect and support, such as traditional family and community services which educate everyone, especially those that are ready for marriage.
5. To establish or ensure existing media watch groups to assist in the elimination of information detrimental to Muslim cultures, particularly the negative portrayal of women and family. This should also be done by utilizing all appropriate possible ways and means to disseminate accurate and supportive information. This should be done through periodic consultation with media authorities.
6. To provide the appropriate training, education, traditional family counselling and community services to women and men so that their families enjoy the necessary physical, psychological and sound moral values as well as harmonious intra-family relationships characterized by mutual care, respect and support, such as traditional family and community services which educate everyone especially those that are ready for marriage.
7. To promote the adoption of family stability and

contentment as one of the main indicators of social and human development along with other current indexes or aspects existing in the international community.

8. To increase awareness and encourage government and international bodies to take practical measures to eliminate global problems on family stability essential for human development.
9. To establish different mechanisms for supporting national, regional and international co-operation through NGO networks working towards the stability of the family.

Religion in the Advancement of Women

To embrace religion as an ideology and manner of life is a sublime, independent and cognizant choice that can satisfy all human dimensions of individual and social life and transcend the limits of time and place. It is by noting this principle that the role of divine religions in the advancement of women finds its real meaning and premise. The history and scriptures of divine religions denote the active and constructive presence of women in various cultural, political, social and economic aspects and this presence has had, and continues to have, certain effects on the process of growth and evolution. Global developments are showing a general turn towards spirituality and introducing the subject of religion at the United Nations after several decades denote a consciousness and active role of religion in society and human development.

Objectives

1. Recognition of the women's status which by divine definition is a being independent in creation, with freedom of choice and the power and ability to make decisions, possessing vast dimensions and the right to benefit and prosper from all divine blessings which have been bestowed for human evolution and which enables her to advance, along side men, to the position of God's representative on earth.
2. Securing social justice is one of the principal goals of

divine religions. The materialization of this goal can lay the grounds to attainment of human for women in all aspects of their lives.

3. Enhancement of the role of women and men in securing and maintaining a tranquil atmosphere for the family and proper advising and rearing of children is an issue which has been recognized by divine religions. In addition, the preservation of her dignity and respect within the frame work of the family as the basic unit in the structure of human societies has always been the concern of religions.
4. Recognizing and fostering the spiritual and religious values inherent in women and men and safeguarding of religious beliefs by governments can create a social environment and lay the foundation for the development of talents and skills of women in all material and spiritual dimensions.
5. Ensuring that women and men enjoy equal rights in all social spheres and that within the family they are entrusted with God-Given responsibilities commensurate with their human status. Women, as will as men can benefit from equitable social, economic and political opportunities.

Obstacles

Obstacles hampering the influence of religion if the social growths of women are:

1. The lack of co-ordination and understanding between "modernism" and timeless religious values has resulted in the belief that religion is incompatible with a modern way of life and isolates progressive religious positions.
2. The combination of human fallibility, historical distortions, erroneous traditions and superstitions or their substitution in the name of religion.
3. The lack of a dynamic and informed vision among policy makers, authorities and religious leaders who are

indifferent to the human and social position of women and their inherent needs.

4. The lack of belief among women themselves as to the creativity and values that religion can bring into their lives which is due to the absence of knowledge or to the false impressions that have been circulated and encouraged on societies.

5. Serious confrontation of governing systems and groups with religious and popular movements through factual fighting imposed domination and use of coercion or violence.

6. Unequal distributions of wealth in society discourages and inhibits the carrying out of religious requirements based on the free activity of women in the economic arena that could result in the improvement of their economic condition.

7. Viewing religion in a manner that limits it to its personal dimension, thereby neutralizing its effect on the development of social order and improvement of the condition of women in the society.

8. Refusal to recognize in the full humanity of woman, which includes the qualities needed for constructive decision-making.

Strategies

1. International societies, governments and NGO's should prepare the ground for the creation of research centres in which researchers and scholars establish comprehensive studies and disseminate findings in order to free genuine religious insights of superstitions relating to women.

2. Noting the inclination towards spirituality of individuals and societies in recent years, it is necessary that governments take action to remove the impediments toward fulfillment of religious practice and create facilities for the spiritual growth of growth of girls of women.

3. In order to increase the level of women's participation in economic, cultural, social and political fields and to eliminate opposition to this participation, it is essential that the laws of each country be reviewed and amended within the framework of religious parameters in such a way as to make feasible the attainment of rights that women deserve.
4. Drawing in their common religious values, women should prepare the ground for convergence and unity among divine religions and move toward the formation of the "International Federation of Women of Divine Religions."
5. Cultural encroachment that isolates and undermines the role of religion in human development must be consistently monitored and challenged.

Unresolved Concerns of Women

Many women in the modern age are familiar with feeling torn between traditional expectations of women and the expectations of the modern working conditions. While traditional expectations require women to be good mothers and housewives, modern impulses put little stress on family roles, compared to the emphasis they make on social roles of individuals. Women's traditional in-home activities include taking care of children, cooking good meals, cleaning and readying the house for guests; and these activities occupy a great deal of their time. Considering that traditional roles of women, compared to men's roles, do not bring money or prestige in the society, there have been reactions that deemed traditional women roles to be the source of men-women inequality. Women looked for appreciation for what they did, and this brought about women employment in good numbers.

The modern equality answer ideally offered that men and women share private roles such as raising children and doing the housework equally so that women can have equal voice in the public space. And in order to prove gender equality, women were pushed into the same working conditions with men. However, this solution was not very practical in reality since women were biologically and emotionally different. Women were bounded to bear children by their biology, and their physiology and psychology were affected by this reality. While modern employment conditions seemed to have ensured gender equality by providing same working conditions for males and females; these conditions, in practice, turned out to work well only for men's adaptation. Working conditions were insufficient for multitasking women and overburd-ened women since women were still expected to shoulder in-home traditional roles much or less.

Women feel physically and emotionally more attached to their children, but when they wanted to extend their commitments to the public realm for social satisfaction, they were- and they still are- faced with either harsh or long hours of modern employment. If they choose not to work, they feel confined at home doing in-home activities all their time. There are not yet notable alternatives for women to be effective in public and private life both. Women have to choose either to be full-time mothers or full-time workers, if they want professional jobs. For Fethullah Gülen, while imprisoning women at home and confining them in the kitchen among 'dirty dishes' oppressed and degraded them; some modern reactions to women's traditional roles have also gone extreme, oppressing and degrading women in another way.

For the sake of proving equality with men, women were pushed into the hard labour force; and in order to demonstrate that women are not machines, some responses rejected the idea of marriage and having and bearing children. If women are not able to bear children that they wish for and if they are not provided a safe environment to raise them; it is as equally unbecoming and unnatural as seeing women as merely child-bearing objects, says Gülen. How safe, one urges to ask, is the modern environment to provide women with a possible child-raising environment, when it forces women to leave their children at day-cares full-time? Gülen's ideas on women's role in private and public spaces offer an avenue between two extremes, both of which, in Gülen's thinking, are oppressive and ignorant of women's unique qualities.

Gülen invites us to give ear to women's primordial nature, physical potentials, spiritual worlds, psychological structures- which are different from men's- when talking about their roles that can bring satisfaction to society and women both. It has been people's cultural heritage that interpreted women's roles confined at home and pushed women into a more restricted area day by day. Gülen believes that "women are responsible for carrying out the duties that befall them in every area of society as long as these duties do not conflict with their primordial nature or with observing religious requirements" Still, in his thinking, exempting women from certain charges like military services and not making women liable for everything men are responsible for is not a disgrace towards women; rather it is Islam's recognition of women's needs and demands.

The modern dilemmas that women suffer from are the result of a lack of recognition of women's multi-roles in their lifetimes. Women, with their various modern-day syndromes, exhibit that they are not at ease with the modern solution of working 'equality'. There are working women syndrome, sacred mother syndrome, super women syndrome and even non-working women syndrome in the modern times.

While working mothers feel guilty about being non-present with their children most of the time, nonworking mothers feel useless at home, especially when mothering is not given its due value in our modern society. Considering these modern dilemmas of women, my paper examines how Gülen's ideas offer solution to women's aforementioned problems. Interviewing 11 women in the Gülen community, I try to bring answers to the following questions: how efficient is the modern working settings for women's expectations?

How much of Gülen's ideas on women's role are effectively put into practice in institutions that follow Gülen's teachings? Is it ever possible to realize Gülen's ideals in today's modern settings, which ignore women's dilemmas? How much satisfaction do working women in the community have in their familial and social roles? Does it make any difference to work at communities' institutions or at any other places? Does being a member of the community help them feel content about women's multi-roles?

The Changing Role of Women

The glass ceiling and the inflexibility of the male-dominated work market meant that the hopes generated in this post-sixties flush of optimism were not realised by many. Instead, women who grew up in that era often passed their dreams onto their daughters.

Social mobility, equal opportunity laws and feminism have introduced opportunities to women today that our grandmothers could never have comprehended. Prepared to compete in the job market under the same terms and adopt the same norms, memes and ethics of our male counterparts, we proved beyond all doubt that we are the equal of men, and that we are able to function as efficient and effective employees at all levels of organisational hierarchy. Dynamic and determined trail-blazers freed us from the confines of traditional nurturing, caring and domestic industries and many women followed in their wake.

Make no mistake here: not all women followed willingly and not all jobs were glittering careers. Women also ended up in dead-end, boring and unfulfilling roles just as men did, but at least now we were demanding a fair crack of the whip. But, of course, there are children to consider. And then some harsh realisations start to hit home. A career means making the same sacrifices in terms of family life that men do: to succeed, work comes first, family second. For many women, this is still a firmly held decision. There are numerous reasons, including economic, vocational and social, why women choose to work and their choices should be neither decried nor devalued. But it cannot be denied that the sixties' ideal of a flexible, dynamic partnership where women could have fulfilling, complete careers and family lives all balanced satisfactorily, was revealed as an impossible illusion - to be pursued, but never quite attained.

Such realisations expose the consequences of the race to achieve workplace equality. Losing women from the home and abandoning the traditional role in which the mother functions as a pivotal member of a community of other mothers has created a generation without a sense of social cohesion. It seems the values, norms and support generated by that web of care, love and attention have been replaced by a howling void in which children and parents are left to navigate their own moral compasses in isolation. Without a cohesive and secure social fabric against which children can test their own developing awareness and maturity, we face disintegration, chaos and conflict. A generation has emerged without a clear cultural identity, the sense of self fashioned out of material possessions and the projection of perfection that those possessions allow them to present to others.

This generation has not been raised with a deep-rooted sense of belonging to a community and place where they are known, accepted and understood. We live in an increasingly fragmented, fearful society in which communication on a personal level is neglected. Working away from home has also resulted in a generation of women dependent on ready-meals and supermarket cheats who have never learned to cook properly, who have lost the ability and knowledge that allows them to feed a family from scratch seven days a week with healthy and nutritious food based on what is seasonal, available and economical. In turn, health has suffered; obesity is at an all-time high and malnutrition is starting to creep back.

This is a generation of women unable to live within their means and who have never been taught how to balance a budget, manage household tasks, how to save and make and re-use so that resources are husbanded and secured rather than squandered and wasted. On top of that, we wallow in the highest level of personal debt ever. It is a bleak picture. So, do our gains compensate for these losses? Some would say yes; others would disagree. I would not advocate for a second that we return to the Victorian era when a woman's place was in the home. Now, there is growing fluidity in gender boundaries and roles which mean that men are just as capable of fulfilling the pivotal household role as women. However, I will assert my opinion that for many families traditional gender roles remain the most effective.

Those trail-blazing women who made sacrifices so that the women of our generation could choose whether or not they wanted to pursue a career are heroes. While raising children will always be, I think, the most challenging thing anyone can do physically, emotionally or mentally - something that no employment can match - it does not have to be a woman's pre-determined fate. There will always be women who gladly fit into corporate roles. The benefits of having a career - engaging with other adults on equal terms, the personal satisfaction of fulfilling potential and realising ambitions - makes it beyond doubt a choice worth having. Women also understand the responsibility of having children and that the merits of the family life our grandmothers knew can not be ignored. Increasingly, women are turning away from conventional work after having children. Many are choosing to contribute to an income flexibly by taking advantage of job shares, part-time positions and working from home.

Some who are able choose not to work at all, prioritising family commitments over a career and accepting the associated reduction in earnings as a necessary price to pay for that freedom. A growing number of women are even finding new and ingenious ways to integrate every area of life into a single, coherent whole by working for themselves and carving out entrepreneurial niches so they can shine without sacrificing family values. This is not a universal change. Women at the highest and lowest levels of society are as unaffected in real terms by this change as they have been by the previous changes; the roles and opportunities (or lack thereof) available to them are much the same as they have always been. But amongst the middleclass, educated, business-competent and energetic women who the pioneers of the sixties produced, there is a clear shift.

Women are now making a statement that they will not be bound by the inflexible practices of large companies. A clear preference has been made for living on our own terms, making small-scale, talent-driven and aspiration-based businesses realistic and desirable because this lifestyle is more compatible with the demands of a family. Women are re-claiming a sense of belonging, self-esteem and self-actualisation without compromising family. Success is defined not in terms of how much is earned, organisational position or excessive and ostentatious status symbols, but in terms of internal satisfaction. The values of our grandmothers - prudence, economy and self-sufficiency - are re-emerging to reunite the fragmented sense of self into a coherent whole and benefit generations to come.

Women in the Family

In that it is, and ought to become, a communion and community of persons, the family finds in love the source and the constant impetus for welcoming, respecting and promoting each one of its members in his or her lofty dignity as a person, that is, as a living image of God. As the synod fathers rightly stated, the moral criterion for the authenticity of conjugal and family relationships consists in fostering the dignity and vocation of the individual persons, who achieve their fullness by sincere self-giving. In this perspective the synod devoted special attention to women, to their rights and role within the family and society. In the same perspective are also to be considered men as husbands and fathers, and likewise children and the elderly.

Above all it is important to underline the equal dignity and responsibility of women with men. This equality is realized in a unique manner in that reciprocal self-giving by each one to the other and by both to the children which is proper to marriage and the family. What human reason intuitively perceives and acknowledges is fully revealed by the word of God: The history of salvation, in fact, is a continuous and luminous testimony to the dignity of women. In creating the human race "male and female", God gives man and woman an equal personality, endowing them the inalienable rights and responsibilities proper to the human person. God then manifests the dignity of women in the highest form possible, by assuming human flesh from the Virgin Mary, whom the church honors as the mother of God, calling her the new Eve and presenting her as the model of redeemed woman.

The sensitive respect of Jesus toward the women that he called to his following and friendship, his appearing on Easter morning to a woman before the other disciples, the mission entrusted to women to carry the good news of the resurrection to the apostles – these are all signs that confirm the special esteem of the Lord Jesus for women. The apostle Paul will say: "In Christ Jesus you are all children of God through faith... There is neither slave nor free, there is neither male nor female; for you are all one in Christ Jesus".

Women and Society

Without intending to deal with all the various aspects of the vast and complex theme of the relationships between women and society and limiting these remarks to a few essential points, one cannot but observe that in the specific area of family life a widespread social and cultural tradition has considered women's role to be exclusively that of wife and mother, without adequate access to public functions, which have generally been reserved for men. There is no doubt that the equal dignity and responsibility of men and women fully justifies women's access to public functions. On the other hand the true advancement of women requires that clear recognition be given to the value of their maternal and family role, by comparison with all other public roles and all other professions. Furthermore, these roles and professions should be harmoniously combined if we wish the evolution of society and culture to be truly and fully human.

This will come about more easily if, in accordance with the wishes expressed by the synod, a renewed "theology of work" can shed light upon and study in depth the meaning of work in the Christian life and determine the fundamental bond between work and the family, and therefore the original and irreplaceable meaning of work in the home be recognized and respected by all in its irreplaceable value. This is of particular importance in education: For possible discrimination between the different types of work and professions is eliminated at its very root once it is clear that all people in every area are working with equal rights and equal responsibilities. The image of God in man and in woman will thus be seen with added luster.

While it must be recognized that women have the same right as men to perform various public functions, society must be structured in such a way that wives and mothers are not in practice compelled to work outside the home, and that their families can live and prosper in a dignified way even when they themselves devote their full time to their own family. Furthermore, the mentality which honors women more for their work outside the home than for their work within the family must be overcome. This requires that men should truly esteem and love women with total respect for their personal dignity, and that society should create and develop conditions favoring work in the home.

With due respect to the different vocations of men and women, the church must in her own life promote as far as possible the equality of rights and dignity: and this for the good of all, the family, the church, and society. But clearly all of this does not mean for women a renunciation of their femininity or an imitation of the male role, but the fullness of true feminine humanity which should be expressed in their activity, whether in the family or outside it, without disregarding the differences of customs and cultures in this sphere.

The Rapid Changes in Women's Roles

Since the beginning of time women have fought to find a lasting and prominent position in their society. In the short span of twenty years, between 1900 and 1920, the roles of women changed dramatically in the United States. Women went from homebound producers to wage-earning consumers to political and social reformers in the short course of these twenty years. Though these women were not always seen as politically productive by men of their time, many women became active and independent and productive in their new found roles by changing what was an acceptable role for a woman to excel in.

At the turn of the century the United States was changing rapidly and the roles of women were not different. As industrialization and immigration changed the face of most cities, women were slowly changing from homebound producers to wage-earning consumers. In Amy Peiss' book *Cheap Amusements* this facet of new women's roles is discussed in detail. Peiss points out that, "By 1900 important changes in the social organization of labour and expanding job opportunities... created new work experiences for women". These new work experiences took them out of the home and gave them a new independence and freedom from their previously male and home dominated lives. It also gave them a new world within which to explore and succeed.

While so many married women barely left the house but the new breed of women left the house for work and leisure as Peiss points out, saying, "many mothers went out no more than twice a week." With incomes of their own, even if they gave most or all of their paychecks to their family, women found a new niche in society as workers and indirectly then as consumers. With money of their own, aside from that spent on family, they were free to buy things that had before been traditionally made at home, such as clothes. As workers, they became more influenced by the society around them, not just influence from family or neighbors and, in turn, led them to realize a change needed to be made in society. This expansion of world brought reform minded women to the front of society. With this new independence in women's roles, women began to explore activeness in society. Women soon became social and even political reformers, dedicated to the Progressive movement and other reform movements that sought to help the good of society. In realizing these new roles expanded women's roles beyond just the local scheme, Kathryn Sklar writes, "Thus although their own communities were essential to their social strength, women were able to realize the full potential of their collective power by reaching outside those boundaries."

The women now had interests outside the home and realized that society not only needed to be reformed, but that if it were to be reformed to their standards it was their responsibility to join together and work to accomplish their goals. Maureen Flanagan supplements this by stating, "the women were asserting their right to involve themselves in every decision made by the Chicago city government, even to restructure that government." Women were developing into political and social activists who worked through public means to reform what they could of society. They did a lot of this through various groups, usually strictly female groups, which worked through the community to better the standard of living where they could. Sklar points out that, "it [social settlement movement] provided those [women] with access to the male political arena while preserving their independence from male-dominated institutions." Women's groups kept independent from men's groups showing not only their independence but also their worth and ability to work without working through men.

These reformers worked to change the face of social and political interaction, widening their role from caretakers of the home and neighborhood, to caretakers of society, striving to better various communities, all the while doing the best they could to separate themselves from the influence of men in order to accomplish their own goals. Despite the rise in women's importance on the economic, social, and political scene, many men still did not see them as strong, productive, or politically active members of society. A leading politician of these two decades, Theodore Roosevelt, on more than one occasion belittled the woman's standing in society. Many men who might have believed that a woman's only role was within the family, it can be assumed, shared Roosevelt's view. Roosevelt is quoted as saying "I am more and more convinced that the great field, the indispensable field for usefulness of woman is as mother of the family.

It is her work in the household, in the home, her work in bearing and rearing the children...which should be normally the woman's special work." Though he tries to make it sound like a noble cause, and in some ways it is, he completely ignores and/or neglects the possibility that women can be anything useful except mothers. His thought, it can be construed, that women in the political arena searching for reform were only a weakness, as politics was a man's role. This viewpoint from such a prominent politician was not an isolated opinion. Many reformers became historical figures of great significance, such as Jane Adams. Also, drawbacks such as political disapproval did nothing to stop the evolution or movement of the role of women. Women's roles were constantly changing, whether men saw it or not.

These changes continue today as women's roles continually change. Women's roles, in this period, had evolved into outside the home and active members of society, not just community.

Despite many obstacles, such as men's popular disbelief and disapproval in their ability to succeed in these roles, women's roles evolved from local to widespread, from producer to consumer, and from homebound to community oriented. Though not all changes in the woman's role in society was a direct product of their changing surroundings, many of the changes can be traced back to the changes in society, economy, and politics during the two decades between 1900 and 1920.

Status of Women in India

Of the several factors that justify the greatness of India's ancient culture, one of the greatest is the honored place ascribed to women. "Where women are respected, there the gods reside, the heavens open up and angels sing paeans of praise" says the Hindu law giver Manu. In ancient India women in many places occupied an equal position to men. Many Hindu religious books like the Vedas, Ramayana etc. have mentioned the names of several women who were great scholars, poets, and philosophers of the time. According to ancient Hindu scriptures no religious rite can be performed with perfection by a man without the participation of his wife. Wife's participation is essential to any religious rite. Married men along with their wives are allowed to perform sacred rites on the occasion of various important festivals. Wives are thus befittingly called 'Ardhangani' (equal half of a man).

During many reigns, the queens held greater power and influence than any of the courtiers. Literary manuscripts tell us about kingdoms gained and lost due to a single woman. However, in the medieval period, the status of women went down considerably. Women were considered to be inferior to men. Many historians have called this age as the 'dark age'.

The woman's position became very miserable. Customs of pardha (a black cloth worn by women to cover their face), sati (burning of widows), child marriage, restrictions on widow marriage, and the prevalence of joint family systems have been the factors responsible for the injustice done towards women. Women were deprived of their rights of equality with men. Raja Ram Mohan Roy started a movement against this inequality and subjugation. The contact of Indian culture with that of the British also brought improvement in the status of women. The third factor in the revival of women's position was the influence of Mahatma Gandhi who induced women to participate in the Freedom Movement.

But in spite of this amelioration in the status of women, the evils of illiteracy, dowry, ignorance, and economic slavery would have to be fully removed in order to give them their rightful place in Indian society. The position of women in modern India has changed considerably. A woman's position in modern Indian society is equal to that of men, socially, economically, educationally, politically, and legally. Women's sufferings from Sati, Child marriage, Institution of Temple prostitution no longer exist. Now women have the right to receive education, inherit and own property, and participate in the public and political life of the nation. Women have become economically independent and can seek employment anywhere, without remaining a domestic slave. As a result of women's newly gained freedom, Indian women have distinguished themselves in various spheres of life as politicians, orators, lawyers, doctors, administrators, and diplomats. They are not only entrusted with great responsibility, but also perform their duties honestly and sincerely. There is hardly any sphere of life in which Indian women have not taken part and shown their worth.

In spite of this, the evils of illiteracy, dowry, ignorance, and economic slavery are not fully removed form the society. Society continues to treat widows, divorcees, and abandoned women with contempt. Widow Remarriage, while it happens frequently, is an uphill task for the couple. Many things are being done to address these problems. The National Human Rights Commission for Women handles all human rights violations against women. The National Council for Women advocates policies for women. There is an entire ministry that manages policies for women. There is also a very large body of educated women in professions. Some statistics quote more women engineers and scientists in India than in the US. Some other advancement includes publications created by women, several vocal women journalists and pundits, special courts for dowry deaths, and countless women specific NGOs. There have been many laudable attempts by successive governments to raise the status of women throughout various legislations and organizations.

Family Formation in Modern Societies

Social historians will generally find this contribution to comparative sociology and demography too demanding of quantitative acumen and too limited in analytic scope. Those who dare it and persist, however, will find in it both ideas and historical information that they will value. The methods are, so far as I am qualified to say, excellently attuned to the effort in the volume to treat an over-time pattern that is generally presumed to be uniform so precisely that the theoretical import of national differences may be explored.

The common social trend to which the essays here are addressed is the restructuring of nuptiality: a delay and/or eschewal of marriage, a rise in non-marital unions, and a loosening of the normative and temporal connection of marriage and childbirth. Commonplace explanations rest on "the new role of women," as indexed by increased formal education and more general employment in the paid labour market. The essays seek to employ both time series data from the national statistics systems of the societies in question, and longitudinal data on individuals available in large multiple-use retrospective samples. Their strategy is to create precisely defined, comparable time series across societies, and examine relatively informally the interconnection of the various aspects of "the new role of women" in each society; and then to use the longitudinal data to test more rigorously in each society a small set of hypotheses drawn, roughly, from Gary Becker's economic theory of the family.

These latter, on the whole, argue a close convergence of national family-formation trends inasmuch as the rise of women's education has brought about women's consequent greater inclination to work gainfully rather than exclusively within the family at childbearing and -rearing, and offer predictions about the propensity of women (of different educational levels, and hence potential earnings), over their life-courses, to cohabit, marry, and give birth. The findings of the national surveys certainly suggest less uniformity than a straightforward application of the Becker-derived hypotheses would indicate. Society-to-society differences in norms regarding control of sexuality, and in economic situation and history, provide ad hoc explanations for the deviations from Becker. Sociology is vindicated as against economics, to this extent; and social historians will probably cheer this result.

Historians will probably enjoy these, and would perhaps be advised to start their reading here, moving then to Blossfeld's introduction. Oppenheimer's chapter on the United States is, to my Americanist eyes, an exceptionally good one, both in terms of measurement and exposition, and in terms of the rather surprising findings she reports. I found the somewhat untypical stories available in the chapters on Italy, Spain, and Hungary among the more interesting for their untypical ness, despite relative deficiencies in data in the first two of these.

The Swedish chapter, placed first because Swedish cohabitation trends (but not patterns) so clearly anticipated that elsewhere, is unfortunately also among those resting upon somewhat weaker data. Unless your undergraduate students are quite different from mine, you will not wish to assign any part of this book to them. Graduate students working in comparative history or recent family history, or with a yen for work in social indicators, might find it useful. But on the whole, even conscientious social historians will define this as a good book for their library to shelve so that they might dip into it some happy day in the indefinite future.

Bibliography

Adepoju, A. (2002). Fostering Free Movement of Persons in West Africa: Achievements, Constraints, and Prospects for Intraregional Migration. *International Migration, 40* (2), 3-28.

Alexander, P. and Frederique D. (Eds.). (1987). *Sex Work: Writings by Women in the Sex Industry.* Pittsburgh: Cleis Press.

Annamanthodo, P. (1992). *Red Light Traffic: The Trade in Nepali Girls.* Kathmandu: ABC/Nepal.

Barry, K. (1995). *The Prostitution of Sexuality.* New York: New York University Press.

Bertone, A. M. (2000). Sexual Trafficking in Women: International Political Economy and the Politics of Sex. *Gender Issues, 18* (1), 4-22.

Biddulph, S. and Cook, S. (1999). Kidnapping and Selling women and Children: The State's Construction and Response. *Violence Against Women, 5* (12), 1437-1468.

Brown, H. (1999*). Sex crimes and tourism in Nepal. International Journal of Contemporary Hospitality Management, 11* (23), 107-110.

Chew, L. (1999). Global Trafficking in Women: Some Issues and Strategies. *Women's Studies Quarterly, 27* (1/2), 11-18.

Chutikul, S. (1995, Spring/Summer). Women and Commercial Sex Trade in Thailand. *Canadian Women's Studies, 15 (2).*

Constable, N. (1996). Jealousy, Charity, and Abuse:

Chinese Maids and Foreign Helpers in Hong Kong. *Modern China, 22* , 448-479.

D'Cunha, J. (1991). *The legalization of Prostitution: A Sociological Inquiry into the Laws Relating to Prostitution in India and the West.* Bangalore: Wordmakers.

D'Cunha, J. (1998). Feminist Perspectives on Prostitution and Trafficking for Prostittuion. In S. Kudchedkar. and S. Al-Issa. (Eds.). *Violence Against Women,_Women Against Violence.* Delhi : Pencraft International.

Eviota, E. U. (1992). *The Political Economy of Gender: Women and the Sexual Division of Labor in the Philippines.* London: Zedbooks.

Farrior, S. (1997, Spring). The International Law on Trafficking in Women and Children for Prostitution: Making it Live Up to its Potential. *Harvard Human Rights Journal, 10* , 213.

Girdler-Brown B. (1998). Eastern and Southern Africa. *International Migration, 36* (4), 513-551.

Hamal, P. (2000). NGOs working Against Trafficking in Girl Children of Nepal. *Population and Development in Nepal, 7,* 219-234.

Hughes, D.M. (2000, Spring). The Internet and Sex Industries: Partners in Globalizing Sexual Exploitation. *IEEE Technology and Society Magazine,* 35-42.

Kempadoo, K. (2001). Women of Color and the Global Sex Trade: Transnational Feminist Perspectives. *Meridians: Feminism, Race, Transnationalism, 1* (2), 28-51.

Kempadoo, K. and Doezema, J. (Eds.). (1998). *Global Sex Workers: Rights, Resistance and Redefinition.* New York: Routledge.

Kyle, D. and Koslowski, R. (Eds.). (2001). *Global Human Smuggling: Comparative Perspectives.* Baltimore: Johns Hopkins University Press.

Lydie, N. and Robinson, N. J. (1998). West and Central Africa. *International Migration, 36* (4), 469-511.

Mensendiek, M. (1996). Women, Migration and Prostitution in Thailand. *International Social Work, 40* (2) 163-176.

Miller, J. and Jayasundara, D. (2001). Prostitution, the Sex Industry, and Sex Tourism. In C. Rezetti, J. Edleson, and R. K. Bergen. (Eds.). *Sourcebook on Violence Against Women,* 459-480. Thousand Oaks, CA: Sage.

Moon, K. (1997). *Sex Among Allies: Military Prostitution in US-Korean Relations.* New York: Columbia University Press.

O'Dea, P. (1993). *Gender Exploitation and Violence: The Market in Women, Girls and Sex in Nepal.* Geneva: UNICEF.

Phizacklea, A. (Eds.). (1983). *One Way Ticket: Migration and Female Labor.* London: Routledge.

Piper, N. (1999). Labor Migration, Trafficking and International Marriage: Female Cross-Border Movements into Japan. *Asian Journal of Women's Studies, 5* (2), 69-99.

Raghu, M. (1997). Sex Trafficking of Thai Women and the United States Asylum Law Response. *Georgetown Immigration Law Journal, 12* (1), 145.

Skrobanek, S. B. S. and Jantateroo, C. (1997). *The Traffic in Women: Human Realities of the International Sex Trade.* New York: Zed Books Ltd.

Sturdevant, S.P. and Stolzfus, B. (1992). *Let the Good Times Roll: Prostitution and the US Military in Asia.* New York: The New Press.

Taylor, I. and Jamieson, R. (1999). Sex trafficking and the mainstream of market culture. *Crime, Law and Social Change, 32* (3), 257-278.

Truong, T.D. (1990). *Sex, Money and Morality: Prostitution and Tourism in Southeast Asia.* London: Zedbooks.

Tzvetkova, M. (2002). NGO Responses to Trafficking in Women. *Gender and Development, 10* (1), 60-68.

Uchida, A. (1998). The Orientalization of Asian Women in America. *Women's Studies International Forum, 21* (2), 161-174.

Williams, P. (Eds.). (1999). *Illegal Immigration and Commercial Sex: The New Slave Trade.* London: Frank Cass Publishers.

Index